MASTERWORKS OF
PHILOSOPHY
VOLUME 3

W9-CII-002

MASTERWORKS OF
PHILOSOPHY
VOLUME 3   EDITED BY S. E. FROST, JR.

DIGESTS OF
ARTHUR SCHOPENHAUER: THE WORLD
                    AS WILL AND IDEA
FRIEDRICH NIETZSCHE: BEYOND GOOD
                    AND EVIL
WILLIAM JAMES: PRAGMATISM
HENRI BERGSON: CREATIVE EVOLUTION

McGraw-Hill Book Company

New York • St. Louis • San Francisco • London • Düsseldorf
Kuala Lumpur • Mexico • Montreal • Panama • Rio de Janeiro
Sydney • Toronto • Johannesburg • New Delhi • Singapore

First McGraw-Hill Paperback Edition, 1972
07-040803-3

   3 4 5 6 7 8 9 MU MU 7 9 8 7 6 5

CONTENTS

ACKNOWLEDGMENTS

THE EDITOR wishes to thank Longmans, Green and Co., Inc., for permission to include our condensation of *Pragmatism* by William James, and Henry Holt and Company for permission to include our condensation of *Creative Evolution* by Henri Bergson.

S. E. F., JR.

THE WORLD AS WILL AND IDEA

by

ARTHUR SCHOPENHAUER

CONTENTS

The World as Will and Idea

ARTHUR SCHOPENHAUER

1788–1860

THE SCHOPENHAUERS were members of the mercantile aristocracy of Danzig, wealthy bankers and traders. Heinrich Floris
Schopenhauer, the philosopher's father, was a man of strong
will and originality. When his town surrendered to the Prus-
sians in 1793, he moved to Hamburg. In 1805 Heinrich began
to show signs of mental deterioration, and in that year he
either fell or threw himself into a canal and died.

Arthur Schopenhauer was born on the twenty-second of
February, 1788. His mother, Johanna, was twenty years younger
than his father and quite different from him temperamentally.
Arthur suffered greatly because of the incompatibility of his
parents and developed a morbid capacity for discontent which
colored his entire life and thought. After the death of his
father he drew away from his mother until, in 1814, he broke
with her completely and never saw her again.

Although his parents urged him to carry on the mercantile
ventures of the family, Schopenhauer had no love for this kind
of life and turned more and more to study. Finally his mother
gave up the idea of forcing him into business, turned over to
him a share of his father's estate, and permitted him to enter
the University of Göttingen, where his studies began in earnest.

At Göttingen he became enthusiastic about the philosophic systems of Plato and of Kant. But a streak of pessimism
began to manifest itself, and morbid fears grew on him. Chief
of these was the fear of being assassinated, which led him to
keep firearms always at hand and ready for use. He had few
intimates and seldom went among people, his closest friend
being a poodle.

From Göttingen he went to the University of Berlin, and

from there to Jena. His fellow students left him severely alone, for he told them that he was unusually sensitive to sound. "Noises torture me. Whenever I am interrupted in my work . . . I feel as if my head were severed from my body under the executioner's ax."

During the years that followed, Schopenhauer received his diploma from Jena and made the acquaintance of F. Mayer, a noted Orientalist who introduced him to the philosophy of ancient India, and to Goethe. It was Goethe who persuaded him to undertake some investigations in color in which he was then interested, and from which came a brilliant essay on the subject of color and light.

But Schopenhauer was chiefly interested in composing a work which would contain his entire philosophy in detail. At Dresden, where he went after a rupture with his mother, he devoted himself almost exclusively to the preparation and the writing of this work. He came more and more to believe that the will and the passions were the determinants of intellectual life, of all life. This was the theme of his greatest work, *The World as Will and Idea,* which was completed in 1818.

But the book did not gain recognition, and Schopenhauer was deeply disappointed. He believed that people were plotting to keep him in obscurity, and this thought preyed upon his mind. His later writings were equally unsuccessful, and he was driven deeper into despair. While he remained unheard, Hegel's philosophy was dominating the intellectual circles of the time. This embittered Schopenhauer against Hegel and his philosophy, which he held to be "three-quarters utter absurdity and one-quarter mere paradox."

Not until 1844, when the second edition of *The World as Will and Idea* appeared in a slightly altered form, did this work really attract attention. It was then that Schopenhauer's fame began to spread and grow. Men of prominence, notably Richard Wagner, sought his advice, and philosophers began to study and interpret his views. This recognition gave some happiness to an otherwise disappointed man. But it came later in life than he would have liked, for his long-nursed bitterness had eaten into his soul.

Early in 1860 Schopenhauer began to be affected by occasional difficulty in breathing and heart palpitations. This continued until the twenty-first of September of that year, when he was found dead in his chair at breakfast.

Schopenhauer's philosophy, like his life, is full of gloom. He was impatient with the "false optimism" of most philosophers. Man, he said, is a creature of pain. His will drives him constantly to attain the objects of his desire. And when he attains them, what then? A terrible boredom, an empty void. So he keeps on desiring, and striving, and complaining, and desiring again. An endless vicious circle of emptiness and pain. In such a world, asks Schopenhauer, is there any place for hope? And his answer is—decidedly no. Nothing but the will to power, and the weariness of acquiring power with the will to further power still unsatisfied.

And what is the end of it all? Is it death? No, not even that. When the individual dies, the universal craving for life goes on. Nature takes care of that. The sex urge is a hunger that is concerned not at all with the individual but with the race. The only things that count—and we can derive no personal comfort out of it—are the will to power and the will to live. The individual is given the power to reproduce his kind, to continue this useless chain of desire and frustration; and then, having fulfilled his function, he is cast upon the rubbish heap like an outworn rag. What a travesty, this meaningless continuation of the race! How stupid it is to marry, to reproduce, to love! "We see the glances of two lovers meet longingly. Yet why so secretly, fearfully, and stealthily? Because these lovers are the traitors who seek to perpetuate the want and the drudgery of the human race which would otherwise speedily come to an end."

The philosophy of Schopenhauer is a depreciation of love by a man who had never been loved.

THE WORLD AS WILL AND IDEA

Part I

FIRST BOOK: THE WORLD AS IDEA

First Aspect: The Idea Subordinated to the Principle of Sufficient Reason: The Object of Experience and Science

"The world is my idea":—this is a truth which holds good for everything that lives and knows, though man alone can bring it into reflective and abstract consciousness. If he really does this, he has attained to philosophical wisdom. It then becomes clear and certain to him that what he knows is not a sun and an earth, but only an eye that sees a sun, a hand that feels an earth; that the world which surrounds him is there only as idea, i.e., only in relation to something else, the consciousness, which is himself. If any truth can be asserted *a priori,* it is this: for it is the expression of the most general form of all possible and thinkable experience: a form which is more general than time, or space, or causality, for they all presuppose it; and each of these, which we have seen to be just so many modes of the principle of sufficient reason, is valid only for a particular class of ideas; whereas the antithesis of object and subject is the common form of all these classes, is that form under which alone any idea of whatever kind it may be, abstract or intuitive, pure or empirical, is possible and thinkable. No truth therefore is more certain, more independent of all others, and less in need of proof than this, that all that exists for knowledge, and therefore this whole world, is only object in relation to subject, perception of a perceiver, in a word, idea. This is obviously true of the past and the future, as well as of the present, of what is farthest off, as of what is near; for it is true of time and space themselves, in which alone these distinctions arise. All that in any way belongs or can belong to the world is inevitably thus conditioned through the subject, and exists only for the subject. The world is idea.

With reference to our exposition up to this point, it must be observed that we did not start either from the object or the subject, but

from the idea, which contains and presupposes them both; for the antithesis of object and subject is its primary, universal, and essential form.

This procedure distinguishes our philosophical method from that
of all former systems. For they all start either from the object or from
the subject, and therefore seek to explain the one from the other, and
this according to the principle of sufficient reason. We, on the contrary,
deny the validity of this principle with reference to the relation of subject
and object, and confine it to the object.

The systems starting from the object had always the whole world
of perception and its constitution as their problem; yet the object which
they take as their starting-point is not always this whole world of perception, nor its fundamental element, matter.

Of all systems of philosophy which start from the object, the most
consistent, and that which may be carried furthest, is simple materialism.
It regards matter, and with it time and space, as existing absolutely, and
ignores the relation to the subject in which alone all this really exists.
It then lays hold of the law of causality as a guiding principle or clue,
regarding it as a self-existent order (or arrangement) of things, *veritas
æterna,* and so fails to take account of the understanding, in which and
for which alone causality is. It seeks the primary and most simple state
of matter, and then tries to develop all the others from it; ascending from
mere mechanism, to chemism, to polarity, to the vegetable and to the
animal kingdom. And if we suppose this to have been done, the last
link in the chain would be animal sensibility—that is, knowledge—which
would consequently now appear as a mere modification or state of matter
produced by causality.

The fundamental absurdity of materialism is that it starts from the
objective, and takes as the ultimate ground of explanation something
objective, whether it be matter in the abstract, simply as it is *thought,* or
after it has taken form, is empirically given—that is to say, is *substance,*
the chemical element with its primary relations. Some such thing it takes,
as existing absolutely and in itself, in order that it may evolve organic
nature and finally the knowing subject from it, and explain them adequately by means of it; whereas in truth all that is objective is already
determined as such in manifold ways by the knowing subject through
its forms of knowing, and presupposes them; and consequently it entirely
disappears if we think the subject away. Thus materialism is the attempt
to explain what is immediately given us by what is given us indirectly.

"No object without a subject," is the principle which renders all
materialism for ever impossible. Suns and planets without an eye that
sees them, and an understanding that knows them, may indeed be spoken
of in words, but for the idea, these words are absolutely meaningless. On
the other hand, the law of causality and the treatment and investigation

of nature which is based upon it, lead us necessarily to the conclusion that, in time, each more highly organised state of matter has succeeded a cruder state: so that the lower animals existed before men, fishes before land animals, plants before fishes, and the unorganised before all that is organised; that, consequently, the original mass had to pass through a long series of changes before the first eye could be opened. And yet, the existence of this whole world remains ever dependent upon the first eye that opened, even if it were that of an insect. For such an eye is a necessary condition of the possibility of knowledge, and the whole world exists only in and for knowledge, and without it is not even thinkable. The world is entirely idea, and as such demands the knowing subject as the supporter of its existence. This long course of time itself, filled with innumerable changes, through which matter rose from form to form till at last the first percipient creature appeared,—this whole time itself is only thinkable in the identity of a consciousness whose succession of ideas, whose form of knowing it is, and apart from which, it loses all meaning and is nothing at all. Thus we see, on the one hand, the existence of the whole world necessarily dependent upon the first conscious being, however undeveloped it may be; on the other hand, this conscious being just as necessarily entirely dependent upon a long chain of causes and effects which have preceded it, and in which it itself appears as a small link. These two contradictory points of view, to each of which we are led with the same necessity, we might again call an *antinomy* in our faculty of knowledge, and set it up as the counterpart of that which we found in the first extreme of natural science.

This explanation at which we have arrived by following the most consistent of the philosophical systems which start from the object, materialism, has brought out clearly the inseparable and reciprocal dependence of subject and object, and at the same time the inevitable antithesis between them. And this knowledge leads us to seek for the inner nature of the world, the thing-in-itself, not in either of the two elements of the idea, but in something quite distinct from it, and which is not encumbered with such a fundamental and insoluble antithesis.

Opposed to the system we have explained, which starts from the object in order to derive the subject from it, is the system which starts from the subject and tries to derive the object from it. The first of these has been of frequent and common occurrence throughout the history of philosophy, but of the second we find only one example, and that a very recent one; the "philosophy of appearance" of J. G. Fichte. He was made a philosopher by Kant's doctrine of the thing-in-itself, and if it had not been for this he would probably have pursued entirely different ends, with far better results, for he certainly possessed remarkable rhetorical talent. If he had only penetrated somewhat deeply into the meaning of the book that made him a philosopher, *The Critique of Pure Reason,* he would have understood that its principal teaching about mind is this. The principle of sufficient reason is not, as all scholastic philosophy maintains, a *veritas æterna*—that is to say, it does not possess an unconditioned validity before, outside of, and above the world. It is relative and conditioned, and valid only in the sphere of phenomena, and thus it may appear as the necessary nexus of space and time, or as the law of causality, or as the law of the ground of knowledge. The inner nature of the world, the thing-in-itself can never be found by the guidance of this principle, for all that it leads to will be found to be dependent and relative and merely phenomenal, not the thing-in-itself. Further, it does not concern the subject, but is only the form of objects, which are therefore not things-in-themselves. The subject must exist along with the object, and the object along with the subject, so that it is impossible that subject and object can stand to each other in a relation of reason and consequent.

The method of our own system is *toto genere* distinct from these two opposite misconceptions, for we start neither from the object nor from the subject, but from the *idea,* as the first fact of consciousness. Its first essential, fundamental form, is the antithesis of subject and object. The form of the object again is the principle of sufficient reason in its various forms. Each of these reigns so absolutely in its own class of ideas that, as we have seen, when the special form of the principle of sufficient reason which governs any class of ideas is known, the nature of the whole class is known also: for the whole class, as idea, is no more than this form of the principle of sufficient reason itself; so that time itself is nothing but the principle of existence in it, i.e., succession; space is nothing but the principle of existence in it, i.e., position; matter is nothing but causality; the concept is nothing but relation to a ground of knowledge. This thorough and consistent relativity of the world as idea, both according to its universal form and according to the form which is subordinate to this, warns us, as we said before, to seek the inner nature of the world in an aspect of it which is *quite different and quite distinct from the idea;* and in the next book we shall find this in a fact which is just as immediate to every living being as the idea.

SECOND BOOK: THE WORLD AS WILL

First Aspect: The Objectification of the Will

In the first book we considered the idea merely as such, that is, only according to its general form.

But what now impels us to inquiry is just that we are not satisfied with knowing that we have ideas, that they are such and such, and that they are connected according to certain laws, the general expression of which is the principle of sufficient reason. We wish to know the significance of these ideas; we ask whether this world is merely idea; in which case it would pass by us like an empty dream or a baseless vision, not worth our notice; or whether it is also something else, something more than idea, and if so, what. Thus much is certain, that this something we seek for must be completely and in its whole nature different from the idea; that the forms and laws of the idea must therefore be completely foreign to it; further, that we cannot arrive at it from the idea under the guidance of the laws which merely combine objects, ideas, among themselves, and which are the forms of the principles of sufficient reason.

In fact, the meaning for which we seek of that world which is present to us only as our idea, or the transition from the world as mere idea of the knowing subject to whatever it may be besides this, would never be found if the investigator himself were nothing more than the pure knowing subject. But he is himself rooted in that world; he finds himself in it as an *individual,* that is to say, his knowledge, which is the necessary supporter of the whole world as idea, is yet always given through the medium of a body, whose affections are, as we have shown, the starting-point for the understanding in the perception of that world. His body is, for the pure knowing subject, an idea like every other idea, an object among objects. Its movements and actions are so far known to him in precisely the same way as the changes of all other perceived objects, and would be just as strange and incomprehensible to him if their meaning were not explained for him in an entirely different way. Otherwise he would see his actions follow upon given motives with the constancy of a law of nature, just as the changes of other objects follow upon causes, stimuli, or motives. But he would not understand the influence of the motives any more than the connection between every other effect which he sees and its cause. He would then call the inner nature of these manifestations and actions of his body which he did not understand a force, a quality, or a character, as he pleased, but he would have no further insight into it. But all this is not the case; indeed the answer to the riddle is given to the subject of knowledge who appears as an individual, and the answer is *will.* This and this alone gives him the key to his own existence, reveals to him the significance, shows him the inner mechanism of his being, of his action, of his movements. The body is given in two entirely different ways to the subject of knowledge, who becomes an individual only through his identity with it. It is given as an idea in intelligent perception, as an object among objects and subject to the laws of objects. And it is also given in quite a different way as that which is immediately known to every one, and is signified by the word *will*. Every true act of his will is also at once and without exception a movement of his body. The act of will and the movement of the body are not two different things objectively known, which the bond of causality unites; they do not stand in the relation of cause and effect; they are one and the same, but they are given in entirely different ways,— immediately, and again in perception for the understanding. The action of the body is nothing but the act of the will objectified, i.e., passed into perception. It will appear later that this is true of every movement of the body, not merely those which follow upon motives, but also involuntary movements which follow upon mere stimuli, and, indeed, that the whole body is nothing but objectified will, i.e., will become idea. All this will be proved and made quite clear in the course of this work. In one respect, therefore, I shall call the body the *objectivity of will;* as in the previous book, and in the essay on the principle of sufficient reason, in accordance with the one-sided point of view intentionally adopted there (that of the idea), I called it *the immediate object.* Thus in a certain sense we may also say that will is the knowledge *a priori* of the body, and the body is the knowledge *a posteriori* of the will.

It is just because of this special relation to one body that the knowing subject is an individual. For regarded apart from this relation, his body is for him only an idea like all other ideas. But the relation through which the knowing subject is an *individual,* is just on that account a relation which subsists only between him and one particular idea of all those which he has. Therefore he is conscious of this one idea, not merely as an idea, but in quite a different way as a will. If, however, he abstracts from that special relation, from that twofold and completely heterogeneous knowledge of what is one and the same, then that *one,* the body, is an idea like all other ideas. Therefore, in order to understand the matter, the individual who knows must either assume that what distinguishes that one idea from others is merely the fact that his knowledge stands in this double relation to it alone; that insight in two ways at the same time is open to him only in the case of this one object of perception, and that this is to be explained not by the difference of this object from all others, but only by the difference between the relation of his knowledge to this one object, and its relation to all other objects. Or else he must assume that this object is essentially different from all others; that it alone of all objects is at once both will and idea, while the rest are only ideas, i.e., only phantoms. Thus he must assume that his body is the only real individual in the world, i.e., the only phenomenon of will and the only immediate object of the subject. That other objects, considered merely as *ideas,* are like his body, that is, like it, fill space (which itself can only be present as idea), and also, like it, are causally active in space, is indeed demonstrably certain from the law of causality which is *a priori* valid for ideas, and which admits of no effect without a cause; but apart from the fact that we can only reason from an effect to a cause generally, and not to a similar cause, we are still in the sphere of mere ideas, in which alone the law of causality is valid, and beyond which it can never take us. But whether the objects known to the individual only as ideas are yet, like his own body, manifestations of a will, is, as was said in the First Book, the proper meaning of the question as to the reality of the external world. To deny this is *theoretical egoism,* which on that account regards all phenomena that are outside its own will as phantoms, just as in a practical reference exactly the same thing is done by practical egoism.

The double knowledge which each of us has of the nature and activity of his own body, and which is given in two completely different ways, has now been clearly brought out. We shall accordingly make further use of it as a key to the nature of every phenomenon in nature, and shall judge of all objects which are not our own bodies, and are consequently not given to our consciousness in a double way but only as ideas, according to the analogy of our own bodies, and shall therefore assume that as in one aspect they are idea, just like our bodies, and in this respect are analogous to them, so in another aspect, what remains of objects when we set aside their existence as idea of the subject, must in its inner nature be the same as that in us which we call *will.* For what other kind of existence or reality should we attribute to the rest of the material world? Whence should we take the elements out of which we construct such a world? Besides will and idea nothing is known to us or thinkable. If we wish to attribute the greatest known reality to the material world which exists immediately only in our idea, we give it the reality which our own body has for each of us; for that is the most real thing for every one. But if we now analyse the reality of this body and its actions, beyond the fact that it is idea, we find nothing in it except the will; with this its reality is exhausted. Therefore we can nowhere find another kind of reality which we can attribute to the material world. Thus if we hold that the material world is something more than merely our idea, we must say that besides being idea, that is, in itself and according to its inmost nature, it is that which we find immediately in ourselves as *will.* I say according to its inmost nature; but we must first come to know more accurately this real nature of the will, in order that we may be able to distinguish from it what does not belong to itself, but to its manifestation, which has many grades. Such, for example, is the circumstance of its being accompanied by knowledge, and the determination by motives which is conditioned by this knowledge. As we shall see farther on, this does not belong to the real nature of will, but merely to its distinct manifestation as an animal or a human being. If, therefore, I say,—the force which attracts a stone to the earth is according to its nature, in itself, and apart from all idea, will, I shall not be supposed to express in this proposition the insane opinion that the stone moves itself in accordance with a known motive, merely because this is the way in which will appears in man. We shall now proceed more clearly and in detail to prove, establish, and develop to its full extent what as yet has only been provisionally and generally explained.

If now every action of my body is the manifestation of an act of will in which my will itself in general, and as a whole, thus my character, expresses itself under given motives, manifestation of the will must be the inevitable condition and presupposition of every action. For the fact of its manifestation cannot depend upon something which does not exist directly and only through it, which consequently is for it merely accidental, and through which its manifestation itself would be merely accidental. Now that condition is just the whole body itself. Thus the body itself must be manifestation of the will, and it must be related to my will as a whole, that is, to my intelligible character, whose phenomenal appearance in time is my empirical character, as the particular action of the body is related to the particular act of the will. The whole body, then, must be simply my will become visible, must be my will itself, so far as this is object of perception, an idea of the first class. It has already been advanced in confirmation of this that every impression upon my body also affects my will at once and immediately, and in this respect is called pain or pleasure, or, in its lower degrees, agreeable or disagreeable sensation; and also, conversely, that every violent movement of the will, every emotion or passion, convulses the body and disturbs the course of its functions. Indeed we can also give an etiological account, though a very incomplete one, of the origin of my body, and a somewhat better account of its development and conservation, and this is the substance of physiology. But physiology merely explains its theme in precisely the same way as motives explain action.

The *will* as a thing-in-itself is quite different from its phenomenal appearance, and entirely free from all the forms of the phenomenal, into which it first passes when it manifests itself, and which therefore only concern its *objectivity,* and are foreign to the will itself. Even the most universal form of all idea, that of being object for a subject, does not concern it; still less the forms which are subordinate to this and which collectively have their common expression in the principle of sufficient reason, to which we know that time and space belong, and consequently multiplicity also, which exists and is possible only through these. In this last regard I shall call time and space the *principium individuationis,* borrowing an expression from the old schoolmen, and I beg to draw attention to this, once for all. For it is only through the medium of time and space that what is one and the same, both according to its nature and to its concept, yet appears as different, as a multiplicity of co-existent and successive phenomena. Thus time and space are the *principium individuationis,* the subject of so many subtleties and disputes among the schoolmen. According to what has been said, the will as a thing-in-itself lies outside the province of the principle of sufficient reason in all its forms, and is consequently completely groundless, although all its manifestations are entirely subordinated to the principle of sufficient reason. Further, it is free from all *multiplicity,* although its manifestations in time and space are innumerable. It is itself one, though not in the sense in which an object is one, for the unity of an object can only be known in opposition to a possible multiplicity; nor yet in the sense in which a concept is one, for the unity of a concept originates only in abstraction from a multiplicity; but it is one as that which lies outside time and space, the *principium individuationis,* i.e., the possibility of multiplicity.

The uncaused nature of will has been actually recognised, where it manifests itself most distinctly, as the will of man, and this has been called free, independent. But on account of the uncaused nature of the will itself, the necessity to which its manifestation is everywhere subjected has been overlooked, and actions are treated as free, which they are not. For every individual action follows with strict necessity from the effect of the motive upon the character. All necessity is, as we have already said, the relation of the consequent to the reason, and nothing more. The principle of sufficient reason is the universal form of all phenomena, and man in his action must be subordinated to it like every other phenomenon. But because in self-consciousness the will is known directly and in itself, in this consciousness lies also the consciousness of freedom. The fact is, however, overlooked that the individual, the person, is not will as a thing-in-itself, but is a *phenomenon* of will, is already determined as such, and has come under the form of the phenomenal, the principle of sufficient reason.

I call a *cause,* in the narrowest sense of the word, that state of matter, which, while it introduces another state with necessity, yet suffers just as great a change itself as that which it causes; which is expressed in the rule, "action and reaction are equal." Further, in the case of what is properly speaking a cause, the effect increases directly in proportion to the cause, and therefore also the reaction. So that, if once the mode of operation be known, the degree of the effect may be measured and calculated from the degree of the intensity of the cause; and conversely the degree of the intensity of the cause may be calculated from the degree of the effect. Such causes, properly so called, operate in all the phenomena of mechanics, chemistry, and so forth; in short, in all the changes of unorganised bodies. On the other hand, I call a *stimulus,* such a cause as sustains no reaction proportional to its effect, and the intensity of which does not vary directly in proportion to the intensity of its effect, so that the effect cannot be measured by it. On the contrary, a small increase of the stimulus may cause a very great increase of the effect, or conversely, it may eliminate the previous effect altogether, and so forth. All effects upon organised bodies as such are of this kind. All properly organic and vegetative changes of the animal body must therefore be referred to stimuli, not to mere causes. But the stimulus, like every cause and motive generally, never determines more than the point of time and space at which the manifestation of every force is to take place, and does not determine the inner nature of the force itself which is manifested. This inner nature we know, from our previous investigation, is will, to which therefore we ascribe both the unconscious and the conscious changes of the body. The stimulus holds the mean, forms the transition between the motive, which is causality accompanied throughout by knowledge, and the cause in the narrowest sense. In particular cases, it is sometimes nearer a motive, sometimes nearer a cause, but yet it can always be distinguished from both.

It only remains for us to take the final step, the extension of our way of looking at things to all those forces which act in nature in accordance with universal, unchangeable laws, in conformity with which the movements of all those bodies take place, which are wholly without organs, and have therefore no susceptibility for stimuli, and have no knowledge, which is the necessary condition of motives. Thus we must also apply the key to the understanding of the inner nature of things, which the immediate knowledge of our own existence alone can give us, to those phenomena of the unorganised world which are most remote from us.

Yet the remoteness, and indeed the appearance of absolute difference between the phenomena of unorganised nature and the will which we know as the inner reality of our own being arises chiefly from the contrast between the completely determined conformity to law of the one species of phenomena, and the apparently unfettered freedom of the other. For in man, individuality makes itself powerfully felt. Every one has a character of his own; and therefore the same motive has not the same influence over all, and a thousand circumstances which exist in the wide sphere of the knowledge of the individual, but are unknown to others, modify its effect. Therefore action cannot be predetermined from the motive alone, for the other factor is wanting, the accurate acquaintance with the individual character, and with the knowledge which accompanies it. On the other hand, the phenomena of the forces of nature illustrate the opposite extreme. They act according to universal laws, without variation, without individuality in accordance with openly manifest circumstances, subject to the most exact predetermination; and the same force of nature appears in its million phenomena in precisely the same way. In order to explain this point and prove the identity of the *one* indivisible will in all its different phenomena, in the weakest as in the strongest, we must first of all consider the relation of the will as thing-in-itself to its phenomena, that is, the relation of the world as will to the world as idea; for this will open to us the best way to a more thorough investigation of the whole subject we are considering in this Second Book.

The lowest grades of the objectification of will are to be found in those most universal forces of nature which partly appear in all matter without exception, as gravity and impenetrability, and partly have shared the given matter among them, so that certain of them reign in one species of matter and others in another species, constituting its specific difference, as rigidity, fluidity, elasticity, electricity, magnetism, chemical properties and qualities of every kind. They are in themselves immediate manifestations of will, just as much as human action; and as such they are groundless, like human character. Only their particular manifestations are subordinated to the principle of sufficient reason, like the particular actions of men. They themselves, on the other hand, can never be called either effect or cause, but are the prior and presupposed conditions of all causes and effects through which their real nature unfolds and reveals itself. It is therefore senseless to demand a cause of gravity or electricity, for they are original forces. Their expressions, indeed, take place in accordance with the law of cause and effect, so that every one of their particular manifestations has a cause, which is itself again just a similar particular manifestation which determines that this force must express itself here, must appear in space and time; but the force itself is by no means the effect of a cause, nor the cause of an effect. It is therefore a mistake to say "gravity is the cause of a stone falling"; for the cause in this case is rather the nearness of the earth, because it attracts the stone. Take the earth away and the stone will not fall, although gravity remains. The force itself lies quite outside the chain of causes and effects, which presupposes time, because it only has meaning in relation to it; but the force lies outside time. The individual change always has for its cause another change just as individual as itself, and not the force of which it is the expression. For that which always gives its efficiency to a cause, however many times it may appear, is a force of nature. As such, it is groundless, i.e., it lies outside the chain of causes and outside the province of the principle of sufficient reason in general, and is philosophically known as the immediate objectivity of will, which is the "in-itself" of the whole of nature; but in etiology, which in this reference is physics, it is set down as an original force.

In the higher grades of the objectivity of will we see individuality occupy a prominent position, especially in the case of man, where it appears as the great difference of individual characters, i.e., as complete personality, outwardly expressed in strongly marked individual physiognomy, which influences the whole bodily form. None of the brutes have this individuality in anything like so high a degree, though the higher species of them have a trace of it; but the character of the species completely predominates over it, and therefore they have little individual physiognomy. The farther down we go, the more completely is every trace of the individual character lost in the common character of the species, and the physiognomy of the species alone remains.

Thus every universal, original force of nature is nothing but a low grade of the objectification of will, and we call every such grade an eternal *Idea* in Plato's sense. But a *law of nature* is the relation of the Idea to the form of its manifestation. This form is time, space, and causality, which are necessarily and inseparably connected and related to each other. Through time and space the Idea multiplies itself in innumerable phenomena, but the order according to which it enters these forms of multiplicity is definitely determined by the law of causality; this law is as it were the norm of the limit of these phenomena of different Ideas, in accordance with which time, space, and matter are assigned to them. This norm is therefore necessarily related to the identity of the aggregate of existing matter, which is the common substratum of all those different phenomena. If all these were not directed to that common matter in the possession of which they must be divided, there would be no need for such a law to decide their claims. They might all at once and together fill a boundless space throughout an endless time. Therefore, because all these phenomena of the eternal Ideas are directed to one and the same matter, must there be a rule for their appearance and disappearance; for if there were not, they would not make way for each other.

If, from the foregoing consideration of the forces of nature and their phenomena, we have come to see clearly how far an explanation from causes can go, and where it must stop if it is not to degenerate into the vain attempt to reduce the content of all phenomena to their mere form, in which case there would ultimately remain nothing but form, we shall be able to settle in general terms what is to be demanded of etiology as a whole. It must seek out the causes of all phenomena in nature, i.e., the circumstances under which they invariably appear. Then it must refer the multitude of phenomena which have various forms in various circumstances to what is active in every phenomenon, and is presupposed in the cause,—original forces of nature. It must correctly distinguish between a difference of the phenomenon which arises from a difference of the force, and one which results merely from a difference of the circumstances under which the force expresses itself; and with equal care it must guard against taking the expressions of one and the same force under different circumstances for the manifestations of different forces, and conversely against taking for manifestations of one and the same force what originally belongs to different forces. For physics demands causes, and the will is never a cause. Its whole relation to the phenomenon is not in accordance with the principle of sufficient reason. But that which in itself is the will exists in another aspect as idea; that is to say, is phenomenon. As such, it obeys the laws which constitute the form of the phenomenon.

It follows from all that has been said that it is certainly an error on the part of natural science to seek to refer the higher grades of the objectification of will to the lower; for the failure to recognise, or the denial of, original and self-existing forces of nature is just as wrong as the groundless assumption of special forces when what occurs is merely a peculiar kind of manifestation of what is already known. Thus Kant rightly says that it would be absurd to hope for a blade of grass from a Newton, that is, from one who reduced the blade of grass to the manifestations of physical and chemical forces, of which it was the chance product, and therefore a mere freak of nature, in which no special Idea appeared, i.e., the will did not directly reveal itself in it in a higher and specific grade, but just as in the phenomena of unorganised nature and by chance in this form.

Now, although the difference between phenomenon and thing-in-itself is never lost sight of, and therefore the identity of the will which objectifies itself in all Ideas can never be distorted to mean identity of the particular Ideas themselves in which it appears, so that, for example, chemical or electrical attraction can never be reduced to the attraction of gravitation, although this inner analogy is known, and the former may be regarded as, so to speak, higher powers of the latter, just as little does the similarity of the construction of all animals warrant us in mixing and identifying the species and explaining the more developed as mere variations of the less developed; and although, finally, the physiological functions are never to be reduced to chemical or physical processes, yet, in justification of this procedure, within certain limits, we may accept the following observations as highly probable.

If several of the phenomena of will in the lower grades of its objectification—that is, in unorganised nature—come into conflict because each of them, under the guidance of causality, seeks to possess a given portion of matter, there arises from the conflict the phenomenon of a higher Idea which prevails over all the less developed phenomena previously there, yet in such a way that it allows the essence of these to continue to exist in a subordinate manner, in that it takes up into itself from them something which is analogous to them. This process is only intelligible from the identity of the will which manifests itself in all the Ideas, and which is always striving after higher objectification. We thus see, for example, in the hardening of the bones, an unmistakable analogy to crystallisation, as the force which originally had possession of the chalk, although ossification is never to be reduced to crystallisation. The analogy shows itself in a weaker degree in the flesh becoming firm. The combination of humours in the animal body and secretion are also analogous to chemical combination and separation. Indeed, the laws of chemistry are still strongly operative in this case, but subordinated, very much modified, and mastered by a higher Idea; therefore mere chemical forces outside the organism will never afford us such humours; but the more developed Idea resulting from this victory over several lower Ideas or objectifications of will, gains an entirely new character by taking up into itself from every Idea over which it has prevailed a strengthened analogy. The will objectifies itself in a new, more distinct way. It originally appears in *generatio æquivoca;* afterwards in assimilation to the given germ, organic moisture, plant, animal, man. Thus from the strife of lower phenomena the higher arise, swallowing them all up, but yet realising in the higher grade the tendency of all the lower.

From grade to grade objectifying itself more distinctly, yet still completely without consciousness as an obscure striving force, the will acts in the vegetable kingdom also, in which the bond of its phenomena consists no longer properly of causes, but of stimuli; and, finally, also in the vegetative part of the animal phenomenon, in the production and maturing of the animal and in sustaining its inner economy, in which the manifestation of will is still always necessarily determined by stimuli. The ever-ascending grades of the objectification of will bring us at last to the point at which the individual that expresses the Idea could no longer receive food for its assimilation through mere movement following upon stimuli.

Thus knowledge generally, rational as well as merely sensuous, proceeds originally from the will itself, belongs to the inner being of the higher grades of its objectification as a means of supporting the individual and the species, just like any organ of the body. Originally destined for the service of the will for the accomplishment of its aims, it remains almost throughout entirely subjected to its service: it is so in all brutes and in almost all men.

We have considered the great multiplicity and diversity of the phenomena in which the will objectifies itself, and we have seen their endless and implacable strife with each other. Yet, according to the whole discussion up to this point, the will itself, as thing-in-itself, is by no means included in that multiplicity and change. The diversity of the Ideas, i.e., grades of objectification, the multitude of individuals in which each of these expresses itself, the struggle of forms for matter,—all this does not concern it, but is only the manner of its objectification, and only through this has an indirect relation to it, by virtue of which it belongs to the expression of the nature of will for the idea. As the magic-lantern shows many different pictures, which are all made visible by one and the same light, so in all the multifarious phenomena which fill the world together or throng after each other as events, only *one will* manifests itself, of which everything is the visibility, the objectivity, and which remains unmoved in the midst of this change; it alone is thing-in-itself; all objects are manifestations, or, to speak the language of Kant, phenomena. Although in man, as Idea, the will finds its clearest and fullest objectification, yet man alone could not express its being. In order to manifest the full significance of the will, the Idea of man would need to appear, not alone and sundered from everything else, but accompanied by the whole series of grades, down through all the forms of animals, through the vegetable kingdom to unorganised nature. All these supplement each other in the complete objectification of will; they are as much presupposed by the Idea of man as the blossoms of a tree presuppose leaves, branches, stem, and root; they form a pyramid, of which man is the apex. We find, however, that the *inner necessity* of the gradation of its manifestations, which is inseparable from the adequate objectification of the will, is expressed by an *outer necessity* in the whole of these manifestations themselves, by reason of which man has need of the beasts for his support, the beasts in their grades have need of each other as well as of plants, which in their turn require the ground, water, chemical elements and their combinations, the planet, the sun, rotation and motion round the sun, the curve of the ellipse, &c., &c. At bottom this results from the fact that the will must live on itself, for there exists nothing beside it, and it is a hungry will. Hence arise eager pursuit, anxiety, and suffering.

It is only the knowledge of the unity of will as thing-in-itself, in the endless diversity and multiplicity of the phenomena, that can afford us the true explanation of that wonderful, unmistakable analogy of all the productions of nature, that family likeness on account of which we may regard them as variations on the same ungiven theme. So in like measure, through the distinct and thoroughly comprehended knowledge of that harmony, that essential connection of all the parts of the world, that necessity of their gradation which we have just been considering, we shall obtain a true and sufficient insight into the inner nature and meaning of the undeniable *teleology* of all organised productions of nature, which, indeed, we presupposed *a priori*, when considering and investigating them.

This *teleology* is of a twofold description; sometimes an *inner teleology*, that is, an agreement of all the parts of a particular organism, so ordered that the sustenance of the individual and the species results from it, and therefore presents itself as the end of that disposition or arrangement. Sometimes, however, there is an *outward teleology,* a relation of unorganised to organised nature in general, or of particular parts of organised nature to each other, which makes the maintenance of the whole of organised nature, or of the particular animal species, possible, and therefore presents itself to our judgment as the means to this end.

I here conclude the second principal division of my exposition, in the hope that, so far as is possible in the case of an entirely new thought, which cannot be quite free from traces of the individuality in which it originated, I have succeeded in conveying to the reader the complete certainty that this world in which we live and have our being is in its whole nature through and through *will,* and at the same time through and through *idea:* that this idea, as such, already presupposes a form, object and subject, is therefore relative; and if we ask what remains if we take away this form, and all those forms which are subordinate to it, and which express the principle of sufficient reason, the answer must be that as something *toto genere* different from idea, this can be nothing but *will,* which is thus properly the *thing-in-itself.* Every one finds that he himself is this will, in which the real nature of the world consists, and he also finds that he is the knowing subject, whose idea the whole world is, the world which exists only in relation to his consciousness, as its necessary supporter. Every one is thus himself in a double aspect the whole world, the microcosm; finds both sides whole and complete in himself. And what he thus recognises as his own real being also exhausts the being of the whole world—the macrocosm; thus the world, like man, is through and through *will,* and through and through *idea,* and nothing more than this.

THIRD BOOK: THE WORLD AS IDEA

SECOND ASPECT: THE IDEA INDEPENDENT OF THE PRINCIPLE OF SUFFICIENT REASON: THE PLATONIC IDEA: THE OBJECT OF ART

IN ORDER to gain a deeper insight into the nature of the world, it is absolutely necessary that we should learn to distinguish the will as thing-in-itself from its adequate objectivity, and also the different grades in which this appears more and more distinctly and fully, i.e., the Ideas themselves, from the merely phenomenal existence of these Ideas in the forms of the principle of sufficient reason, the restricted method of knowledge of the individual. We shall then agree with Plato when he attributes actual being only to the Ideas, and allows only an illusive, dreamlike existence to things in space and time, the real world for the individual. Then we shall understand how one and the same Idea reveals itself in so many phenomena, and presents its nature only bit by bit to the individual, one side after another. Then we shall also distinguish the Idea itself from the way in which its manifestation appears in the observation of the individual, and recognise the former as essential and the latter as unessential.

To him who has thoroughly grasped this, and can distinguish between the will and the Idea, and between the Idea and its manifestation, the events of the world will have significance only so far as they are the letters out of which we may read the Idea of man, but not in and for themselves. He will not believe with the vulgar that time may produce something actually new and significant; that through it, or in it, something absolutely real may attain to existence, or indeed that it itself as a whole has beginning and end, plan and development, and in some way has for its final aim the highest perfection (according to their conception) of the last generation of man, whose life is a brief thirty years.

History follows the thread of events; it is pragmatic so far as it deduces them in accordance with the law of motivation, a law that determines the self-manifesting will wherever it is enlightened by knowledge. At the lowest grades of its objectivity, where it still acts without knowledge, natural science, in the form of etiology, treats of the laws of the changes of its phenomena, and, in the form of morphology, of what is permanent in them. This almost endless task is lightened by the aid of concepts, which comprehend what is general in order that we may deduce what is particular from it. Lastly, mathematics treats of the mere forms, time and space, in which the Ideas, broken up into multiplicity, appear for the knowledge of the subject as individual. All these, of which the common name is science, proceed according to the principle of sufficient reason in its different forms, and their theme is always the phenomenon, its laws, connections, and the relations which result from them. But what kind of knowledge is concerned with that which is outside and independent of all relations, that which alone is really essential to the world, the true content of its phenomena, that which is subject to no change, and therefore is known with equal truth for all time, in a word, the *Ideas,* which are the direct and adequate objectivity of the thing-in-itself, the will? We answer, *Art,* the work of genius. It repeats or reproduces the eternal Ideas grasped through pure contemplation, the essential and abiding in all the phenomena of the world; and according to what the material is in which it reproduces, it is sculpture or painting, poetry or music. Its one source is the knowledge of Ideas; its one aim the communication of this knowledge. While science, following the unresting and inconstant stream of the fourfold forms of reason and consequent, with each end attained sees further, and can never reach a final goal nor attain full satisfaction, any more than by running we can reach the place where the clouds touch the horizon; art, on the contrary, is everywhere at its goal. For it plucks the object of its contemplation out of the stream of the world's course, and has it isolated before it. And this particular thing, which in that stream was a small perishing part, becomes to art the representative of the whole, an equivalent of the endless multitude in space and time. It therefore pauses at this particular thing; the course of time stops; the relations vanish for it; only the essential, the Idea, is its object. We may, therefore, accurately define it as the *way of viewing things independent of the principle of sufficient reason,* in opposition to the way of viewing them which proceeds in accordance with that principle, and which is the method of experience and of science. This last method of considering things may be compared to a line infinitely extended in a horizontal direction, and the former to a vertical line which cuts it at any point. The method of viewing things which proceeds in accordance with the principle of sufficient reason is the rational method, and it alone is valid and of use in practical life and in science. The method which looks away from the content of this principle is the method of genius, which is only valid and of use in art.

Imagination has rightly been recognised as an essential element of genius; it has sometimes even been regarded as identical with it; but this is a mistake. As the objects of genius are the eternal Ideas, the permanent, essential forms of the world and all its phenomena, and as the knowledge of the Idea is necessarily knowledge through perception, is not abstract, the knowledge of the genius would be limited to the Ideas of the objects actually present to his person, and dependent upon the chain of circumstances that brought these objects to him, if his imagination did not extend his horizon far beyond the limits of his actual personal existence, and thus enable him to construct the whole out of the little that comes into his own actual apperception, and so to let almost all possible scenes of life pass before him in his own consciousness. Further, the actual objects are almost always very imperfect copies of the Ideas expressed in them; therefore the man of genius requires imagination in order to see in things, not that which Nature has actually made, but that which she endeavoured to make, yet could not because of that conflict of her forms among themselves which we referred to in the last book. The imagination then extends the intellectual horizon of the man of genius beyond the objects which actually present themselves to him, both as regards quality and quantity. Therefore extraordinary strength of imagination accompanies, and is indeed a necessary condition of genius. But the converse does not hold, for strength of imagination does not indicate genius; on the contrary, men who have no touch of genius may have much imagination. For as it is possible to consider a real object in two opposite ways, purely objectively, the way of genius grasping its Idea, or in the common way, merely in the relations in which it stands to other objects and to one's own will, in accordance with the principle of sufficient reason, it is also possible to perceive an imaginary object in both of these ways. Regarded in the first way, it is a means to the knowledge of the Idea, the communication of which is the work of art; in the second case, the imaginary object is used to build castles in the air congenial to egotism and the individual humour, and which for the moment delude and gratify; thus only the relations of the phantasies so linked together are known. The man who indulges in such an amusement is a dreamer; he will easily mingle those fancies that delight his solitude with reality, and so unfit himself for real life: perhaps he will write them down, and then we shall have the ordinary novel of every description, which entertains those who are like him and the public at large, for the readers imagine themselves in the place of the hero, and then find the story very agreeable.

The knowledge of the beautiful always supposes at once and inseparably the pure knowing subject and the known Idea as object. Yet the source of æsthetic satisfaction will sometimes lie more in the comprehension of the known idea, sometimes more in the blessedness and spiritual peace of the pure knowing subject freed from all willing, and therefore from all individuality, and the pain that proceeds from it. And, indeed, this predominance of one or the other constituent part of æsthetic feeling will depend upon whether the intuitively grasped Idea is a higher or a lower grade of the objectivity of will. Thus in æsthetic contemplation (in the real, or through the medium of art) of the beauty of Nature in the inorganic and vegetable worlds, or in works of architecture, the pleasure of pure will-less knowing will predominate, because the Ideas which are here apprehended are only low grades of the objectivity of will, and are therefore not manifestations of deep significance and rich content. On the other hand, if animals and man are the objects of æsthetic contemplation or representation, the pleasure will consist rather in the comprehension of these Ideas, which are the most distinct revelation of will; for they exhibit the greatest multiplicity of forms, the greatest richness and deep significance of phenomena, and reveal to us most completely the nature of will, whether in its violence, its terribleness, its satisfaction or its aberration (the latter in tragic situations), or finally in its change and self-surrender, which is the peculiar theme of Christian painting; as the Idea of the will enlightened by full knowledge is the object of historical painting in general, and of the drama. We shall now go through the fine arts one by one, and this will give completeness and distinctness to the theory of the beautiful which we have advanced.

The great problem of historical painting and sculpture is to express directly and for perception the Idea in which the will reaches the highest grade of its objectification. The objective side of the pleasure afforded by the beautiful is here always predominant, and the subjective side has retired into the background. It is further to be observed that at the next grade below this, animal painting, the characteristic is entirely one with the beautiful; the most characteristic lion, wolf, horse, sheep, or ox, was always the most beautiful also. The reason of this is that animals have only the character of their species, no individual character. In the representation of men the character of the species is separated from that of the individual; the former is now called beauty (entirely in the objective sense), but the latter retains the name, character, or expression, and the new difficulty arises of representing both, at once and completely, in the same individual.

Human beauty is an objective expression, which means the fullest objectification of will at the highest grade at which it is knowable, the Idea of man in general, completely expressed in the sensible form. But however much the objective side of the beautiful appears here, the subjective side still always accompanies it. And just because no object transports us so quickly into pure æsthetic contemplation, as the most beautiful human countenance and form, at the sight of which we are instantly filled with unspeakable satisfaction, and raised above ourselves and all that troubles us; this is only possible because this most distinct and purest knowledge of will raises us most easily and quickly to the state of pure knowing, in which our personality, our will with its constant pain, disappears, so long as the pure æsthetic pleasure lasts. Therefore it is that Goethe says: "No evil can touch him who looks on human beauty; he feels himself at one with himself and with the world." That a beautiful human form is produced by Nature must be explained in this way. At this its highest grade the will objectifies itself in an individual; and therefore through circumstances and its own power it completely overcomes all the hindrances and opposition which the phenomena of the lower grades present to it. Such are the forces of Nature, from which the will must always first extort and win back the matter that belongs to all its manifestations. Further, the phenomenon of will at its higher grades always has multiplicity in its form. Even the tree is only a systematic aggregate of innumerably repeated sprouting fibres. This combination assumes greater complexity in higher forms and the human body is an exceedingly complex system of different parts, each of which has a peculiar life of its own, *vita propria,* subordinate to the whole. Now that all these parts are in the proper fashion subordinate to the whole, and co-ordinate to each other, that they all work together harmoniously for the expression of the whole, nothing superfluous, nothing restricted; all these are the rare conditions, whose result is beauty, the completely expressed character of the species. So is it in Nature. But how in art? One would suppose that art achieved the beautiful by imitating Nature. But how is the artist to recognise the perfect work which is to be imitated, and distinguish it from the failures, if he does not anticipate the beautiful *before experience?* And besides this, has Nature ever produced a human being perfectly beautiful in all his parts? It has accordingly been thought that the artist must seek out the beautiful parts, distributed among a number of different human beings, and out of them construct a beautiful whole; a perverse and foolish opinion. For it will be asked, how is he to know that just these forms and not others are beautiful? We also see what kind of success attended the efforts of the old German painters to achieve the beautiful by imitating Nature. Observe their naked figures. No knowledge of the beautiful is possible purely *a posteriori*, and from mere experience; it is always, at least in part, *a priori*, although quite different in kind, from the forms of the principle of sufficient reason, of which we are conscious *a priori*. These concern the universal form of phenomena as such, as it constitutes the possibility of knowledge in general, the universal *how* of all phenomena, and from this knowledge proceed mathematics and pure natural science. But this other kind of knowledge *a priori*, which makes it possible to express the beautiful, concerns, not the form but the content of phenomena, not the *how* but the *what* of the phenomenon. That we all recognise human beauty when we see it, but that in the true artist this takes place with such clearness that he shows it as he has never seen it, and surpasses Nature in his representation; this is only possible because *we ourselves are* the will whose adequate objectification at its highest grade is here to be judged and discovered. Thus alone have we in fact an anticipation of that which Nature (which is just the will that constitutes our own being) strives to express. And in the true genius this anticipation is accompanied by so great a degree of intelligence that he recognises the Idea in the particular thing, and thus, as it were, *understands the half-uttered speech of Nature,* and articulates clearly what she only stammered forth. He expresses in the hard marble that beauty of form which in a thousand attempts she failed to produce, he presents it to Nature, saying, as it were, to her, "That is what you wanted to say!" And whoever is able to judge replies, "Yes, that is it." Only in this way was it possible for the genius of the Greeks to find the type of human beauty and establish it as a canon for the school of sculpture; and only by virtue of such an anticipation is it possible for all of us to recognise beauty, when it has actually been achieved by Nature in the particular case. This anticipation is the *Ideal.* It is the *Idea* so far as it is known *a priori,* at least half, and it becomes practical for art, because it corresponds to and completes what is given *a posteriori* through Nature. The possibility of such an anticipation of the beautiful *a priori* in the artist, and of its recognition *a posteriori* by the critic, lies in the fact that the artist and the critic are themselves the "in-itself" of Nature, the will which objectifies itself. For, as Empedocles said, like can only be known by like: only Nature can understand itself: only Nature can fathom itself; but only spirit also can understand spirit.

FOURTH BOOK: THE WORLD AS WILL

SECOND ASPECT: THE ASSERTION AND DENIAL OF THE WILL TO LIVE, WHEN SELF-CONSCIOUSNESS HAS BEEN ATTAINED

THE WILL, which, considered purely in itself, is without knowledge, and is merely a blind incessant impulse, as we see it appear in unorganised and vegetable nature and their laws, and also in the vegetative part of our own life, receives through the addition of the world as idea, which is developed in subjection to it, the knowledge of its own willing and of what it is that it wills. And this is nothing else than the world as idea, life, precisely as it exists. Therefore we called the phenomenal world the mirror of the will, its objectivity. And since what the will wills is always life, just because life is nothing but the representation of that willing for the idea, it is all one and a mere pleonasm if, instead of simply saying "the will," we say, "the will to live."

Will is the thing-in-itself, the inner content, the essence of the world. Life, the visible world, the phenomenon, is only the mirror of the will. Therefore life accompanies the will as inseparably as the shadow accompanies the body; and if will exists, so will life, the world, exist. Life is, therefore, assured to the will to live; and so long as we are filled with the will to live we need have no fear for our existence, even in the presence of death. It is true we see the individual come into being and pass away; but the individual is only phenomenal, exists only for the knowledge which is bound to the principle of sufficient reason, to the *principium individuationis*. Certainly, for this kind of knowledge, the individual receives his life as a gift, rises out of nothing, then suffers the loss of this gift through death, and returns again to nothing. But we desire to consider life philosophically, i.e., according to its Ideas, and in this sphere we shall find that neither the will, the thing-in-itself in all phenomena, nor the subject of knowing, that which perceives all phenomena, is affected at all by birth or by death. Birth and death belong merely to the phenomenon of will, thus to life; and it is essential to this to exhibit itself in individuals which come into being and pass away, as fleeting phenomena appearing in the form of time—phenomena of that which in itself knows no time, but must exhibit itself precisely in the way we have said, in order to objectify its peculiar nature. Birth and death belong in like manner to life, and hold the balance as reciprocal conditions of each other, or, if one likes the expression, as poles of the whole phenomenon of life. The form of this phenomenon is time, space, and causality, and by means of these individuation, which carries with it that the individual must come into being and pass away. But this no more affects the will to live, of whose manifestation the individual is, as it were, only a particular example or specimen, than the death of an individual injures the whole of Nature. For it is not the individual, but only the species that Nature cares for, and for the preservation of which she so earnestly strives, providing for it with the utmost prodigality through the vast surplus of the seed and the great strength of the fructifying impulse. The individual, on the contrary, neither has nor can have any value for Nature, for her kingdom is infinite time and infinite space, and in these infinite multiplicity of possible individuals. Therefore she is always ready to let the individual fall, and hence it is not only exposed to destruction in a thousand ways by the most insignificant accident, but originally destined for it, and conducted towards it by Nature herself from the moment it has served its end of maintaining the species. Thus Nature naïvely expresses the great truth that only the Ideas, not the individuals, have, properly speaking, reality, i.e., are complete objectivity of the will. Now, since man is Nature itself, and indeed Nature at the highest grade of its self-consciousness, but Nature is only the objectified will to live, the man who has comprehended and retained this point of view may well console himself, when contemplating his own death and that of his friends, by turning his eyes to the immortal life of Nature, which he himself is. This is the significance of Siva with the lingam, and of those ancient sarcophagi with their pic- tures of glowing life, which say to the mourning beholder, *Natura non contristatur.*

Above all things, we must distinctly recognise that the form of the phenomenon of will, the form of life or reality, is really only the *present,* not the future nor the past. The latter are only in the conception, exist only in the connection of knowledge, so far as it follows the principle of sufficient reason. No man has ever lived in the past, and none will live in the future; the *present* alone is the form of all life, and is its sure possession which can never be taken from it. The present always exists, together with its content. Both remain fixed without wavering, like the rainbow on the waterfall. For life is firm and certain in the will, and the present is firm and certain in life.

The present alone is that which always exists and remains immovable. That which, empirically apprehended, is the most transitory of all, presents itself to the metaphysical vision, which sees beyond the forms of empirical perception, as that which alone endures, the *nunc stans* of the schoolmen. The source and the supporter of its content is the will to live or the thing-in-itself,—which we are. That which constantly becomes and passes away, in that it has either already been or is still to be, belongs to the phenomenon as such on account of its forms, which make coming into being and passing away possible. Life is certain to the will, and the present is certain to life. Thus it is that every one can say, "I am once for all lord of the present, and through all eternity it will accompany me as my shadow: therefore I do not wonder where it has come from, and how it happens that it is exactly now." We might compare time to a constantly revolving sphere; the half that was always sinking would be the past, that which was always rising would be the future; but the indivisible point at the top, where the tangent touches, would be the extensionless present. As the tangent does not revolve with the sphere, neither does the present, the point of contact of the object, the form of which is time, with the subject, which has no form, because it does not belong to the knowable, but is the condition of all that is knowable. Or, time is like an unceasing stream, and the present a rock on which the stream breaks itself, but does not carry away with it. The will, as thing-in-itself, is just as little subordinate to the principle of sufficient reason as the subject of knowledge, which, finally, in a certain regard is the will itself or its expression. And as life, its own phenomenon, is assured to the will, so is the present, the single form of real life. Therefore we have not to investigate the past before life, nor the future after death: we have rather to know the *present,* the one form in which the will manifests itself. It will not escape from the will, but neither will the will escape from it. If, therefore, life as it is satis- fies, whoever affirms it in every way may regard it with confidence as endless, and banish the fear of death as an illusion that inspires him with the foolish dread that he can ever be robbed of the present, and fore- shadows a time in which there is no present; an illusion with regard to time analogous to the illusion with regard to space through which every one imagines the position on the globe he happens to occupy as above, and all other places as below. In the same way every one links the present to his own individuality, and imagines that all present is extinguished with it; that then past and future might be without a present. But as on the surface of the globe every place is above, so the form of all life is the *present,* and to fear death because it robs us of the present, is just as foolish as to fear that we may slip down from the round globe upon which we have now the good fortune to occupy the upper surface. The present is the form essential to the objectification of the will. It cuts time, which extends infinitely in both directions, as a mathematical point, and stands immovably fixed, like an everlasting mid-day with no cool evening, as the actual sun burns without intermission, while it only seems to sink into the bosom of night. Therefore, if a man fears death as his annihila- tion, it is just as if he were to think that the sun cries out at evening, "Woe is me! for I go down into eternal night." And conversely, whoever is oppressed with the burden of life, whoever desires life and affirms it, but abhors its torments, and especially can no longer endure the hard lot that has fallen to himself, such a man has no deliverance to hope for from death, and cannot right himself by suicide. The cool shades of Orcus allure him only with the false appearance of a haven of rest. The earth rolls from day into night, the individual dies, but the sun itself shines without intermission, an eternal noon. Life is assured to the will to live; the form of life is an endless present, no matter how the individuals, the phenomena of the Idea, arise and pass away in time, like fleeting dreams. Thus even already suicide appears to us as a vain and therefore a foolish action; when we have carried our investigation further it will appear to us in a still less favourable light.

That the will as such is *free*, follows from the fact that, according to our view, it is the thing-in-itself, the content of all phenomena. The phenomena, on the other hand, we recognise as absolutely subordinate to the principle of sufficient reason in its four forms. And since we know that necessity is throughout identical with following from given grounds, and that these are convertible conceptions, all that belongs to the phenomenon, i.e., all that is object for the knowing subject as individual, is in one aspect reason, and in another aspect consequent; and in this last capacity is determined with absolute necessity, and can, therefore, in no respect be other than it is. The whole content of Nature, the collective sum of its phenomena, is thus throughout necessary, and the necessity of every part, of every phenomenon, of every event, can always be proved, because it must be possible to find the reason from which it follows as a consequent. This admits of no exception: it follows from the unrestricted validity of the principle of sufficient reason. In another aspect, however, the same world is for us, in all its phenomena, objectivity of will. And the will, since it is not phenomenon, is not idea or object, but thing-in-itself, and is not subordinate to the principle of sufficient reason, the form of all object; thus is not determined as a consequent through any reason, knows no necessity, i.e., is *free*. The concept of freedom is thus properly a negative concept, for its content is merely the denial of necessity, i.e., the relation of consequent to its reason, according to the principle of sufficient reason. Now here lies before us in its most distinct form the solution of that great contradiction, the union of freedom with necessity, which has so often been discussed in recent times, yet, so far as I know, never clearly and adequately. Everything is as phenomenon, as object, absolutely necessary: *in itself* it is will, which is perfectly free to all eternity. The phenomenon, the object, is necessarily and unalterably determined in that chain of causes and effects which admits of no interruption. But the existence in general of this object, and its specific nature, i.e., the Idea which reveals itself in it, or, in other words, its character, is a direct manifestation of will. Thus, in conformity with the freedom of this will, the object might not be at all, or it might be originally and essentially something quite different from what it is, in which case, however, the whole chain of which it is a link, and which is itself a manifestation of the same will, would be quite different also. But once there and existing, it has entered the chain of causes and effects, is always necessarily determined in it, and can, therefore, neither become something else, i.e., change itself, nor yet escape from the chain, i.e., vanish. Man, like every other part of Nature, is objectivity of the will; therefore all that has been said holds good of him. As everything in Nature has its forces and qualities, which react in a definite way when definitely affected, and constitute its character, man also has his *character,* from which the motives call forth his actions with necessity. In this manner of conduct his empirical character reveals itself, but in this again his intelligible character, the will in itself, whose determined phenomenon he is. But man is the most complete phenomenon of will, and he had to be enlightened with so high a degree of knowledge in order to maintain himself in existence, that in it a perfectly adequate copy or repetition of the nature of the world under the form of the idea became possible: this is the comprehension of the Ideas, the pure mirror of the world. Thus in man the will can attain to full self-consciousness, to distinct and exhaustive knowledge of its own nature, as it mirrors itself in the whole world. We saw in the preceding book that art springs from the actual presence of this degree of knowledge; and at the end of our whole work it will further appear that, through the same knowledge, in that the will relates it to itself, a suppression and self-denial of the will in its most perfect manifestation is possible. So that the freedom which otherwise, as belonging to the thing-in-itself, can never show itself in the phenomenon, in such a case does also appear in it, and, by abolishing the nature which lies at the foundation of the phenomenon, while the latter itself still continues to exist in time, it brings about a contradiction of the phenomenon with itself, and in this way exhibits the phenomena of holiness and self-renunciation. But all this can only be fully understood at the end of this book. What has just been said merely affords a preliminary and general indication of how man is distinguished from all the other phenomena of will by the fact that freedom, i.e., independence of the principle of sufficient reason, which only belongs to the will as thing-in-itself, and contradicts the phenomenon, may yet possibly, in his case, appear in the phenomenon also, where, however, it necessarily exhibits itself as a contradiction of the phenomenon with itself. In this sense, not only the will in itself, but man also may certainly be called free, and thus distinguished from all other beings. But how this is to be understood can only become clear through all that is to follow, and for the present we must turn away from it altogether. For, in the first place, we must beware of the error that the action of the individual definite man is subject to no necessity, i.e., that the power of the motive is less certain than the power of the cause, or the following of the conclusion from the premises. The freedom of the will as thing-in-itself, if, as has been said, we abstract from the entirely exceptional case mentioned above, by no means extends directly to its phenomenon, not even in the case in which this reaches the highest grade of its visibility, and thus does not extend to the rational animal endowed with individual character, i.e., the person. The person is never free although he is the phenomenon of a free will; for he is already the determined phenomenon of the free volition of this will, and, because he enters the form of every object, the principle of sufficient reason, he develops indeed the unity of that will in a multiplicity of actions, but on account of the timeless unity of that volition in itself, this multiplicity exhibits in itself the regular conformity to law of a force of nature. Since, however, it is that free volition that becomes visible in the person and the whole of his conduct, relating itself to him as the concept to the definition, every individual action of the person is to be ascribed to the free will, and directly proclaims itself as such in consciousness.

The assertion of an empirical freedom of the will agrees precisely with the doctrine that places the inner nature of man in a *soul,* which is originally a *knowing,* and indeed really an abstract *thinking* nature, and only in consequence of this a *willing* nature—a doctrine which thus regards the will as of a secondary or derivative nature, instead of knowledge which is really so. The will indeed came to be regarded as an act of thought, and to be identified with the judgment, especially by Descartes and Spinoza. According to this doctrine every man must become what he is only through his knowledge; he must enter the world as a moral cipher come to know the things in it, and thereupon determine to be this or that, to act thus or thus, and may also through new knowledge achieve a new course of action, that is to say, become another person. Further, he must first know a thing to be *good,* and in consequence of this will it, instead of first *willing* it, and in consequence of this calling it *good.* According to my fundamental point of view, all this is a reversal of the true relation. Will is first and original; knowledge is merely added to it as an instrument belonging to the phenomenon of will. Therefore every man is what he is through his will, and his character is original, for willing is the basis of his nature. Through the knowledge which is added to it he comes to know in the course of experience *what he is,* i.e., he learns his character. Thus he *knows* himself in consequence of and in accordance with the nature of his will, instead of *willing* in consequence of and in accordance with his knowing. According to the latter view, he would only require to consider how he would like best to be, and he would be it; that is its doctrine of the freedom of the will. Thus it consists really in this, that a man is his own work guided by the light of knowledge. I, on the contrary, say that he is his own work before all knowledge, and knowledge is merely added to it to enlighten it. Therefore he cannot resolve to be this or that, nor can he become other than he is; but he *is* once for all, and he knows in the course of experience *what* he is. According to one doctrine he *wills* what he knows, and according to the other he *knows* what he wills.

As the result of the whole of this discussion of the freedom of the will and what relates to it, we find that although the will may, in itself and apart from the phenomenon, be called free and even omnipotent, yet in its particular phenomena enlightened by knowledge, as in men and brutes, it is determined by motives to which the special character regularly and necessarily responds, and always in the same way. We see that because of the possession on his part of abstract or rational knowledge, man, as distinguished from the brutes, has a *choice,* which only makes him the scene of the conflict of his motives, without withdrawing him from their control. This choice is therefore certainly the condition of the possibility of the complete expression of the individual character, but is by no means to be regarded as freedom of the particular volition, i.e., independence of the law of causality, the necessity of which extends to man as to every other phenomenon. Thus the difference between human volition and that of the brutes, which is introduced by reason or knowledge through concepts, extends to the point we have indicated, and no farther. But, what is quite a different thing, there may arise a phenomenon of the human will which is quite impossible in the brute creation, if man altogether lays aside the knowledge of particular things as such which is subordinate to the principle of sufficient reason, and by means of his knowledge of the Ideas sees through the *principium individuationis.* Then an actual appearance of the real freedom of the will as a thing-in-itself is possible, by which the phenomenon comes into a sort of contradiction with itself, as is indicated by the word *self-renunciation;* and, finally, the "in-itself" of its nature suppresses itself.

Though everything may be regarded as irrevocably predetermined by fate, yet it is so only through the medium of the chain of causes; therefore in no case can it be determined that an effect shall appear without its cause. Thus it is not simply the event that is predetermined, but the event as the consequence of preceding causes; so that fate does not decide the consequence alone, but also the means as the consequence of which it is destined to appear. Accordingly, if some means is not present, it is certain that the consequence also will not be present: each is always present in accordance with the determination of fate, but this is never known to us till afterwards.

As events always take place according to fate, i.e., according to the infinite concatenation of causes, so our actions always take place according to our intelligible character. But just as we do not know the former beforehand, so no *a priori* insight is given us into the latter, but we only come to know ourselves as we come to know other persons *a posteriori* through experience. If the intelligible character involved that we could only form a good resolution after a long conflict with a bad disposition, this conflict would have to come first and be waited for. Reflection on the unalterable nature of the character, on the unity of the source from which all our actions flow, must not mislead us into claiming the decision of the character in favour of one side or the other; it is in the resolve that follows that we shall see what manner of men we are, and mirror ourselves in our actions. This is the explanation of the satisfaction or the anguish of soul with which we look back on the course of our past life. Both are experienced, not because these past deeds have still an existence; they are past, they have been, and now are no more; but their great importance for us lies in their significance, lies in the fact that these deeds are the expression of the character, the mirror of the will, in which we look and recognise our inmost self, the kernel of our will. Because we experience this not before, but only after, it behoves us to strive and fight in time, in order that the picture we produce by our deeds may be such that the contemplation of it may calm us as much as possible, instead of harassing us. The significance of this consolation or anguish of soul will, as we have said, be inquired into farther on; but to this place there belongs the inquiry which follows, and which stands by itself.

This freedom, this omnipotence, as the expression of which the whole visible world exists and progressively develops in accordance with the laws which belong to the form of knowledge, can now, at the point at which in its most perfect manifestation it has attained to the completely adequate knowledge of its own nature, express itself anew in two ways. Either it wills here, at the summit of mental endowment and self-consciousness, simply what it willed before blindly and unconsciously, and if so, knowledge always remains its *motive* in the whole as in the particular case. Or, conversely, this knowledge becomes for it a *quieter,* which appeases and suppresses all willing. This is that assertion and denial of the will to live which was stated above in general terms. As, in the reference of individual conduct, a general, not a particular manifestation of will, it does not disturb and modify the development of the character, nor does it find its expression in particular actions; but, either by an ever more marked appearance of the whole method of action it has followed hitherto, or conversely by the entire suppression of it, it expresses in a living form the maxims which the will has freely adopted in accordance with the knowledge it has now attained to. By the explanations we have just given of freedom, necessity, and character, we have somewhat facilitated and prepared the way for the clearer development of all this, which is the principal subject of this last book. But we shall have done so still more when we have turned our attention to life itself, the willing or not willing of which is the great question, and have endeavoured to find out generally what the will itself, which is everywhere the inmost nature of this life, will really attain by its assertion—in what way and to what extent this assertion satisfies or can satisfy the will; in short, what is generally and mainly to be regarded as its position in this its own world, which in every relation belongs to it.

At every grade that is enlightened by knowledge, the will appears as an individual. The human individual finds himself as finite in infinite space and time, and consequently as a vanishing quantity compared with them. He is projected into them, and, on account of their unlimited nature, he has always a merely relative, never absolute *when* and *where* of his existence; for his place and duration are finite parts of what is infinite and boundless. His real existence is only in the present, whose unchecked flight into the past is a constant transition into death, a constant dying. For his past life, apart from its possible consequences for the present, and the testimony regarding the will that is expressed in it, is now entirely done with, dead, and no longer anything; and, therefore, it must be, as a matter of reason, indifferent to him whether the content of that past was pain or pleasure. But the present is always passing through his hands into the past; the future is quite uncertain and always short. Thus his existence, even when we consider only its formal side, is a constant hurrying of the present into the dead past, a constant dying. But if we look at it from the physical side; it is clear that, as our walking is admittedly merely a constantly prevented falling, the life of our body is only a constantly prevented dying, an ever-postponed death: finally, in the same way, the activity of our mind is a constantly deferred ennui. Every breath we draw wards off the death that is constantly intruding upon us. In this way we fight with it every moment, and again, at longer intervals, through every meal we eat, every sleep we take, every time we warm ourselves, &c. In the end, Death must conquer, for we became subject to him through birth, and he only plays for a little while with his prey before he swallows it up. We pursue our life, however, with great interest and much solicitude as long as possible, as we blow out a soap-bubble as long and as large as possible, although we know perfectly well that it will burst.

All satisfaction, or what is commonly called happiness, is always really and essentially only *negative,* and never positive. It is not an original gratification coming to us of itself, but must always be the satisfaction of a wish. The wish, i.e., some want, is the condition which precedes every pleasure. But with the satisfaction the wish and therefore the pleasure cease. Thus the satisfaction or the pleasing can never be more than the deliverance from a pain, from a want; for such is not only every actual, open sorrow, but every desire, the importunity of which disturbs our peace, and, indeed, the deadening ennui also that makes life a burden to us. It is, however, so hard to attain or achieve anything; difficulties and troubles without end are opposed to every purpose, and at every step hindrances accumulate. But when finally everything is overcome and attained, nothing can ever be gained but deliverance from some sorrow or desire, so that we find ourselves just in the same position as we occupied before this sorrow or desire appeared. All that is even directly given us is merely the want, i.e., the pain. The satisfaction and the pleasure we can only know indirectly through the remembrance of the preceding suffering and want, which ceases with its appearance. Hence it arises that we are not properly conscious of the blessings and advantages we actually possess, nor do we prize them, but think of them merely as a matter of course, for they gratify us only negatively by restraining suffering. Only when we have lost them do we become sensible of their value; for the want, the privation, the sorrow, is the positive, communicating itself directly to us.

That all happiness is only of a negative, not a positive, nature, that just on this account it cannot be lasting satisfaction and gratification, but merely delivers us from some pain or want which must be followed either by a new pain, or by languor, empty longing, and ennui; this finds support in art, that true mirror of the world and life, and especially in poetry. Every epic and dramatic poem can only represent a struggle, an effort, and fight for happiness, never enduring and complete happiness itself. It conducts its heroes through a thousand difficulties and dangers to the goal; as soon as this is reached, it hastens to let the curtain fall; for now there would remain nothing for it to do but to show that the glittering goal in which the hero expected to find happiness had only disappointed him, and that after its attainment he was no better off than before. Because a genuine enduring happiness is not possible, it cannot be the subject of art. Certainly the aim of the idyll is the description of such a happiness, but one also sees that the idyll as such cannot continue. The poet always finds that it either becomes epical in his hands, and in this case it is a very insignificant epic, made up of trifling sorrows, trifling delights, and trifling efforts—this is the commonest case—or else it becomes a merely descriptive poem, describing the beauty of nature, i.e., pure knowing free from will, which certainly, as a matter of fact, is the only pure happiness, which is neither preceded by suffering or want, nor necessarily followed by repentance, sorrow, emptiness, or satiety; but this happiness cannot fill the whole life, but is only possible at moments. What we see in poetry we find again in music; in the melodies of which we have recognised the universal expression of the inmost history of the self-conscious will, the most secret life, longing, suffering, and delight; the ebb and flow of the human heart. Melody is always a deviation from the keynote through a thousand capricious wanderings, even to the most painful discord, and then a final return to the keynote which expresses the satisfaction and appeasing of the will, but with which nothing more can then be done, and the continuance of which any longer would only be a wearisome and unmeaning monotony corresponding to ennui.

We now wish to discover the significance of the concept *good*, which can be done with very little trouble. This concept is essentially relative, and signifies *the conformity of an object to any definite effort of the will.* Accordingly everything that corresponds to the will in any of its expressions and fulfils its end is thought through the concept *good,* however different such things may be in other respects. Thus we speak of good eating, good roads, good weather, good weapons, good omens, and so on; in short, we call everything good that is just as we wish it to be; and therefore that may be good in the eyes of one man which is just the reverse in those of another. The conception of the good divides itself into two sub-species—that of the direct and present satisfaction of any volition, and that of its indirect satisfaction which has reference to the future, i.e., the agreeable, and the useful. The conception of the opposite, so long as we are speaking of unconscious existence, is expressed by the word *bad,* more rarely and abstractly by the word *evil,* which thus denotes everything that does not correspond to any effort of the will. Like all other things that can come into relation to the will, men who are favourable to the ends which happen to be desired, who further and befriend them, are called good in the same sense, and always with that relative limitation, which shows itself, for example, in the expression, "I find this good, but you don't." Those, however, who are naturally disposed not to hinder the endeavours of others, but rather to assist them, and who are thus consistently helpful, benevolent, friendly, and charitable, are called *good* men, on account of this relation of their conduct to the will of others in general. Thus, having started entirely from the passive element to the good, the inquiry could only proceed later to the active element, and investigate the conduct of the man who is called good, no longer with reference to others, but to himself; specially setting itself the task of explaining both the purely objective respect which such conduct produces in others, and the peculiar contentment with himself which it clearly produces in the man himself, since he purchases it with sacrifices of another kind; and also, on the other hand, the inner pain which accompanies the bad disposition, whatever outward advantages it brings to him who entertains it. It was from this source that the ethical systems, both the philosophical and those which are supported by systems of religion, took their rise. Both seek constantly in some way or other to connect happiness with virtue, the former either by means of the principle of contradiction or that of sufficient reason, and thus to make happiness either identical with or the consequence of virtue, always sophistically; the latter, by asserting the existence of other worlds than that which alone can be known to experience. In our system, on the contrary, virtue will show itself, not as a striving after happiness, that is, well-being and life, but as an effort in quite an opposite direction.

Absolute good is, therefore, a contradiction in terms; highest good, *summum bonum,* really signifies the same thing—a final satisfaction of the will, after which no new desire could arise,—a last motive, the attainment of which would afford enduring satisfaction of the will. But such a consummation is not even thinkable. The will can just as little cease from willing altogether on account of some particular satisfaction, as time can end or begin; for it there is no such thing as a permanent fulfilment which shall completely and for ever satisfy its craving. It is the vessel of the Danaides; for it there is no highest good, no absolute good, but always a merely temporary good. If, however, we wish to give an honorary position, as it were emeritus, to an old expression, which from custom we do not like to discard altogether, we may, metaphorically and figuratively, call the complete self-effacement and denial of the will, the true absence of will, which alone for ever stills and silences its struggle, alone gives that contentment which can never again be disturbed, alone redeems the world, and which we shall now soon consider at the close of our whole investigation—the absolute good, the *summum bonum*—and regard it as the only radical cure of the disease of which all other means are only palliations or anodynes.

If a man is always disposed to do *wrong* whenever the opportunity presents itself, and there is no external power to restrain him, we call him *bad.* According to our doctrine of wrong, this means that such a man does not merely assert the will to live as it appears in his own body, but in this assertion goes so far that he denies the will which appears in other individuals. This is shown by the fact that he desires their powers for the service of his own will, and seeks to destroy their existence when they stand in the way of its efforts. The ultimate source of this is a high degree of egoism, the nature of which has been already explained. Two things are here apparent. In the first place, that in such a man an excessively vehement will to live expresses itself, extending far beyond the assertion of his own body; and, in the second place, that his knowledge, entirely given up to the principle of sufficient reason and involved in the *principium individuationis,* cannot get beyond the difference which this latter principle establishes between his own person and every one else. Therefore he seeks his own well-being alone, completely indifferent to that of all others, whose existence is to him altogether foreign and divided from his own by a wide gulf, and who are indeed regarded by him as mere masks with no reality behind them. And these two qualities are the constituent elements of the bad character.

This great intensity of will is in itself and directly a constant source of suffering. In the first place, because all volition as such arises from want; that is, suffering. (Therefore, as will be remembered, from the Third Book, the momentary cessation of all volition, which takes place whenever we give ourselves up to æsthetic contemplation, as pure will-less subject of knowledge, the correlative of the Idea, is one of the principal elements in our pleasure in the beautiful.) Secondly, because, through the causal connection of things, most of our desires must remain unfulfilled, and the will is oftener crossed than satisfied, and therefore much intense volition carries with it much intense suffering. For all suffering is simply unfulfilled and crossed volition; and even the pain of the body when it is injured or destroyed is as such only possible through the fact that the body is nothing but the will itself become object. Now on this account, because much intense suffering is inseparable from much intense volition, very bad men bear the stamp of inward suffering in the very expression of the countenance; even when they have attained every external happiness, they always look unhappy so long as they are not transported by some momentary ecstasy and are not dissembling. From this inward torment, which is absolutely and directly essential to them, there finally proceeds that delight in the suffering of others which does not spring from mere egoism, but is disinterested, and which constitutes *wickedness* proper, rising to the pitch of *cruelty*. For this the suffering of others is not a means for the attainment of the ends of its own will, but an end in itself. The more definite explanation of this phenomenon is as follows:—Since man is a manifestation of will illuminated by the clearest knowledge, he is always contrasting the actual and felt satisfaction of his will with the merely possible satisfaction of it which knowledge presents to him. Hence arises envy: every privation is infinitely increased by the enjoyment of others, and relieved by the knowledge that others also suffer the same privation. Those ills which are common to all and inseparable from human life trouble us little, just as those which belong to the climate, to the whole country. The recollection of greater sufferings than our own stills our pain; the sight of the sufferings of others soothes our own. If, now, a man is filled with an exceptionally intense pressure of will,—if with burning eagerness he seeks to accumulate everything to slake the thirst of his egoism, and thus experiences, as he inevitably must, that all satisfaction is merely apparent, that the attained end never fulfils the promise of the desired object, the final appeasing of the fierce pressure of will, but that when fulfilled the wish only changes its form, and now torments him in a new one; and indeed that if at last all wishes are exhausted, the pressure of will itself remains without any conscious motive, and makes itself known to him with fearful pain as a feeling of terrible desolation and emptiness; if from all this, which in the case of the ordinary degrees of volition is only felt in a small measure, and only produces the ordinary degree of melancholy, in the case of him who is a manifestation of will reaching the point of extraordinary wickedness, there necessarily springs an excessive inward misery, an eternal unrest, an incurable pain; he seeks indirectly the alleviation which directly is denied him,—seeks to mitigate his own suffering by the sight of the suffering of others, which at the same time he recognises as an expression of his power. The suffering of others now becomes for him an end in itself, and is a spectacle in which he delights; and thus arises the phenomenon of pure cruelty, blood-thirstiness, which history exhibits so often in the Neros and Domitians, in the African Deis, in Robespierre, and the like.

Suicide, the actual doing away with the individual manifestation of will, differs most widely from the denial of the will to live, which is the single outstanding act of free will in the manifestation, and is therefore, as Asmus calls it, the transcendental change. This last has been fully considered in the course of our work. Far from being denial of the will, suicide is a phenomenon of strong assertion of will; for the essence of negation lies in this, that the joys of life are shunned, not its sorrows. The suicide wills life, and is only dissatisfied with the conditions under which it has presented itself to him. He therefore by no means surrenders the will to live, but only life, in that he destroys the individual manifestation. He wills life—wills the unrestricted existence and assertion of the body; but the complication of circumstances does not allow this, and there results for him great suffering. The very will to live finds itself so much hampered in this particular manifestation that it cannot put forth its energies. It therefore comes to such a determination as is in conformity with its own nature, which lies outside the conditions of the principle of sufficient reason, and to which, therefore, all particular manifestations are alike indifferent, inasmuch as it itself remains unaffected by all appearing and passing away, and is the inner life of all things; for that firm inward assurance by reason of which we all live free from the constant dread of death, the assurance that a phenomenal existence can never be wanting to the will, supports our action even in the case of suicide. Thus the will to live appears just as much in suicide as in the satisfaction of self-preservation and in the sensual pleasure of procreation. This is the inner meaning of the unity of the Trimurti, which is embodied in its entirety in every human being, though in time it raises now one, now another, of its three heads. Suicide stands in the same relation to the denial of the will as the individual thing does to the Idea. The suicide denies only the individual, not the species. We have already seen that as life is always assured to the will to live, and as sorrow is inseparable from life, suicide, the wilful destruction of the single phenomenal existence, is a vain and foolish act; for the thing-in-itself remains unaffected by it, even as the rainbow endures however fast the drops which support it for the moment may change. But, more than this, it is also the masterpiece of Mâyâ, as the most flagrant example of the contradiction of the will to live with itself. As we found this contradiction in the case of the lowest manifestations of will, in the permanent struggle of all the forces of nature, and of all organic individuals for matter and time and space; and as we saw this antagonism come ever more to the front with terrible distinctness in the ascending grades of the objectification of the will, so at last in the highest grade, the Idea of man, it reaches the point at which, not only the individuals which express the same Idea extirpate each other, but even the same individual declares war against itself. The vehemence with which it wills life, and revolts against what hinders it, namely, suffering, brings it to the point of destroying itself; so that the individual will, by its own act, puts an end to that body which is merely its particular visible expression, rather than permit suffering to break the will. Just because the suicide cannot give up willing, he gives up living. The will asserts itself here even in putting an end to its own manifestation, because it can no longer assert itself otherwise. As, however, it was just the suffering which it so shuns that was able, as mortification of the will, to bring it to the denial of itself, and hence to freedom, so in this respect the suicide is like a sick man, who, after a painful operation which would entirely cure him has been begun, will not allow it to be completed, but prefers to retain his disease. Suffering approaches and reveals itself as the possibility of the denial of will; but the will rejects it, in that it destroys the body, the manifestation of itself, in order that it may remain unbroken. This is the reason why almost all ethical teachers, whether philosophical or religious, condemn suicide, although they themselves can only give far-fetched sophistical reasons for their opinion. But if a human being was ever restrained from committing suicide by purely moral motives, the inmost meaning of this self-conquest (in whatever ideas his reason may have clothed it) was this: "I will not shun suffering, in order that it may help to put an end to the will to live, whose manifestation is so wretched, by so strengthening the knowledge of the real nature of the world which is already beginning to dawn upon me, that it may become the final quieter of my will, and may free me for ever."

I now end the general account of ethics, and with it the whole development of that one thought which it has been my object to impart; and I by no means desire to conceal here an objection which concerns this last part of my exposition, but rather to point out that it lies in the nature of the question, and that it is quite impossible to remove it. It is this, that after our investigation has brought us to the point at which we have before our eyes perfect holiness, the denial and surrender of all volition, and thus the deliverance from a world whose whole existence we have found to be suffering, this appears to us as a passing away into empty nothingness.

That which is generally received as positive, which we call the real, and the negation of which the concept nothing in its most general significance expresses, is just the world as idea, which I have shown to be the objectivity and mirror of the will. Moreover, we ourselves are just this will and this world, and to them belongs the idea in general, as one aspect of them. The form of the idea is space and time, therefore for this point of view all that is real must be in some place and at some time. Denial, abolition, conversion of the will, is also the abolition and the vanishing of the world, its mirror. If we no longer perceive it in this mirror, we ask in vain where it has gone, and then, because it has no longer any where and when, complain that it has vanished into nothing.

A reversed point of view, if it were possible for us, would reverse the signs and show the real for us as nothing, and that nothing as the real. But as long as we ourselves are the will to live, this last—nothing as the real—can only be known and signified by us negatively, because the old saying of Empedocles, that like can only be known by like, deprives us here of all knowledge, as, conversely, upon it finally rests the possibility of all our actual knowledge, i.e., the world as idea; for the world is the self-knowledge of the will.

If, however, it should be absolutely insisted upon that in some way or other a positive knowledge should be attained of that which philosophy can only express negatively as the denial of the will, there would be nothing for it but to refer to that state which all those who have attained to complete denial of the will have experienced, and which has been variously denoted by the names ecstasy, rapture, illumination, union with God, and so forth; a state, however, which cannot properly be called knowledge, because it has not the form of subject and object, and is, moreover, only attainable in one's own experience and cannot be further communicated.

We, however, who consistently occupy the standpoint of philosophy, must be satisfied here with negative knowledge, content to have reached the utmost limit of the positive. We have recognised the inmost nature of the world as will, and all its phenomena as only the objectivity of will; and we have followed this objectivity from the unconscious working of obscure forces of Nature up to the completely conscious action of man. Therefore we shall by no means evade the consequence, that with the free denial, the surrender of the will, all those phenomena are also abolished; that constant strain and effort without end and without rest at all the grades of objectivity, in which and through which the world consists; the multifarious forms succeeding each other in gradation; the whole manifestation of the will; and, finally, also the universal forms of this manifestation, time and space, and also its last fundamental form, subject and object; all are abolished. No will: no idea, no world.

Before us there is certainly only nothingness. But that which resists this passing into nothing, our nature, is indeed just the will to live, which we ourselves are as it is our world. That we abhor annihilation so greatly, is simply another expression of the fact that we so strenuously will life, and are nothing but this will, and know nothing besides it. But if we turn our glance from our own needy and embarrassed condition to those who have overcome the world, in whom the will, having attained to perfect self-knowledge, found itself again in all, and then freely denied itself, and who then merely wait to see the last trace of it vanish with the body which it animates; then, instead of the restless striving and effort, instead of the constant transition from wish to fruition, and from joy to sorrow, instead of the never-satisfied and never-dying hope which constitutes the life of the man who wills, we shall see that peace which is above all reason, that perfect calm of the spirit, that deep rest, that inviolable confidence and serenity, the mere reflection of which in the countenance, as Raphael and Correggio have represented it, is an entire and certain gospel; only knowledge remains, the will has vanished. We look with deep and painful longing upon this state, beside which the misery and wretchedness of our own is brought out clearly by the contrast. Yet this is the only consideration which can afford us lasting consolation, when, on the one hand, we have recognised incurable suffering and endless misery as essential to the manifestation of will, the world; and, on the other hand, see the world pass away with the abolition of will, and retain before us only empty nothingness. Thus, in this way, by contemplation of the life and conduct of saints, whom it is certainly rarely granted us to meet with in our own experience, but who are brought before our eyes by their written history, and, with the stamp of inner truth, by art, we must banish the dark impression of that nothingness which we discern behind all virtue and holiness as their final goal, and which we fear as children fear the dark; we must not even evade it like the Indians, through myths and meaningless words, such as reabsorption in Brahma or the Nirvana of the Buddhists. Rather do we freely acknowledge that what remains after the entire abolition of will is for all those who are still full of will certainly nothing; but, conversely, to those in whom the will has turned and has denied itself, this our world, which is so real, with all its suns and milky-ways—is nothing.

Part II: Selections

I. ON MAN'S NEED OF METAPHYSICS

WITH the exception of man, no being wonders at its own existence; but it is to them all so much a matter of course that they do not observe it. The wisdom of nature speaks out of the peaceful glance of the brutes; for in them the will and the intellect are not yet so widely separated that they can be astonished at each other when they meet again. Thus here the whole phenomenon is still firmly attached to the stem of nature from which it has come, and is partaker of the unconscious omniscience of the great mother. Only after the inner being of nature (the will to live in its objectification) has ascended, vigorous and cheerful, through the two series of unconscious existences, and then through the long and broad series of animals, does it attain at last to reflection for the first time on the entrance of reason, thus in man. Then it marvels at its own works, and asks itself what it itself is. Its wonder however is the more serious, as it here stands for the first time consciously in the presence of *death*, and besides the finiteness of all existence, the vanity of all effort forces itself more or less upon it. With this reflection and this wonder there arises therefore in man alone, the need *for a metaphysic;* he is accordingly an *animal metaphysicum.* At the beginning of his consciousness certainly he also accepts himself as a matter of course. This does not last long however, but very early, with the first dawn of reflection, that wonder already appears, which is some day to become the mother of metaphysics. The lower a man stands in an intellectual regard the less of a problem is existence itself for him; everything, how it is, and that it is, appears to him rather a matter of course. This rests upon the fact that his intellect still remains perfectly true to its original destiny of being serviceable to the will as the medium of motives, and therefore is closely bound up with the world and nature, as an integral part of them. Consequently it is very far from comprehending the world in a purely objective manner, freeing itself, so to speak, from the whole of things, opposing itself to this whole, and so for a while becoming as if self-existent. On the other hand, the philosophical wonder which springs from this is conditioned in the individual by higher development of the intellect, yet in general not by this alone; but without doubt it is the knowledge of death, and along with this the consideration of the suffering and misery of life, which gives the strongest impulse to philosophical reflection and metaphysical explanation of the world. If our life were endless and painless, it would perhaps occur to no one to ask why the world exists, and is just the kind of world it is; but everything would just be taken as a matter of course.

Temples and churches, pagodas and mosques, in all lands and in all ages, in splendour and vastness, testify to the metaphysical need of man, which, strong and ineradicable, follows close upon his physical need. Certainly whoever is satirically inclined might add that this metaphysical need is a modest fellow who is content with poor fare. It sometimes allows itself to be satisfied with clumsy fables and insipid tales. If only imprinted early enough, they are for a man adequate explanations of his existence and supports of his morality.

On the other hand, there have never been wanting persons who were interested in deriving their living from that metaphysical need, and in making the utmost they could out of it. Therefore among all nations there are monopolists and farmers-general of it—the priests. Yet their trade had everywhere to be assured to them in this way, that they received the right to impart their metaphysical dogmas to men at a very early age, before the judgment has awakened from its morning slumber, thus in early childhood; for then every well-impressed dogma, however senseless it may be, remains for ever. If they had to wait till the judgment is ripe, their privileges could not continue.

A second, though not a numerous class of persons, who derive their support from the metaphysical need of man, is constituted by those who live by *philosophy*. By the Greeks they were called Sophists, by the moderns they are called Professors of Philosophy.

By *metaphysics* I understand all knowledge that pretends to transcend the possibility of experience, thus to transcend nature or the given phenomenal appearance of things, in order to give an explanation of that by which, in some sense or other, this experience or nature is conditioned; or, to speak in popular language, of that which is behind nature, and makes it possible. But the great original diversity in the power of understanding, besides the cultivation of it, which demands much leisure, makes so great a difference between men, that as soon as a people has emerged from the state of savages, no *one* metaphysic can serve for them all. Therefore among civilised nations we find throughout two different kinds of metaphysics, which are distinguished by the fact that the one has its evidence *in itself,* the other *outside itself.* Since the metaphysical systems of the first kind require reflection, culture, and leisure for the recognition of their evidence, they can be accessible only to a very small number of men; and, moreover, they can only arise and maintain their existence in the case of advanced civilisation. On the other hand, the systems of the second kind exclusively are for the great majority of men who are not capable of thinking, but only of believing, and who are not accessible to reasons, but only to authority. These systems may therefore be called metaphysics of the people, after the analogy of poetry of the people, and also wisdom of the people, by which is understood proverbs.

To the distinction established above between metaphysics of the first and of the second kind, we have yet to add the following:—A system of the first kind, thus a philosophy, makes the claim, and has therefore the obligation, in everything that it says, *sensu stricto et proprio,* to be true, for it appeals to thought and conviction. A religion, on the other hand, being intended for the innumerable multitude who, since they are incapable of examination and thought, would never comprehend the profoundest and most difficult truths *sensu proprio,* has only the obligation to be true *sensu allegorico.* Truth cannot appear naked before the people. A symptom of this *allegorical* nature of religions is the *mysteries* which are to be found perhaps in them all, certain dogmas which cannot even be distinctly thought, not to speak of being literally true.

It would be most beneficial to both kinds of metaphysics that each of them should remain clearly separated from the other and confine itself to its own province, that it may there be able to develop its nature fully. Instead of which, through the whole Christian era, the endeavour has been to bring about a fusion of the two, for the dogmas and conceptions of the one have been carried over into the other, whereby both are spoiled. This has taken place in the most open manner in our own day in that strange hermaphrodite or centaur, the so-called philosophy of religion, which, as a kind of gnosis, endeavours to interpret the given religion, and to explain what is true *sensu allegorico* through something which is true *sensu proprio.* But for this we would have to know and possess the truth *sensu proprio* already; and in that case such an interpretation would be superfluous.

Religions, being calculated with reference to the power of comprehension of the great mass of men, can only have indirect, not immediate truth. To require of them the latter is as if one wished to read the letters set up in the form-chase, instead of their impression. The value of a religion will accordingly depend upon the greater or less content of truth which it contains under the veil of allegory, and then upon the greater or less distinctness with which it becomes visible through this veil, thus upon the transparency of the latter. It almost seems that, as the oldest languages are the most perfect, so also are the oldest religions. If I were to take the results of my philosophy as the standard of truth, I would be obliged to concede to Buddhism the pre-eminence over the rest. In any case it must be a satisfaction to me to see my teaching in such close agreement with a religion which the majority of men upon the earth hold as their own; for it numbers far more adherents than any other.

I cannot place, as is always done, the fundamental difference of all religions in the questions whether they are monotheistic, polytheistic, pantheistic, or atheistic, but only in the question whether they are optimistic or pessimistic, that is, whether they present the existence of the world as justified by itself, and therefore praise and value it, or regard it as something that can only be conceived as the consequence of our guilt, and therefore properly ought not to be, because they recognise that pain and death cannot lie in the eternal, original, and immutable order of things, in that which in every respect ought to be. The power by virtue of which Christianity was able to overcome first Judaism, and then the heathenism of Greece and Rome, lies solely in its pessimism, in the confession that our state is both exceedingly wretched and sinful, while Judaism and heathenism were optimistic. That truth, profoundly and painfully felt by all, penetrated, and bore in its train the need of redemption.

I turn to a general consideration of the other kind of metaphysics, that which has its authentication in itself, and is called *philosophy*. I remind the reader of its origin, mentioned above, in a *wonder* concerning the world and our own existence, inasmuch as these press upon the intellect as a riddle, the solution of which therefore occupies mankind without intermission.

Only to the brutes, who are without thought, does the world and existence appear as a matter of course; to man, on the contrary, it is a problem, of which even the most uneducated and narrow-minded becomes vividly conscious in certain brighter moments, but which enters more distinctly and more permanently into the consciousness of each one of us the clearer and more enlightened that consciousness is, and the more material for thought it has acquired through culture, which all ultimately rises, in minds that are naturally adapted for philosophising, to Plato's *wonder* which comprehends in its whole magnitude that problem which unceasingly occupies the nobler portion of mankind in every age and in every land, and gives it no rest. In fact, the pendulum which keeps in motion the clock of metaphysics, that never runs down, is the consciousness that the non-existence of this world is just as possible as its existence.

We find *physics* also (in the widest sense of the word) occupied with the explanation of the phenomena in the world. But it lies in the very nature of its explanations themselves that they cannot be sufficient. Physics cannot stand on its own feet, but requires a metaphysic to lean upon, whatever airs it may give itself towards the latter. For it explains the phenomena by something still more unknown than they are themselves; by laws of nature, resting upon forces of nature, to which the power of life also belongs. Certainly the whole present condition of all things in the world, or in nature, must necessarily be explicable from purely physical causes.

With naturalism, then, or the purely physical way of looking at things, we shall never attain our end; it is like a sum that never comes out. Causal series without beginning or end, fundamental forces which are inscrutable, endless space, beginningless time, infinite divisibility of matter, and all this further conditioned by a knowing brain, in which alone it exists just like a dream, and without which it vanishes—constitute the labyrinth in which naturalism leads us ceaselessly round. The height to which in our time the natural sciences have risen in this respect entirely throws into the shade all previous centuries, and is a summit which mankind reaches for the first time. But however great are the advances which *physics* (understood in the wide sense of the ancients) may make, not the smallest step towards *metaphysics* is thereby taken, just as a plane can never obtain cubical content by being indefinitely extended. For all such advances will only perfect our knowledge of the *phenomenon;* while *metaphysics* strives to pass beyond the phenomenal appearance itself, to that which so appears. And if indeed it had the assistance of an entire and complete experience, it would, as regards the main point, be in no way advantaged by it. Nay, even if one wandered through all the planets and fixed stars, one would thereby have made no step in *metaphysics.* It is rather the case that the greatest advances of physics will make the need of metaphysics ever more felt; for it is just the corrected, extended, and more thorough knowledge of nature which, on the one hand, always undermines and ultimately over-throws the metaphysical assumptions which till then have prevailed, but, on the other hand, presents the problem of metaphysics itself more distinctly, more correctly, and more fully, and separates it more clearly from all that is merely physical; moreover, the more perfectly and accurately known nature of the particular thing more pressingly demands the explanation of the whole and the general, which, the more correctly, thoroughly, and completely it is known empirically, only presents itself as the more mysterious.

The origin of metaphysics in empirical sources of knowledge, which is here set forth, and which cannot fairly be denied, deprives it certainly of that kind of apodictic certainty which is only possible through knowledge *a priori.* This remains the possession of logic and mathematics—sciences, however, which really only teach what every one knows already, though not distinctly. At most the primary elements of natural science may also be deduced from knowledge *a priori.* By this confession metaphysics only surrenders an ancient claim, which, according to what has been said above, rested upon misunderstanding, and against which the great diversity and changeableness of metaphysical systems, and also the constantly accompanying scepticism, in every age has testified. Yet against the possibility of metaphysics in general this changeableness cannot be urged, for the same thing effects just as much all branches of natural science, chemistry, physics, geology, zoology, &c., and even history has not remained exempt from it. But when once, as far as the limits of human intellect allow, a true system of metaphysics shall have been found, the unchangeableness of a science which is known *a priori* will yet belong to it; for its foundation can only be *experience in general,* and not the particular and special experiences by which, on the other hand, the natural sciences are constantly modified and new material is always being provided for history. For experience as a whole and in general will never change its character for a new one.

If, as so often happens, metaphysics is reproached with having made so little progress, it ought also to be considered that no other science has grown up like it under constant oppression, none has been so hampered and hindered from without as it has always been by the religion of every land, which, everywhere in possession of a monopoly of metaphysical knowledge, regards metaphysics as a weed growing beside it, as an unlicensed worker, as a horde of gipsies, and as a rule tolerates it only under the condition that it accommodates itself to serve and follow it. For where has there ever been true freedom of thought? It has been vaunted sufficiently; but whenever it wishes to go further than perhaps to differ about the subordinate dogmas of the religion of the country, a holy shudder seizes the prophets of tolerance, and they say: "Not a step further!" What progress of metaphysics was possible under such oppression? Nay, this constraint which the privileged metaphysics exercises is not confined to the *communication* of thoughts, but extends to *thinking* itself, for its dogmas are so firmly imprinted in the tender, plastic, trustful, and thoughtless age of childhood, with studied solemnity and serious airs, that from that time forward they grow with the brain, and almost assume the nature of innate thoughts, which some philosophers have therefore really held them to be, and still more have pretended to do so. Yet nothing can so firmly resist the comprehension of even the *problem* of metaphysics as a previous solution of it intruded upon and early implanted in the mind. For the necessary starting-point for all genuine philosophy is the deep feeling of the Socratic: "This one thing I know, that I know nothing."

Whenever metaphysics is reproached with its small progress, and with not having yet reached its goal in spite of such sustained efforts, one ought further to consider that in the meanwhile it has constantly performed the invaluable service of limiting the boundless claims of the privileged metaphysics, and yet at the same time combatting naturalism and materialism proper, which are called forth by it as an inevitable reaction. Consider to what a pitch the arrogance of the priesthood of every religion would rise if the belief in their doctrines was as firm and blind as they really wish. Look back also at the wars, disturbances, rebellions, and revolutions in Europe from the eighth to the eighteenth century; how few will be found that have not had as their essence, or their pretext, some controversy about beliefs, thus a metaphysical problem, which became the occasion of exciting nations against each other. Yet is that whole thousand years a continual slaughter, now on the battlefield, now on the scaffold, now in the streets, in metaphysical interests! I wish I had an authentic list of all crimes which Christianity has really prevented, and all good deeds it has really performed, that I might be able to place them in the other scale of the balance.

Lastly, as regards the *obligations* of metaphysics, it has only one; for it is one which endures no other beside it—the obligation to be *true.* If one would impose other obligations upon it besides this, such as to be spiritualistic, optimistic, monotheistic, or even only to be moral, one cannot know beforehand whether this would not interfere with the fulfilment of that first obligation, without which all its other achievements must clearly be worthless. A given philosophy has accordingly no other standard of its value than that of truth. For the rest, philosophy is essentially *world-wisdom:* its problem is the world. It has to do with this alone, and leaves the gods in peace—expects, however, in return, to be left in peace by them.

II. ON THE POSSIBILITY OF KNOWING THE THING IN ITSELF

I WISH NOW first of all to make a few preliminary observations from a general point of view as to the sense in which we can speak of a knowledge of the thing in itself and of its necessary limitation.

What is *knowledge?* It is primarily and essentially *idea.* What is *Idea?* A very complicated *physiological* process in the brain of an animal, the result of which is the consciousness of a *picture* there. Clearly the relation between such a picture and something entirely different from the animal in whose brain it exists can only be a very indirect one. This is perhaps the simplest and most comprehensible way of disclosing the *deep gulf between the ideal and the real.* This belongs to the things of which, like the motion of the earth, we are not directly conscious; therefore the ancients did not observe it, just as they did not observe the motion of the earth. Once pointed out, on the other hand, first by Descartes, it has ever since given philosophers no rest. But after Kant had at last proved in the most thorough manner the complete diversity of the ideal and the real, it was an attempt, as bold as it was absurd, yet perfectly correctly calculated with reference to the philosophical public in Germany, and consequently crowned with brilliant results, to try to assert the *absolute identity* of the two by dogmatic utterances, on the strength of a pretended intellectual intuition. In truth, on the contrary, a subjective and an objective existence, a being for self and a being for others, a consciousness of one's own self, and a consciousness of other things, is given us directly, and the two are given in such a fundamentally different manner that no other difference can compare with this. About himself every one knows directly, about all others only very indirectly. This is the fact and the problem.

Whether, on the other hand, through further processes in the interior of a brain, general conceptions are abstracted from the perceptible ideas or images that have arisen within it, for the assistance of further combinations, whereby knowledge becomes *rational,* and is now called *thinking*—this is here no longer the essential question, but is of subordinate significance. For all such *conceptions* receive their content only from the perceptible idea, which is therefore *primary knowledge,* and has consequently alone to be taken account of in an investigation of the relation between the ideal and the real. It therefore shows entire ignorance of the problem, or at least it is very inept, to wish to define that relation as that between *being* and *thinking.* Thinking has primarily only a relation to *perceiving,* but *perception* has a relation to the *real being* of what is perceived, and this last is the great problem with which we are here concerned. Empirical being, on the other hand, as it lies before us, is nothing else than simply being given in perception; but the relation of the latter to *thinking* is no riddle, for the conceptions, thus the immediate materials of thought, are obviously *abstracted* from perception, which no reasonable man can doubt. It may be said in passing that one can see how important the choice of expressions in philosophy is from the fact that that inept expression condemned above, and the misunderstanding which arose from it, became the foundation of the whole Hegelian pseudo-philosophy, which has occupied the German public for twenty-five years.

If, however, it should be said: "The perception is itself the knowledge of the thing in itself: for it is the effect of that which is outside of us, and as this *acts,* so it *is:* its action is just its being;" to this we reply: (1.) that the law of causality, as has been sufficiently proved, is of subjective origin, as well as the sensation from which the perception arises; (2.) that at any rate time and space, in which the object presents itself, are of subjective origin; (3.) that if the being of the object consists simply in its action, this means that it consists merely in the changes which it brings about in others; therefore itself and in itself it is nothing at all. Only of *matter* is it true, that its being consists in its action, that it is through and through only causality, thus is itself causality objectively regarded; hence, however, it is also nothing in itself, but as an ingredient in the perceived object, is a mere abstraction, which for itself alone can be given in no experience. The perceived object must be something *in itself;* not merely something *for others.* For otherwise it would be altogether merely idea, and we would have an absolute idealism, which would ultimately become theoretical egoism, with which all reality disappears and the world becomes a mere subjective phantasm. If, however, without further question, we stop altogether at the *world as idea,* then certainly it is all one whether I explain objects as ideas in my head or as phenomena exhibiting themselves in time and space; for time and space themselves exist only in my head. In this sense, then, an identity of the ideal and the real might always be affirmed; only, after Kant, this would not be saying anything new. Besides this, however, the nature of things and of the phenomenal world would clearly not be thereby exhausted; but with it we would always remain still upon the ideal side. The *real* side must be something *toto genere* different from *the world as idea,* it must be that which things are *in themselves;* and it is this entire diversity between the ideal and the real which Kant has proved in the most thorough manner.

Locke had denied to the senses the knowledge of things as they are in themselves; but Kant denied this also to the perceiving *understanding,* under which name I here comprehend what he calls the *pure* sensibility, and, as it is given *a priori,* the law of causality which brings about the empirical perception. Not only are both right, but we can also see quite directly that a contradiction lies in the assertion that a thing is known as it is in and for itself, i.e., outside of knowledge. For all knowing is, as we have said, essentially a perceiving of ideas; but my perception of ideas, just because it is mine, can never be identical with the inner nature of the thing outside of me. The being in and for itself, of everything, must necessarily be *subjective;* in the idea of another, however, it exists just as necessarily as *objective*—a difference which can never be fully reconciled. For by it the whole nature of its existence is fundamentally changed; as objective it presupposes a foreign subject, as whose idea it exists, and, moreover, as Kant has shown, has entered forms which are foreign to its own nature, just because they belong to that foreign subject, whose knowledge is only possible by means of them. If I, absorbed in this reflection, perceive, let us say lifeless bodies, of easily surveyed magnitude and regular, comprehensible form, and now attempt to conceive this spatial existence, in its three dimensions, as their being in itself, consequently as the existence which to the things is subjective, the impossibility of the thing is at once apparent to me, for I can never think those objective forms as the being which to the things is subjective, rather I become directly conscious that what I there perceive is only a picture produced in my brain, and existing only for me as the knowing subject, which cannot constitute the ultimate, and therefore subjective, being in and for itself of even these lifeless bodies. But, on the other hand, I must not assume that even these lifeless bodies exist only in my idea, but, since they have inscrutable qualities, and, by virtue of these, activity, I must concede to them a *being in itself* of some kind. But this very inscrutableness of the properties, while, on the one hand, it certainly points to something which exists independently of our knowledge, gives also, on the other hand, the empirical proof that our knowledge, because it consists simply in *framing ideas* by means of subjective forms, affords us always mere *phenomena,* not the true being of things. This is the explanation of the fact that in all that we know there remains hidden from us a certain something, as quite inscrutable, and we are obliged to confess that we cannot thoroughly understand even the commonest and simplest phenomena. For it is not merely the highest productions of nature, living creatures, or the *complicated* phenomena of the unorganised world that remain inscrutable to us, but even every rock-crystal, every iron-pyrite, by reason of its crystallographical, optical, chemical, and electrical properties, is to the searching consideration and investigation an abyss of incomprehensibilities and mysteries. This could not be the case if we knew things as they are in themselves; for then at least the simpler phenomena, the path to whose qualities was not barred for us by ignorance, would necessarily be thoroughly comprehensible to us, and their whole being and nature would be able to pass over into our knowledge. Thus it lies not in the defectiveness of our acquaintance with things, but in the nature of knowledge itself. For if our perception, and consequently the whole empirical comprehension of the things that present themselves to us, is already essentially and in the main determined by our faculty of knowledge, and conditioned by its forms and functions, it cannot but be that things exhibit themselves in a manner which is quite different from their own inner nature, and therefore appear as in a mask, which allows us merely to assume what is concealed beneath it, but never to know it; hence, then, it gleams through as an inscrutable mystery, and never can the nature of anything entire and without reserve pass over into knowledge; but much less can any real thing be construed *a priori,* like a mathematical problem. Thus the empirical inscrutableness of all natural things is a proof *a posteriori* of the ideality and merely phenomenal-actuality of their empirical existence.

According to all this, upon the path of *objective knowledge,* hence starting from the *idea,* one will never get beyond the idea, i.e., the phenomenon. One will thus remain at the outside of things, and will never be able to penetrate to their inner nature and investigate what they are in themselves, i.e., for themselves. So far I agree with Kant. But, as the counterpart of this truth, I have given prominence to this other truth, that we are not merely the *knowing subject,* but, in another aspect, we ourselves also belong to the inner nature that is to be known, *we ourselves are the thing in itself;* that therefore a *way from within* stands open for us to that inner nature belonging to things themselves, to which we cannot penetrate *from without,* as it were a subterranean passage, a secret alliance, which, as if by treachery, places us at once within the fortress which it was impossible to take by assault from without. The thing in itself can, as such, only come into consciousness quite directly, in this way, that *it is itself conscious of itself;* to wish to know it objectively is to desire something contradictory. Everything objective is idea, therefore appearance, mere phenomenon of the brain.

Kant's chief result may in substance be thus concisely stated: "All conceptions which have not at their foundation a perception in space and time (sensuous intuition) that is to say then, which have not been drawn from such a perception, are absolutely empty, i.e., give no knowledge. But since now perception can afford us only *phenomena,* not things in themselves, we have also absolutely no knowledge of things in themselves." I grant this of everything, with the single exception of the knowledge which each of us has of his own *willing:* this is neither a perception (for all perception is spatial) nor is it empty; rather it is more real than any other. Further, it is not *a priori,* like merely formal knowledge, but entirely *a posteriori;* hence also we cannot anticipate it in the particular case, but are hereby often convicted of error concerning ourselves. In fact, our *willing* is the one opportunity which we have of understanding from within any event which exhibits itself without, consequently the one thing which is known to us *immediately,* and not, like all the rest, merely given in the idea. Here, then, lies the datum which alone is able to become the key to everything else, or, as I have said, the single narrow door to the truth. Accordingly we must learn to understand nature from ourselves, not conversely ourselves from nature. What is known to us immediately must give us the explanation of what we only know indirectly, not conversely. Do we perhaps understand the rolling of a ball when it has received an impulse more thoroughly than our movement when we feel a motive? Many may imagine so, but I say it is the reverse. Yet we shall attain to the knowledge that what is essential in both the occurrences just mentioned is identical; although identical in the same way as the lowest audible note of harmony is the same as the note of the same name ten octaves higher.

Meanwhile it should be carefully observed, and I have always kept it in mind, that even the inward experience which we have of our own will by no means affords us an exhaustive and adequate knowledge of the thing in itself. This would be thé case if it were entirely an immediate experience; but it is effected in this way: the will, with and by means of the corporisation, provides itself also with an intellect (for the sake of its relations to the external world), and through this now knows itself as will in self-consciousness (the necessary counterpart of the external world); this knowledge therefore of the thing in itself is not fully adequate. First of all, it is bound to the form of the idea, it is apprehension, and as such falls asunder into subject and object. For even in self-consciousness the I is not absolutely simple, but consists of a knower, the intellect, and a known, the will. The former is not known, and the latter does not know, though both unite in the consciousness of an I. But just on this account that I is not thoroughly *intimate* with itself, as it were transparent, but is opaque, and therefore remains a riddle to itself, thus even in inner knowledge there also exists a difference between the true being of its object and the apprehension of it in the knowing subject. Yet inner knowledge is free from two forms which belong to outer knowledge, the form of *space* and the form of *causality,* which is the means of effecting all sense-perception. On the other hand, there still remains the form of *time,* and that of being known and knowing in general. Accordingly in this inner knowledge the thing in itself has indeed in great measure thrown off its veil, but still does not yet appear quite naked. In consequence of the form of time which still adheres to it, every one knows his will only in its successive *acts,* and not as a whole, in and for itself: therefore no one knows his character *a priori,* but only learns it through experience and always incompletely. But yet the apprehension, in which we know the affections and acts of our own will, is far more immediate than any other. It is the point at which the thing in itself most directly enters the phenomenon and is most closely examined by the knowing subject; therefore the event thus intimately known is alone fitted to become the interpreter of all others.

For in every emergence of an act of will from the obscure depths of our inner being into the knowing consciousness a direct transition occurs of the thing in itself, which lies outside time, into the phenomenal world. Accordingly the act of will is indeed only the closest and most distinct *manifestation* of the thing in itself; yet it follows from this that if all other manifestations or phenomena could be known by us as directly and inwardly, we would be obliged to assert them to be that which the will is in us. Thus in this sense I teach that the inner nature of everything is *will,* and I call will the thing in itself. Kant's doctrine of the unknowableness of the thing in itself is hereby modified to this extent, that the thing in itself is only not absolutely and from the very foundation knowable, that yet by far the most immediate of its phenomena, which by this immediateness is *toto genere* distinguished from all the rest, represents it for us; and accordingly we have to refer the whole world of phenomena to that one in which the thing in itself appears in the very thinnest of veils, and only still remains phenomenon in so far as my intellect, which alone is capable of knowledge, remains ever distinguished from me as the willing subject, and moreover does not even in *inner* perfection put off the form of knowledge of *time*.

Accordingly, even after this last and furthest step, the question may still be raised, what that will, which exhibits itself in the world and as the world, ultimately and absolutely is in itself? i.e., what it is, regarded altogether apart from the fact that it exhibits itself as will, or in general *appears,* i.e., in general is *known*. This question can never be answered: because, as we have said, becoming known is itself the contradictory of being in itself, and everything that is known is as such only phenomenal. But the possibility of this question shows that the thing in itself, which we know most directly in the will, may have, entirely outside all possible phenomenal appearance, ways of existing, determinations, qualities, which are absolutely unknowable and incomprehensible to us, and which remain as the nature of the thing in itself, when, as is explained in the Fourth Book, it has voluntarily abrogated itself as *will,* and has therefore retired altogether from the phenomenon, and for our knowledge, i.e., as regards the world of phenomena, has passed into empty nothingness. If the will were simply and absolutely the thing in itself this nothing would also be *absolute,* instead of which it expressly presents itself to us there as only *relative*.

I now proceed to supplement with a few considerations pertinent to the subject the exposition given both in our Second Book and in the work *On the Will in Nature,* of the doctrine that what makes itself known to us in the most immediate knowledge as will is also that which objectifies itself at different grades in all the phenomena of this world; and I shall begin by citing a number of psychological facts which prove that first of all in our own consciousness the will always appears as primary and fundamental, and throughout asserts its superiority to the intellect, which, on the other hand, always presents itself as secondary, subordinate and conditioned. This proof is the more necessary as all philosophers before me, from the first to the last, place the true being or the kernel of man in the *knowing* consciousness, and accordingly have conceived and explained the I, or, in the case of many of them, its transcendental hypostasis called soul, as primarily and essentially *knowing,* nay, *thinking,* and only in consequence of this, secondarily and derivatively, as *willing*. This ancient and universal radical error must before everything be set aside, and instead of it the true state of the case must be brought to perfectly distinct consciousness. Since, however, this is done here for the first time, after thousands of years of philosophising, some fulness of statement will be appropriate. The remarkable phenomenon, that in this most essential point all philosophers have erred, nay, have exactly reversed the truth, might, especially in the case of those of the Christian era, be partly explicable from the fact that they all had the intention of presenting man as distinguished as widely as possible from the brutes, yet at the same time obscurely felt that the difference between them lies in the intellect, not in the will; whence there arose unconsciously within them an inclination to make the intellect the essential and principal thing, and even to explain volition as a mere function of the intellect. Hence also the conception of a soul is not only inadmissible, because it is a transcendent hypostasis, as is proved by the *Critique of Pure Reason,* but it becomes the source of irremediable errors, because in its "simple substance" it establishes beforehand an indivisible unity of knowledge and will, the separation of which is just the path to the truth. That conception must therefore appear no more in philosophy, but may be left to German doctors and physiologists, who, after they have laid aside scalpel and spattle, amuse themselves by philosophising with the conceptions they received when they were confirmed. They might certainly try their luck in England. The French physiologists and zootomists have (till lately) kept themselves free from that reproach.

The first consequence of their common fundamental error, which is very inconvenient to all these philosophers, is this: since in death the knowing consciousness obviously perishes, they must either allow death to be the annihilation of the man, to which our inner being is opposed, or they must have recourse to the assumption of a continued existence of the knowing consciousness, which requires a strong faith, for his own experience has sufficiently proved to every one the thorough and complete dependence of the knowing consciousness upon the brain, and one can just as easily believe in digestion without a stomach as in a knowing consciousness without a brain. My philosophy alone leads out of this dilemma, for it for the first time places the true being of man not in the consciousness but in the will, which is not essentially bound up with consciousness, but is related to consciousness, i.e., to knowledge, as substance to accident, as something illuminated to the light, as the string to the resounding-board, and which enters consciousness from within as the corporeal world does from without. Now we can comprehend the indestructibleness of this our real kernel and true being, in spite of the evident ceasing of consciousness in death, and the corresponding non-existence of it before birth. For the intellect is as perishable as the brain, whose product or rather whose action it is. But the brain, like the whole organism, is the product or phenomenon, in short, the subordinate of the will, which alone is imperishable.

III. THE METAPHYSICS OF THE LOVE OF THE SEXES

WE ARE ACCUSTOMED to see poets principally occupied with describing the love of the sexes. This is as a rule the chief theme of all dramatic works, tragical as well as comical, romantic as well as classical, Indian as well as European. Not less is it the material of by far the largest part of lyrical and also of epic poetry, especially if we class with the latter the enormous piles of romances which for centuries every year has produced in all the civilised countries of Europe as regularly as the fruits of the earth. As regards their main contents, all these works are nothing else than many-sided brief or lengthly descriptions of the passion we are speaking of.

After what has here been called to mind, no one can doubt either the reality or the importance of the matter; and therefore, instead of wondering that a philosophy should also for once make its own this constant theme of all poets, one ought rather to be surprised that a thing which plays throughout so important a part in human life has hitherto practically been disregarded by philosophers altogether, and lies before us as raw material.

All love, however ethereally it may bear itself, is rooted in the sexual impulse alone, nay, it absolutely is only a more definitely determined, specialised, and indeed in the strictest sense individualised sexual impulse. If now, keeping this in view, one considers the important part which the sexual impulse in all its degrees and nuances plays not only on the stage and in novels, but also in the real world, where, next to the love of life, it shows itself the strongest and most powerful of motives, constantly lays claim to half the powers and thoughts of the younger portion of mankind, is the ultimate goal of almost all human effort, exerts an adverse influence on the most important events, interrupts the most serious occupations every hour, sometimes embarrasses for a while even the greatest minds, does not hesitate to intrude with its trash interfering with the negotiations of statesmen and the investigations of men of learning, knows how to slip its love letters and locks of hair even into ministerial portfolios and philosophical manuscripts, and no less devises daily the most entangled and the worst actions, destroys the most valuable relationships, breaks the firmest bonds, demands the sacrifice sometimes of life or health, sometimes of wealth, rank, and happiness, nay, robs those who are otherwise honest of all conscience, makes those who have hitherto been faithful, traitors; accordingly, on the whole, appears as a malevolent demon that strives to pervert, confuse, and overthrow everything;—then one will be forced to cry, Wherefore all this noise? Wherefore the straining and storming, the anxiety and want? It is merely a question of every Hans finding his Grethe. Why should such a trifle play so important a part, and constantly introduce disturbance and confusion into the well-regulated life of man? But to the earnest investigator the spirit of truth gradually reveals the answer. It is no trifle that is in question here; on the contrary, the importance of the matter is quite proportionate to the seriousness and ardour of the effort. The ultimate end of all love affairs, whether they are played in sock or cothurnus, is really more important than all other ends of human life, and is therefore quite worthy of the profound seriousness with which every one pursues it. That which is decided by it is nothing less than *the composition of the next generation.*

The collective love affairs of the present generation taken together are accordingly, of the whole human race, the serious *meditation on the composition of the future generation.* This high importance of the matter, in which it is not a question of individual weal or woe, as in all other matters, but of the existence and special nature of the human race in future times, and therefore the will of the individual appears at a higher power as the will of the species;—this it is on which the pathetic and sublime elements in affairs of love depend, which for thousands of years poets have never wearied of representing in innumerable examples; because no theme can equal in interest this one, which stands to all others which only concern the welfare of individuals as the solid body to the surface, because it concerns the weal and woe of the species. Just on this account, then, is it so difficult to impart interest to a drama without the element of love, and, on the other hand, this theme is never worn out even by daily use.

That which presents itself in the individual consciousness as sexual impulse in general, without being directed towards a definite individual of the other sex, is in itself, and apart from the phenomenon, simply the will to live. But what appears in consciousness as a sexual impulse directed to a definite individual is in itself the will to live as a definitely determined individual. Now in this case the sexual impulse, although in itself a subjective need, knows how to assume very skilfully the mask of an objective admiration, and thus to deceive our consciousness; for nature requires this stratagem to attain its ends. But yet that in every case of falling in love, however objective and sublime this admiration may appear, what alone is looked to is the production of an individual of a definite nature is primarily confirmed by the fact that the essential matter is not the reciprocation of love, but possession, i.e., the physical enjoyment. The certainty of the former can therefore by no means console us for the want of the latter; on the contrary, in such a situation many a man has shot himself. On the other hand, persons who are deeply in love, and can obtain no return of it, are contented with possession, i.e., with the physical enjoyment. This is proved by all forced marriages, and also by the frequent purchase of the favour of a woman, in spite of her dislike, by large presents or other sacrifices, nay, even by cases of rape. That this particular child shall be begotten is, although unknown to the parties concerned, the true end of the whole love story; the manner in which it is attained is a secondary consideration. Now, however loudly persons of lofty and sentimental soul, and especially those who are in love, may cry out here about the gross realism of my view, they are yet in error. For is not the definite determination of the individualities of the next generation a much higher and more worthy end than those exuberant feelings and supersensible soap bubbles of theirs? Nay, among earthly aims, can there be one which is greater or more important? It alone corresponds to the profoundness with which passionate love is felt, to the seriousness with which it appears, and the importance which it attributes even to the trifling details of its sphere and occasion. Only so far as this end is assumed as the true one do the difficulties encountered, the infinite exertions and annoyances made and endured for the attainment of the loved object, appear proportionate to the matter. For it is the future generation, in its whole individual determinateness, that presses into existence by means of those efforts and toils. Nay, it is itself already active in that careful, definite, and arbitrary choice for the satisfaction of the sexual impulse which we call love. The growing inclination of two lovers is really already the will to live of the new individual which they can and desire to produce; nay, even in the meeting of their longing glances its new life breaks out, and announces itself as a future individuality harmoniously and well composed. They feel the longing for an actual union and fusing together into a single being, in order to live on only as this; and this longing receives its fulfilment in the child which is produced by them, as that in which the qualities transmitted by them both, fused and united in one being, live on. Conversely, the mutual, decided, and persistent aversion between a man and a maid is a sign that what they could produce would only be a badly organised, in itself inharmonious and unhappy, being.

But, finally, what draws two individuals of different sex exclusively to each other with such power is the will to live, which exhibits itself in the whole species, and which here anticipates in the individual which these two can produce an objectification of its nature answering to its aims. This individual will have the will, or character, from the father, the intellect from the mother, and the corporisation from both; yet, for the most part, the figure will take more after the father, the size after the mother,—according to the law which comes out in the breeding of hybrids among the brutes, and principally depends upon the fact that the size of the fœtus must conform to the size of the uterus. Just as inexplicable as the quite special individuality of any man, which is exclusively peculiar to him, is also the quite special and individual passion of two lovers; indeed at bottom the two are one and the same: the former is explicit while the latter is implicit.

Let us now set about the more thorough investigation of the matter. Egoism is so deeply rooted a quality of all individuals in general, that in order to arouse the activity of an individual being egoistical ends are the only ones upon which we can count with certainty. Certainly the species has an earlier, closer, and greater claim upon the individual than the perishable individuality itself. Yet when the individual has to act, and even make sacrifices for the continuance and quality of the species, the importance of the matter cannot be made so comprehensible to his intellect, which is calculated merely with regard to individual ends, as to have its proportionate effect. Therefore in such a case nature can only attain its ends by implanting a certain illusion in the individual, on account of which that which is only a good for the species appears to him as a good for himself, so that when he serves the species he imagines he is serving himself; in which process a mere chimera, which vanishes immediately afterwards, floats before him, and takes the place of a real thing as a motive. This illusion is instinct. In the great majority of cases this is to be regarded as the sense of the species, which presents what is of benefit to *it* to the will. Since, however, the will has here become individual, it must be so deluded that it apprehends through the sense of the individual what the sense of the species presents to it, thus imagines it is following individual ends while in truth it is pursuing ends which are merely general (taking this word in its strictest sense).

Hitherto I have only taken account of the *absolute* considerations, i.e., those which hold good for every one: I come now to the *relative* considerations, which are individual, because in their case what is looked to is the rectification of the type of the species, which is already defectively presented, the correction of the divergences from it which the chooser's own person already bears in itself, and thus the return to the pure presentation of the type. Here, then, each one loves what he lacks. Starting from the individual constitution, and directed to the individual constitution, the choice which rests upon such relative considerations is much more definite, decided, and exclusive than that which proceeds merely from the absolute considerations; therefore the source of really passionate love will lie, as a rule, in these relative considerations, and only that of the ordinary and slighter inclination in the absolute considerations.

Accordingly it is not generally precisely correct and perfect beauties that kindle great passions. For such a truly passionate inclination to arise something is required which can only be expressed by a chemical metaphor: two persons must neutralise each other, like acid and alkali, to a neutral salt.

We have seen in the above that the intensity of love increases with its individualisation, because we have shown that the physical qualities of two individuals can be such that, for the purpose of restoring as far as possible the type of the species, the one is quite specially and perfectly the completion or supplement of the other, which therefore desires it exclusively. Already in this case a considerable passion arises, which at once gains a nobler and more sublime appearance from the fact that it is directed to an individual object, and to it alone; thus, as it were, arises at the special order of the species. For the opposite reason, the mere sexual impulse is ignoble, because without individualisation it is directed to all, and strives to maintain the species only as regards quantity, with little respect to quality. But the individualising, and with it the intensity of the love, can reach so high a degree that without its satisfaction all the good things in the world, and even life itself, lose their value. It is then a wish which attains a vehemence that no other wish ever reaches, and therefore makes one ready for any sacrifice, and in case its fulfilment remains unalterably denied, may lead to madness or suicide. At the foundation of such an excessive passion there must lie, besides the considerations we have shown above, still others which we have not thus before our eyes. We must therefore assume that here not only the corporisation, but the *will* of the man and the *intellect* of the woman are specially suitable to each other, in consequence of which a perfectly definite individual can be produced by them alone, whose existence the genius of the species has here in view, for reasons which are inaccessible to us, since they lie in the nature of the thing in itself. Or, to speak more exactly, the will to live desires here to objectify itself in a perfectly definite individual, which can only be produced by this father with this mother. This metaphysical desire of the will in itself has primarily no other sphere of action in the series of existences than the hearts of the future parents, which accordingly are seized with this ardent longing, and now imagine themselves to desire on their own account what really for the present has only a purely metaphysical end, i.e., an end which lies outside the series of actually existing things. Thus it is the ardent longing to enter existence of the future individual which has first become possible here, a longing which proceeds from the primary source of all being, and exhibits itself in the phenomenal world as the lofty passion of the future parents for each other, paying little regard to all that is outside itself; in fact, as an unparalleled illusion, on account of which such a lover would give up all the good things of this world to enjoy the possession of this woman, who yet can really give him nothing more than any other.

Because the passion depended upon an illusion, which represented that which has only value for the species as valuable for the individual, the deception must vanish after the attainment of the end of the species. The spirit of the species which took possession of the individual sets it free again. Forsaken by this spirit, the individual falls back into its original limitation and narrowness, and sees with wonder that after such a high, heroic, and infinite effort nothing has resulted for its pleasure but what every sexual gratification affords. Contrary to expectation, it finds itself no happier than before. It observes that it has been the dupe of the will of the species. Therefore, as a rule, a Theseus who has been made happy will forsake his Ariadne. If Petrarch's passion had been satisfied, his song would have been silenced from that time forth, like that of the bird as soon as the eggs are laid.

Marriages from love are made in the interest of the species, not of the individuals. Certainly the persons concerned imagine they are advancing their own happiness; but their real end is one which is foreign to themselves, for it lies in the production of an individual which is only possible through them. Brought together by this aim, they ought henceforth to try to get on together as well as possible. But very often the pair brought together by that instinctive illusion, which is the essence of passionate love, will, in other respects, be of very different natures. This comes to light when the illusion vanishes, as it necessarily must. Accordingly love marriages, as a rule, turn out unhappy; for through them the coming generation is cared for at the expense of the present. The opposite is the case with marriages contracted for purposes of convenience, generally in accordance with the choice of the parents. The considerations prevailing here, of whatever kind they may be, are at least real, and cannot vanish of themselves. Through them, however, the happiness of the present generation is certainly cared for, to the disadvantage of the coming generation, and notwithstanding this it remains problematical.

The whole metaphysics of love here dealt with stands in close connection with my metaphysics in general, and the light which it throws upon this may be summed up as follows:

We have seen that the careful selection for the satisfaction of the sexual impulse, a selection which rises through innumerable degrees up to that of passionate love, depends upon the highly serious interest which man takes in the special personal constitution of the next generation. Now this exceedingly remarkable interest confirms two truths which have been set forth in the preceding chapters. (1) The indestructibility of the true nature of man, which lives on in that coming generation. For that interest which is so lively and eager, and does not spring from reflection and intention, but from the inmost characteristics and tendencies of our nature, could not be so indelibly present and exercise such great power over man if he were absolutely perishable, and were merely followed in time by a race actually and entirely different from him. (2) That his true nature lies more in the species than in the individual. For that interest in the special nature of the species, which is the root of all love, from the passing inclination to the serious passion, is for every one really the highest concern, the success or failure of which touches him most sensibly; therefore it is called *par excellence* the affair of the heart. Moreover, when this interest has expressed itself strongly and decidedly, everything which merely concerns one's own person is postponed and necessarily sacrificed to it. Through this, then, man shows that the species lies closer to him than the individual, and he lives more immediately in the former than in the latter. Why does the lover hang with complete abandonment on the eyes of his chosen one, and is ready to make every sacrifice for her? Because it is his immortal part that longs after her; while it is only his mortal part that desires everything else. That vehement or intense longing directed to a particular woman is accordingly an immediate pledge of the indestructibility of the kernel of our being, and of its continued existence in the species. But to regard this continued existence as something trifling and insufficient is an error which arises from the fact that under the conception of the continued life of the species one thinks nothing more than the future existence of beings similar to us, but in no regard identical with us; and this again because, starting from knowledge directed towards without, one takes into consideration only the external form of the species as we apprehend it in perception, and not its inner nature. But it is just this inner nature which lies at the foundation of our own consciousness as its kernel, and hence indeed is more immediate than this itself, and, as thing in itself, free from the principle of individuation, is really the same and identical in all individuals, whether they exist together or after each other. Now this is the will to live, thus just that which desires life and continuance so vehemently. This accordingly is spared and unaffected by death. It can attain to no better state than its present one; and consequently for it, with life, the constant suffering and striving of the individuals is certain. To free it from this is reserved for the denial of the will to live, as the means by which the individual will breaks away from the stem of the species, and surrenders that existence in it. We lack conceptions for that which it now is; indeed all data for such conceptions are wanting. We can only describe it as that which is free to be will to live or not. Buddhism denotes the latter case by the word Nirvana. It is the point which remains for ever unattainable to all human knowledge, just as such.

If now, from the standpoint of this last consideration, we contemplate the turmoil of life, we behold all occupied with its want and misery, straining all their powers to satisfy its infinite needs and to ward off its multifarious sorrows, yet without daring to hope anything else than simply the preservation of this tormented existence for a short span of time. In between, however, in the midst of the tumult, we see the glances of two lovers meet longingly: yet why so secretly, fearfully, and stealthily? Because these lovers are the traitors who seek to perpetuate the whole want and drudgery, which would otherwise speedily reach an end; this they wish to frustrate, as others like them have frustrated it before.

IV. EPIPHILOSOPHY

AT THE CONCLUSION of my exposition a few reflections concerning my philosophy itself may find their place. My philosophy does not pretend to explain the existence of the world in its ultimate grounds: it rather sticks to the facts of external and internal experience as they are accessible to every one, and shows the true and deepest connection of them without really going beyond them to any extra-mundane things and their relations to the world. It therefore arrives at no conclusions as to what lies beyond all possible experience, but affords merely an exposition of what is given in the external world and in self-consciousness, thus contents itself with comprehending the nature of the world in its inner connection with itself. It is consequently *immanent,* in the Kantian sense of the word. But just on this account it leaves many questions untouched; for example, why what is proved as a fact is as it is and not otherwise, &c. All such questions, however, or rather the answers to them, are really transcendent, i.e., they cannot be thought by the forms and functions of our intellect, do not enter into these; it is therefore related to them as our sensibility is related to the possible properties of bodies for which we have no senses. After all my explanations one may still ask, for example, whence has sprung this will that is free to assert itself, the manifestation of which is the world, or to deny itself, the manifestation of which we do not know. What is the fatality lying beyond all experience which has placed it in the very doubtful dilemma of either appearing as a world in which suffering and death reign, or else denying its very being?—or again, what can have prevailed upon it to forsake the infinitely preferable peace of blessed nothingness? An individual will, one may add, can only turn to its own destruction through error in the choice, thus through the fault of knowledge; but the will in itself, before all manifestation, consequently still without knowledge, how could it go astray and fall into the ruin of its present condition? Whence in general is the great discord that permeates this world? It may, further, be asked how deep into the true being of the world the roots of individuality go; to which it may certainly be answered: they go as deep as the assertion of the will to live; where the denial of the will appears they cease, for they have arisen with the assertion. But one might indeed even put the question, "What would I be if I were not will to live?" and more of the same kind. To all such questions we would first have to reply that the expression of the most universal and general form of our intellect is the *principle of sufficient reason;* but that just on this account that principle finds application only to the phenomenon, not to the being in itself of things. Yet all whence and why depend upon that principle alone. As a result of the Kantian philosophy it is no longer an *æterna veritas,* but merely the form, i.e., the function, of our intellect, which is essentially cerebral, and originally a mere tool in the service of the will, which it therefore presupposes together with all its objectifications. But our whole knowing and conceiving is bound to its forms; accordingly we must conceive everything in time, consequently as a before and after, then as cause and effect, and also as above and below, whole and part, &c., and cannot by any means escape from this sphere in which all possibility of our knowledge lies. Now these forms are utterly unsuited to the problems raised here, nor are they fit or able to comprehend their solution even if it were given. Therefore with our intellect, this mere tool of the will, we are everywhere striking upon insoluble problems, as against the walls of our prison. But, besides this, it may at least be assumed as probable that not only *for us* is knowledge of all that has been asked about impossible, but no such knowledge is possible in general, thus never and in no way; that these relations are not only relatively but absolutely insusceptible of investigation; that not only does no one know them, but that they are in themselves unknowable, because they do not enter into the form of knowledge in general. For knowableness in general, with its most essential, and therefore constantly necessary form of subject and object, belongs merely to the phenomenal appearance, not to the being in itself of things. Where knowledge, and consequently idea, is, there is also only phenomenon, and we stand there already in the province of the phenomenal; nay, knowledge in general is known to us only as a phenomenon of brain, and we are not only unjustified in conceiving it otherwise, but also incapable of doing so. What the world is as world may be understood: it is phenomenal manifestation; and we can know that which manifests itself in it, directly from ourselves, by means of a thorough analysis of self-consciousness. Then, however, by means of this key to the nature of the world, the whole phenomenal manifestation can be deciphered, as I believe I have succeeded in doing. But if we leave the world in order to answer the questions indicated above, we have also left the whole sphere in which not only connection according to reason and consequent, but even knowledge itself is possible. The nature of things before or beyond the world, and consequently beyond the will, is open to no investigation; because knowledge in general is itself only a phenomenon, and therefore exists only in the world as the world exists only in it. The inner being in itself of things is nothing that knows, no intellect, but an unconscious; knowledge is only added as an accident, a means of assistance to the phenomenon of that inner being, and can therefore apprehend that being itself only in proportion to its own nature, which is designed with reference to quite different ends (those of the individual will), consequently very imperfectly. Here lies the reason why a perfect understanding of the existence, nature, and origin of the world, extending to its ultimate ground and satisfying all demands, is impossible. So much as to the limits of my philosophy, and indeed of all philosophy.

The "One and All," i.e., that the inner nature in all things is absolutely one and the same, my age had already grasped and understood, after the Eleatics, Scotus Erigena, Giordano Bruno, and Spinoza had thoroughly taught, and Schelling had revived this doctrine. But *what* this one is, and how it is able to exhibit itself as the many, is a problem the solution of which is first found in my philosophy. Certainly from the most ancient times man had been called the microcosm. I have reversed the proposition, and shown the world as the macranthropos: because will and idea exhaust its nature as they do that of man. But it is clearly more correct to learn to understand the world from man than man from the world; for one has to explain what is indirectly given, thus external perception from what is directly given, thus self-consciousness—not conversely.

With the Pantheists, then, I have certainly that "One and All" in common, but not the "All God"; because I do not go beyond experience (taken in its widest sense), and still less do I put myself in contradiction with the data which lie before me. Scotus Erigena, quite consistently with the spirit of Pantheism, explains every phenomenon as a theophany; but then this conception must also be applied to the most terrible and abominable phenomena. Fine theophanies! What further distinguishes me from Pantheism is principally the following: (1) That their "God" is an x, an unknown quantity; the will, on the other hand, is of all possible things the one that is known to us most exactly, the only thing given immediately, and therefore exclusively fitted for the explanation of the rest. For what is unknown must always be explained by what is better known; not conversely. (2) That their "God" manifests himself to unfold his glory, or, indeed, to let himself be admired. Apart from the vanity here attributed to him, they are placed in the position of being obliged to sophisticate away the colossal evil of the world; but the world remains in glaring and terrible contradiction with that imagined excellence. With me, on the contrary, the *will* arrives through its objectification, however this may occur, at self-knowledge, whereby its abolition, conversion, salvation becomes possible. And accordingly, with me alone ethics has a sure foundation and is completely worked out in agreement with the sublime and profound religions, Brahmanism, Buddhism, and Christianity, not merely with Judaism and Mohammedanism. The metaphysic of the beautiful also is first fully cleared up as a result of my fundamental truth, and no longer requires to take refuge behind empty words. With me alone is the evil of the world honestly confessed in its whole magnitude: this is rendered possible by the fact that the answer to the question as to its origin coincides with the answer to the question as to the origin of the world. On the other hand, in all other systems, since they are all optimistic, the question as to the origin of evil is the incurable disease, ever breaking out anew, with which they are affected, and in consequence of which they struggle along with palliatives and quack remedies. (3) That I start from experience and the natural self-consciousness given to every one, and lead to the will as that which alone is metaphysical; thus I adopt the ascending, analytical method. The Pantheists, again, adopt the opposite method, the descending or synthetical. They start from their "God," which they beg or take by force, although sometimes under the name substance, or absolute, and this unknown is then supposed to explain everything that is better known. (4) That with me the world does not fill the whole possibility of all being, but in this there still remains much room for that which we denote only negatively as the denial of the will to live. Pantheism, on the other hand, is essentially optimism: but if the world is what is best, then the matter may rest there. (5) That to the Pantheists the perceptible world, thus the world of idea, is just the intentional manifestation of the God indwelling in it, which contains no real explanation of its appearance, but rather requires to be explained itself. With me, on the other hand, the world as idea appears merely *per accidens,* because the intellect, with its external perception, is primarily only the medium of motives for the more perfect phenomena of will, which gradually rises to that objectivity of perceptibility, in which the world exists. In this sense its origin, as an object of perception, is really accounted for, and not, as with the Pantheists, by means of untenable fictions.

Since, in consequence of the Kantian criticism of all speculative theology, the philosophers of Germany almost all threw themselves back upon Spinoza, so that the whole series of futile attempts known by the name of the post-Kantian philosophy are simply Spinozism tastelessly dressed up, veiled in all kinds of unintelligible language, and otherwise distorted, I wish, now that I have explained the relation of my philosophy to Pantheism in general, to point out its relation to Spinozism in particular. It stands, then, to Spinozism as the New Testament stands to the Old. What the Old Testament has in common with the New is the same God-Creator. Analogous to this, the world exists, with me as with Spinoza, by its inner power and through itself. But with Spinoza his eternal substance, the inner nature of the world, which he himself calls God, is also, as regards its moral character and worth, Jehovah, the God-Creator, who applauds His own creation, and finds that all is very good. Spinoza has deprived Him of nothing but personality. Thus, according to him also, the world and all in it is wholly excellent and as it ought to be; he is even to rejoice in his life as long as it lasts; entirely in accordance with Ecclesiastes ix, 7-10. In short, it is optimism: therefore its ethical side is weak, as in the Old Testament; nay, it is even false, and in part revolting. With me, on the other hand, the will, or the inner nature of the world, is by no means Jehovah, it is rather, as it were, the crucified Saviour, or the crucified thief, according as it resolves. Therefore my ethical teaching agrees with that of Christianity, completely and in its highest tendencies, and not less with that of Brahmanism and Buddhism. Spinoza could not get rid of the Jews. His contempt for the brutes, which, as mere things for our use, he also declares to be without rights, is thoroughly Jewish, and, in union with Pantheism, is at the same time absurd and detestable (*Eth.*, iv., appendix, c. 27). With all this Spinoza remains a very great man. But in order to estimate his work correctly we must keep in view his relation to Descartes. The latter had sharply divided nature into mind and matter, i.e., thinking and extended substance, and had also placed God and the world in complete opposition to each other; Spinoza also, so long as he was a Cartesian, taught all that in his *Cogitatis Metaphysics,* 1665. Only in his later years did he see the fundamental falseness of that double dualism; and accordingly his own philosophy principally consists of the indirect abolition of these two antitheses. Yet partly to avoid injuring his teacher, partly in order to be less offensive, he gave it a positive appearance by means of a strictly dogmatic form, although its content is chiefly negative. His identification of the world with God has also this negative significance alone. For to call the world God is not to explain it: it remains a riddle under the one name as under the other. But these two negative truths had value for their age, as for every age in which there still are conscious or unconscious Cartesians. He makes the mistake, common to all philosophers before Locke, of starting from conceptions, without having previously investigated their origin, such, for example, as substance, cause, &c., and in such a method of procedure these conceptions then receive a much too extensive validity. Those who in the most recent times refused to acknowledge the Neo-Spinozism which had appeared, for example, Jacobi, were principally deterred from doing so by the bugbear of fatalism. By this is to be understood every doctrine which refers the existence of the world, together with the critical position of mankind in it, to any absolute necessity, i.e., to a necessity that cannot be further explained. Those who feared fatalism, again, believed that all that was of importance was to deduce the world from the free act of will of a being existing outside it; as if it were antecedently certain which of the two was more correct, or even better merely in relation to us. What is, however, especially assumed here is the *there is no third*, and accordingly hitherto every philosophy has represented one or the other. I am the first to depart from this; for I have actually established the *Third:* the act of will from which the world arises is our own. It is free; for the principle of sufficient reason, from which alone all necessity derives its significance, is merely the form of its phenomenon. Just on this account this phenomenon, if it once exists, is absolutely necessary in its course; in consequence of this alone we can recognise in it the nature of the act of will, and accordingly *eventualiter* will otherwise.

BEYOND GOOD AND EVIL

by

FRIEDRICH WILHELM NIETZSCHE

CONTENTS

Beyond Good and Evil

FRIEDRICH WILHELM NIETZSCHE

1844–1900

REVOLT is the key word to any understanding of the life and writings of Friedrich Wilhelm Nietzsche—a revolt that was born of a brilliant but sick mind, and of a life which began with great promise and concluded in hopeless insanity.

The son of the pastor at Röcken, near Leipzig, Nietzsche was born on October 15, 1844. He received his education at Schulpforta and at the universities of Bonn and Leipzig. His college work was confined largely to the classics—the ancient civilizations of Greece and Rome.

While still an undergraduate, Nietzsche was appointed (in 1869) to an extraordinary professorship in classical philology at the University of Basel. Here began his famous literary career and his gradual but definite attraction toward the field of philosophy. He was soon promoted to a full professorship, and his popularity grew enormously.

But the rise of this meteoric career was as brief as it was rapid. Just seven years later (1876) eye and brain trouble made it necessary for him to take sick leave from the university. His condition became steadily worse, and he was pensioned in 1879, while yet a young man of only thirty-five.

Nietzsche spent the next few years visiting health resorts and consulting with physicians in an effort to obtain some relief from his steadily growing pain. He tells us that more than two hundred days of every year were spent in "pure pain."

As time went on, Nietzsche's condition became progressively worse. But it could not prevent him from producing many of his most famous essays, most of which were dashed off at high pressure and between moments of the most violent head pains.

Finally, in 1888, Nietzsche was pronounced hopelessly insane and remained in that condition until his death on the twenty-fifth of August, 1900.

The "injustice" of his physical condition dominated Nietzsche's thinking. He could not accept his suffering as a "fair deal." Furthermore, he was a man of intensely emotional temperament. These two factors colored all that he wrote. Since it was possible for him to work only during occasional periods of surcease from pain, his writings are not systematic, but consist rather of frequently inconsistent aphorisms, epigrams, and short essays.

Yet we can find the general trace of a method in the "madness" of Nietzsche's philosophy. It is the method of a man who tries to find happiness through the battle against pain. Accepting in part the philosophy of Schopenhauer, whom he greatly admired, he transformed Schopenhauer's *will to live* from a negative *rejection* of the world into a positive *defiance* of the world. If Nietzsche could will strongly enough, he would overcome his pain. "The will alone can make men free." You must *fight* for your freedom, the right to emancipate yourself from the shackles of your pain. "The strongest and highest will to life is a will to war, a will to power, a will to *overpower*." To overpower suffering, so that you can stand forth as a man among men. Nay, as a *Superman* among men! "I say unto you, what is the ape to man? A laughingstock, a thing of shame. And so too shall man be to Superman. A laughingstock, a thing of shame." "I announce the day," declared Nietzsche, "when man shall disappear from the earth and Superman shall be enthroned in his place."

Thus spake Nietzsche, a pathetic cripple of a man who in his suffering dreamed that some day he might become a god.

BEYOND GOOD AND EVIL

I. PREJUDICES OF PHILOSOPHERS

I

HAVING KEPT a sharp eye on philosophers, and having read between their lines long enough, I now say to myself that the greater part of conscious thinking must be counted amongst the instinctive functions, and it is so even in the case of philosophical thinking; one has here to learn anew, as one learned anew about heredity and "innateness." As little as the act of birth comes into consideration in the whole process and procedure of heredity, just as little is "being-conscious" *opposed* to the instinctive in any decisive sense; the greater part of the conscious thinking of a philosopher is secretly influenced by his instincts, and forced into definite channels. And behind all logic and its seeming sovereignty of movement, there are valuations, or to speak more plainly, physiological demands, for the maintenance of a definite mode of life. For example, that the certain is worth more than the uncertain, that illusion is less valuable than "truth": such valuations, in spite of their regulative importance for *us,* might notwithstanding be only superficial valuations, special kinds of *niaiserie,* such as may be necessary for the maintenance of beings such as ourselves. Supposing, in effect, that man is not just the "measure of things." . . .

II

That which causes philosophers to be regarded half-distrustfully and half-mockingly, is not the oft-repeated discovery how innocent they are—how often and easily they make mistakes and lose their way, in short, how childish and childlike they are,—but that there is not enough honest dealing with them, whereas they all raise a loud and virtuous outcry when the problem of truthfulness is even hinted at in the remotest manner. They all pose as though their real opinions had been discovered and attained through the self-evolving of a cold, pure, divinely indifferent dialectic (in contrast to all sorts of mystics, who, fairer and foolisher, talk of "inspiration"); whereas, in fact, a prejudiced proposition, idea, or "suggestion," which is generally their heart's desire abstracted and refined, is defended by them with arguments sought out after the event. They are all advocates who do not wish to be regarded as such, generally astute defenders, also, of their prejudices, which they dub "truths,"—and *very* far from having the conscience which bravely admits this to itself; very far from having the good taste of the courage which goes so far as to let this be understood, perhaps to warn friend or foe, or in cheerful confidence and self-ridicule.

III

It has gradually become clear to me what every great philosophy up till now has consisted of—namely, the confession of its originator, and a species of involuntary and unconscious auto-biography; and moreover that the moral (or immoral) purpose in every philosophy has constituted the true vital germ out of which the entire plant has always grown. Indeed, to understand how the abstrusest metaphysical assertions of a philosopher have been arrived at, it is always well (and wise) to first ask oneself: "What morality do they (or does he) aim at?" Accordingly, I do not believe that an "impulse to knowledge" is the father of philosophy; but that another impulse, here as elsewhere, has only made use of knowledge (and mistaken knowledge!) as an instrument. But whoever considers the fundamental impulses of man with a view to determining how far they may have here acted as *inspiring* genii (or as demons and cobolds), will find that they have all practised philosophy at one time or another, and that each one of them would have been only too glad to look upon itself as the ultimate end of existence and the legitimate *lord* over all the other impulses. For every impulse is imperious, and as *such,* attempts to philosophise. To be sure, in the case of scholars, in the case of really scientific men, it may be otherwise—"better," if you will; there there may really be such a thing as an "impulse to knowledge," some kind of small, independent clock-work, which, when well wound up, works away industriously to that end, *without* the rest of the scholarly impulses taking any material part therein. The actual "interests" of the scholar, therefore, are generally in quite another direction—in the family, perhaps, or in money-making, or in politics; it is, in fact, almost indifferent at what point of research his little machine is placed, and whether the hopeful young worker becomes a good philologist, a mushroom specialist, or a chemist; he is not *characterised* by becoming this or that. In the philosopher, on the contrary, there is absolutely nothing impersonal; and above all, his morality furnishes a decided and decisive testimony as to *who he is,*—that is to say, in what order the deepest impulses of his nature stand to each other.

IV

Psychologists should bethink themselves before putting down the instinct of self-preservation as the cardinal instinct of an organic being. A living thing seeks above all to *discharge* its strength—life itself is *Will to Power;* self-preservation is only one of the indirect and most frequent *results* thereof. In short, here, as everywhere else, let us beware of *superfluous* teleological principles!—one of which is the instinct of self-preservation (we owe it to Spinoza's inconsistency). It is thus, in effect, that method ordains, which must be essentially economy of principles.

V

To study physiology with a clear conscience, one must insist on the fact that the sense-organs are *not* phenomena in the sense of the idealistic philosophy; as such they certainly could not be causes! Sensualism, therefore, at least as regulative hypothesis, if not as heuristic principle. What? And others say even that the external world is the work of our organs? But then our body, as a part of this external world, would be the work of our organs! But then our organs themselves would be the work of our organs! It seems to me that this is a complete *reductio ad absurdum,* if the conception *causa sui* is something fundamentally absurd. Consequently, the external world is *not* the work of our organs—?

VI

That the separate philosophical ideas are not anything optional or autonomously evolving, but grow up in connection and relationship with each other; that, however suddenly and arbitrarily they seem to appear in the history of thought, they nevertheless belong just as much to a system as the collective members of the fauna of a Continent—is betrayed in the end by the circumstance: how unfailingly the most diverse philosophers always fill in again a definite fundamental scheme of *possible* philosophies. Under an invisible spell, they always revolve once more in the same orbit; however independent of each other they may feel themselves with their critical or systematic wills, something within them leads them, something impels them in definite order the one after the other— to wit, the innate methodology and relationship of their ideas. Their thinking is, in fact, far less a discovery than a re-recognising, a remember-

ing, a return and a home-coming to a far-off, ancient common-household
of the soul, out of which those ideas formerly grew: philosophising is so
far a kind of atavism of the highest order. The wonderful family resemblance of all Indian, Greek, and German philosophising is easily
enough explained. In fact, where there is affinity of language, owing to the
common philosophy of grammar—I mean owing to the unconscious dom-
ination and guidance of similar grammatical functions—it cannot but be
that everything is prepared at the outset for a similar development and
succession of philosophical systems; just as the way seems barred against
certain other possibilities of world-interpretation. It is highly probable
that philosophers within the domain of the Ural-Altaic languages (where
the conception of the subject is least developed) look otherwise "into
the world," and will be found on paths of thought different from those
of the Indo Germans and Mussulmans, the spell of certain grammatical
functions is ultimately also the spell of *physiological* valuations and racial
conditions.—So much by way of rejecting Locke's superficiality with regard to the origin of ideas.

VII

All psychology hitherto has run aground on moral prejudices and
timidities, it has not dared to launch out into the depths. In so far as it
is allowable to recognise in that which has hitherto been written, evidence
of that which has hitherto been kept silent, it seems as if nobody had
yet harboured the notion of psychology as the Morphology and *Develop-
ment-doctrine of the Will to Power,* as I conceive of it. The power of
moral prejudices has penetrated deeply into the most intellectual world,
the world apparently most indifferent and unprejudiced, and has obviously
operated in an injurious, obstructive, blinding, and distorting manner.
A proper physio-psychology has to contend with unconscious antagonism
in the heart of the investigator, it has "the heart" against it: even a
doctrine of the reciprocal conditionalness of the "good" and the "bad"
impulses, causes (as refined immorality) distress and aversion in a still
strong and manly conscience—still more so, a doctrine of the derivation
of all good impulses from bad ones. If, however, a person should regard
even the emotions of hatred, envy, covetousness, and imperiousness as
life-conditioning emotions, as factors which must be present, fundamentally and essentially, in the general economy of life (which must,
therefore, be further developed if life is to be further developed), he will
suffer from such a view of things as from sea-sickness. And yet this
hypothesis is far from being the strangest and most painful in this immense and almost new domain of dangerous knowledge; and there are
in fact a hundred good reasons why every one should keep away from it

who *can* do so! On the other hand, if one has once drifted hither with
one's bark, well! very good! now let us set our teeth firmly! let us open
our eyes and keep our hand fast on the helm! We sail away right *over*
morality, we crush out, we destroy perhaps the remains of our own
morality by daring to make our voyage thither—but what do *we* matter!
Never yet did a *profounder* world of insight reveal itself to daring travel-
lers and adventurers, and the psychologist who thus "makes a sacrifice"
—it is *not* the *sacrifizio dell' intelletto,* on the contrary!—will at least be
entitled to demand in return that psychology shall once more be recognised as the queen of the sciences, for whose service and equipment the
other sciences exist. For psychology is once more the path to the fundamental problems.

II. THE FREE SPIRIT

I

EVERY SELECT MAN strives instinctively for a citadel and a privacy, where
he is *free* from the crowd, the many, the majority—where he may forget
"men who are the rule," as their exception;—exclusive only of the case
in which he is pushed straight to such men by a still stronger instinct,
as a discerner in the great and exceptional sense. Whoever, in intercourse
with men, does not occasionally glisten in all the green and grey colours
of distress, owing to disgust, satiety, sympathy, gloominess, and solitari-
ness, is assuredly not a man of elevated tastes; supposing, however, that
he does not voluntarily take all this burden and disgust upon himself,
that he persistently avoids it, and remains, as I said, quietly and proudly
hidden in his citadel, one thing is then certain: he was not made, he was
not predestined for knowledge. For as such, he would one day have to
say to himself: "The devil take my good taste! but 'the rule' is more
interesting than the exception—than myself, the exception!" And he would
go *down,* and above all, he would go "inside." The long and serious study
of the *average* man—and consequently much disguise, self-overcoming,
familiarity, and bad intercourse (all intercourse is bad intercourse except with one's equals):—that constitutes a necessary part of the life-
history of every philosopher; perhaps the most disagreeable, odious, and
disappointing part. If he is fortunate, however, as a favourite child of
knowledge should be, he will meet with suitable auxiliaries who will
shorten and lighten his task; I mean so-called cynics, those who simply
recognise the animal, the common-place and "the rule" in themselves,
and at the same time have so much spirituality and ticklishness as to make
them talk of themselves and their like *before witnesses*—sometimes they
wallow, even in books, as on their own dung-hill. Cynicism is the only

form in which base souls approach what is called honesty; and the higher man must open his ears to all the coarser or finer cynicism, and congratulate himself when the clown becomes shameless right before him, or the scientific satyr speaks out. There are even cases where enchantment mixes with the disgust—namely, where by a freak of nature, genius is bound to some such indiscreet billy-goat and ape, as in the case of the Abbe Galiani, the profoundest, acutest, and perhaps also filthiest man of his century—he was far profounder than Voltaire, and consequently also, a good deal more silent. It happens more frequently, as has been hinted, that a scientific head is placed on an ape's body, a fine exceptional understanding in a base soul, an occurrence by no means rare, especially amongst doctors and moral physiologists. And whenever anyone speaks without bitterness, or rather quite innocently, of man as a belly with two requirements, and a head with one; whenever anyone sees, seeks, and *wants* to see only hunger, sexual instinct, and vanity as the real and only motives of human actions; in short, when anyone speaks "badly"—and not even "ill"—of man, then ought the lover of knowledge to hearken attentively and diligently; he ought, in general, to have an open ear wherever there is talk without indignation. For the indignant man, and he who perpetually tears and lacerates himself with his own teeth (or, in place of himself, the world, God, or society), may indeed, morally speaking, stand higher than the laughing and self-satisfied satyr, but in every other sense he is the more ordinary, more indifferent, and less instructive case. And no one is such a *liar* as the indignant man.

II

It is the business of the very few to be independent; it is a privilege of the strong. And whoever attempts it, even with the best right, but without being *obliged* to do so, proves that he is probably not only strong, but also daring beyond measure. He enters into a labyrinth, he multiplies a thousandfold the dangers which life in itself already brings with it; not the least of which is that no one can see how and where he loses his way, becomes isolated, and is torn piece-meal by some minotaur of conscience. Supposing such a one comes to grief, it is so far from the comprehension of men that they neither feel it, nor sympathise with it. And he cannot any longer go back! He cannot even go back again to the sympathy of men!

III

At whatever standpoint of philosophy one may place oneself nowadays, seen from every position, the *erroneousness* of the world in which we think we live is the surest and most certain thing our eyes can light upon: we find proof after proof thereof, which would fain allure us into surmises concerning a deceptive principle in the "nature of things." He, however, who makes thinking itself, and consequently "the spirit," responsible for the falseness of the world—an honourable exit, which every conscious or unconscious *advocatus dei* avails himself of—he who regards this world, including space, time, form, and movement, as falsely *deduced,* would have at least good reason in the end to become distrustful also of all thinking; has it not hitherto been playing upon us the worst of scurvy tricks? and what guarantee would it give that it would not continue to do what it has always been doing? In all seriousness, the innocence of thinkers has something touching and respect-inspiring in it, which even nowadays permits them to wait upon consciousness with the request that it will give them *honest* answers: for example whether it be "real" or not, and why it keeps the outer world so resolutely at a distance, and other questions of the same description. The belief in "immediate certainties" is a *moral naïveté* which does honour to us philosophers; but—we have now to cease being *"merely* moral" men! Apart from morality, such belief is a folly which does little honour to us! If in middle-class life an ever-ready distrust is regarded as the sign of a "bad character," and consequently as an imprudence, here amongst us, beyond the middle-class world and its Yeas and Nays, what should prevent our being imprudent and saying: the philosopher has at length a *right* to "bad character," as the being who has hitherto been most befooled on earth—he is now under *obligation* to distrustfulness, to the wickedest squinting out of every abyss of suspicion.—Forgive me the joke of this gloomy grimace and turn of expression; for I myself have long ago learned to think and estimate differently with regard to deceiving and being deceived, and I keep at least a couple of pokes in the ribs ready for the blind rage with which philosophers struggle against being deceived. Why *not?* It is nothing more than a moral prejudice that truth is worth more than semblance; it is, in fact, the worst proved supposition in the world. *So* much must be conceded: there could have been no life at all except upon the basis of perspective estimates and semblances; and if, with the virtuous enthusiasm and stupidity of many philosophers, one wished to do away altogether with the "seeming world"—well, granted that *you* could do that,—at least nothing of your "truth" would thereby remain! Indeed, what is it that forces us in general to the supposition that there is an essential opposition of "true" and "false"? Is it not enough to suppose degrees of seemingness, and as it were lighter and darker shades and tones of semblance—different *valeurs,* as the painters say? Why might not the world *which concerns us*—be a fiction? And to anyone who suggested: "But to a fiction belongs an originator?"—might it not be bluntly replied: *Why?* May not this "belong" also belong to the fiction?

Is it not at length permitted to be a little ironical towards the subject, just as towards the predicate and object? Might not the philosopher elevate himself above faith in grammar? All respect to governesses, but is it not time that philosophy should renounce governess-faith?

IV

Supposing that nothing else is "given" as real but our world of desires and passions, that we cannot sink or rise to any other "reality" but just that of our impulses—for thinking is only a relation of these impulses to one another:—are we not permitted to make the attempt and to ask the question whether this which is "given" does not *suffice*, by means of our counterparts, for the understanding even of the so-called mechanical (or "material") world? I do not mean as an illusion, a "semblance," a "representation" (in the Berkeleyan and Schopenhauerian sense), but as possessing the same degree of reality as our emotions themselves—as a more primitive form of the world of emotions, in which everything still lies locked in a mighty unity, which afterwards branches off and develops itself in organic processes (naturally also, refines and debilitates)—as a kind of instinctive life in which all organic functions, including self-regulation, assimilation, nutrition, secretion, and change of matter, are still synthetically united with one another—as a *primary form* of life?—In the end, it is not only permitted to make this attempt, it is commanded by the conscience of *logical method*. Not to assume several kinds of causality, so long as the attempt to get along with a single one has not been pushed to its furtherest extent (to absurdity, if I may be allowed to say so): that is a morality of method which one may not repudiate nowadays—it follows "from its definition," as mathematicians say. The question is ultimately whether we really recognise the will as *operating*, whether we believe in the causality of the will; if we do so—and fundamentally our belief *in this* is just our belief in causality itself—we *must* make the attempt to posit hypothetically the causality of the will as the only causality. "Will" can naturally only operate on "will"—and not on "matter" (not on "nerves," for instance): in short, the hypothesis must be hazarded, whether will does not operate on will wherever "effects" are recognised—and whether all mechanical action, inasmuch as a power operates therein, is not just the power of will, the effect of will. Granted, finally, that we succeeded in explaining our entire instinctive life as the development and ramification of one fundamental form of will—namely, the Will to Power, as *my* thesis puts it; granted that all organic functions could be traced back to this Will to Power, and that the solution of the problem of generation and nutrition—it is one problem—could also be found therein: one would thus have acquired the right to define *all* active force unequivocally as *Will to Power*. The world seen from within, the world defined and designated according to its "intelligible character"—it would simply be "Will to Power," and nothing else.

V

One must subject oneself to one's own tests that one is destined for independence and command, and do so at the right time. One must not avoid one's tests, although they constitute perhaps the most dangerous game one can play, and are in the end tests made only before ourselves and before no other judge. Not to cleave to any person, be it even the dearest—every person is a prison and also a recess. Not to cleave to a fatherland, be it even the most suffering and necessitous—it is even less difficult to detach one's heart from a victorious fatherland. Not to cleave to a sympathy, be it even for higher men, into whose peculiar torture and helplessness chance has given us an insight. Not to cleave to a science, though it tempt one with the most valuable discoveries, apparently specially reserved for *us*. Not to cleave to one's own liberation, to the voluptuous distance and remoteness of the bird, which always flies further aloft in order always to see more under it—the danger of the flier. Not to cleave to our own virtues, nor become as a whole a victim to any of our specialties, to our "hospitality" for instance, which is the danger of dangers for highly developed and wealthy souls, who deal prodigally, almost indifferently with themselves, and push the virtue of liberality so far that it becomes a vice. One must know how *to conserve oneself*— the best test of independence.

III. THE RELIGIOUS MOOD

I

Faith, such as early Christianity desired, and not infrequently achieved in the midst of a sceptical and southernly free-spirited world, which had centuries of struggle between philosophical schools behind it and in it, counting besides the education in tolerance which the *imperium Romanum* gave—this faith is *not* that sincere, austere slave-faith by which perhaps a Luther or a Cromwell, or some other northern barbarian of the spirit remained attached to his God and Christianity; it is much rather the faith of Pascal, which resembles in a terrible manner a continuous suicide of reason—a tough, long-lived, wormlike reason, which is not to be slain at once and with a single blow. The Christian faith, from the beginning, is sacrifice: the sacrifice of all freedom, all pride, all self-confidence of spirit; it is at the same time subjection, self-derision, and self-mutilation. There is cruelty and religious Phœnicianism in this faith, which is adapted to a tender, many-sided, and very fastidious conscience; it takes for granted that the subjection of the spirit is indescribably *painful,* that all the past and all the habits of such a spirit resist the *absurdissimum,* in the form of which "faith" comes to it. Modern men, with their obtuseness as regards all Christian nomenclature, have no longer the sense for the terribly superlative conception which was implied to an antique taste by the paradox of the formula, "God on the Cross." Hitherto there had never and nowhere been such boldness in inversion, nor anything at once so dreadful, questioning, and questionable as this formula: it promised a transvaluation of all ancient values.—It was the Orient, the *profound* Orient, it was the Oriental slave who thus took revenge on Rome and its noble, light-minded toleration, on the Roman "Catholicism" of non-faith; and it was always, not the faith, but the freedom from the faith, the half-stoical and smiling indifference to the seriousness of the faith, which made the slaves indignant at their masters and revolt against them. "Enlightenment" causes revolt: for the slave desires the unconditioned, he understands nothing but the tyrannous, even in morals; he loves as he hates, without *nuance,* to the very depths, to the point of pain, to the point of sickness—his many *hidden* sufferings make him revolt against the noble taste which seems to *deny* suffering. The scepticism with regard to suffering, fundamentally only an attitude of aristocratic morality, was not the least of the causes, also, of the last great slave-insurrection which began with the French Revolution.

II

Wherever the religious neurosis has appeared on the earth so far, we find it connected with three dangerous prescriptions as to regimen: solitude, fasting, and sexual abstinence—but without its being possible to determine with certainty which is cause and which is effect, or *if* any relation at all of cause and effect exists there. This latter doubt is justified by the fact that one of the most regular symptoms among savage as well as among civilised peoples is the most sudden and excessive sensuality; which then with equal suddenness transforms into penitential paroxysms, world-renunciation, and will-renunciation: both symptoms perhaps explainable as disguised epilepsy? But nowhere is it *more* obligatory to put aside explanations: around no other type has there grown such a mass of absurdity and superstition, no other type seems to have been more interesting to men and even to philosophers—perhaps it is time to become just a little indifferent here, to learn caution, or, better still, to look away, *to go away.*—Yet in the background of the most recent philosophy, that of Schopenhauer, we find, almost as the problem in itself, this terrible note of interrogation of the religious crisis and awakening. How is the negation of will *possible?* how is the saint possible?—that seems to have been the very question with which Schopenhauer made a start and became a philosopher. And thus it was a genuine Schopenhauerian consequence, that his most convinced adherent (perhaps also his last, as far as Germany is concerned), namely, Richard Wagner, should bring his own life-work to an end just here, and should finally put that terrible and eternal type upon the stage as Kundry, *type vécu,* and as it loved and lived, at the very time that the mad-doctors in almost all European countries had an opportunity to study the type close at hand, wherever the religious neurosis —or as I call it, "the religious mood"—made its latest epidemical outbreak and display as the "Salvation Army."—If it be a question, however, as to what has been so extremely interesting to men of all sorts in all ages, and even to philosophers, in the whole phenomenon of the saint, it is undoubtedly the appearance of the miraculous therein—namely, the immediate *succession of opposites,* of states of the soul regarded as morally antithetical: it was believed here to be self-evident that a "bad man" was all at once turned into a "saint," a good man. The hitherto existing psychology was wrecked at this point; is it not possible it may have happened principally because psychology had placed itself under the dominion of morals, because it *believed* in oppositions of moral values, and saw, read, and *interpreted* these oppositions into the text and facts of the case? What? "Miracle" only an error of interpretation? A lack of philology?

III

There is a great ladder of religious cruelty, with many rounds; but three of these are the most important. Once on a time men sacrificed human beings to their God, and perhaps just those they loved the best —to this category belong the firstling sacrifices of all primitive religions, and also the sacrifice of the Emperor Tiberius in the Mithra-Grotto on the Island of Capri, that most terrible of all Roman anachronisms. Then, during the moral epoch of mankind, they sacrificed to their God the strongest instincts they possessed, their "nature"; *this* festal joy shines in the cruel glances of ascetics and "anti-natural" fanatics. Finally, what still remained to be sacrificed? Was it not necessary in the end for men to sacrifice everything comforting, holy, healing, all hope, all faith in hidden harmonies, in future blessedness and justice? Was it not necessary to sacrifice God himself, and out of cruelty to themselves to worship stone, stupidity, gravity, fate, nothingness? To sacrifice God for nothingness—this paradoxical mystery of the ultimate cruelty has been reserved for the rising generation; we all know something thereof already.

IV

Has it been observed to what extent outward idleness, or semi-idleness, is necessary to a real religious life (alike for its favourite microscopic labour of self-examination, and for its soft placidity called "prayer," the state of perpetual readiness for the "coming of God"), I mean the idleness with a good conscience, the idleness of olden times and of blood, to which the aristocratic sentiment that work is *dishonouring*—that it vulgarises body and soul—is not quite unfamiliar? And that consequently the modern, noisy, time-engrossing, conceited, foolishly proud laboriousness educates and prepares for "unbelief" more than anything else? Amongst these, for instance, who are at present living apart from religion in Germany, I find "free-thinkers" of diversified species and origin, but above all a majority of those in whom laboriousness from generation to generation has dissolved the religious instincts; so that they no longer know what purpose religions serve, and only note their existence in the world with a kind of dull astonishment. They feel themselves already fully occupied, these good people, be it by their business or by their pleasures, not to mention the "Fatherland," and the newspapers, and their "family duties"; it seems that they have no time whatever left for religion; and above all, it is not obvious to them whether it is a question of a new business or a new pleasure—for it is impossible, they say to themselves, that people should go to church merely to spoil their tempers. They are by no means enemies of religious customs; should certain circumstances, State affairs perhaps, require their participation in such customs, they do what is required, as so many things are done—with a patient and unassuming seriousness, and without much curiosity or discomfort;—they live too much apart and outside to feel even the necessity for a *for* or *against* in such matters. Among those indifferent persons may be reckoned nowadays the majority of German Protestants of the middle classes, especially in the great laborious centres of trade and commerce; also the majority of laborious scholars, and the entire University personnel (with the exception of the theologians, whose existence and possibility there always give psychologists new and more subtle puzzles to solve). On the part of pious, or merely church-going people, there is seldom any idea of *how much* good will, one might say arbitrary will, is now necessary for a German scholar to take the problem of religion seriously; his whole profession (and as I have said, his whole workmanlike laboriousness, to which he is compelled by his modern conscience) inclines him to a lofty and almost charitable serenity as regards religion, with which is occasionally mingled a slight disdain for the "uncleanliness" of spirit which he takes for granted wherever anyone still professes to belong to the Church. It is only with the help of history (*not* through his own personal experience, therefore) that the scholar succeeds in bringing himself to a respectful seriousness, and to a certain timid deference in presence of religions; but even when his sentiments have reached the stage of gratitude towards them, he has not personally advanced one step nearer to that which still maintains itself as Church or as piety; perhaps even the contrary. The practical indifference to religious matters in the midst of which he has been born and brought up, usually sublimates itself in his case into circumspection and cleanliness, which shuns contact with religious men and things; and it may be just the depth of his tolerance and humanity which prompts him to avoid the delicate trouble which tolerance itself brings with it.—Every age has its own divine type of naïveté, for the discovery of which other ages may envy it: and how much naïveté—adorable, childlike, and boundlessly foolish naïveté—is involved in this belief of the scholar in his superiority, in the good conscience of his tolerance, in the unsuspecting, simple certainty with which his instinct treats the religious man as a lower and less valuable type, beyond, before, and *above* which he himself has developed —he, the little arrogant dwarf and mob-man, the sedulously alert, head-and-hand drudge of "ideas," of "modern ideas"!

V

The philosopher, as *we* free spirits understand him—as the man of the greatest responsibility, who has the conscience for the general development of mankind,—will use religion for his disciplining and educating work, just as he will use the contemporary political and economic conditions. The selecting and disciplining influence—destructive, as well as creative and fashioning—which can be exercised by means of religion is manifold and varied, according to the sort of people placed under its spell and protection. For those who are strong and independent, destined and trained to command, in whom the judgment and skill of a ruling race is incorporated, religion is an additional means for overcoming resistance in the exercise of authority—as a bond which binds rulers and subjects in common, betraying and surrendering to the former the conscience of the latter, their inmost heart, which would fain escape obedience. And in the case of the unique natures of noble origin, if by virtue of superior spirituality they should incline to a more retired and contemplative life, reserving to themselves only the more refined forms of government (over chosen disciples or members of an order), religion itself may be used as a means for obtaining peace from the noise and trouble of managing *grosser* affairs, and for securing immunity from the *unavoidable* filth of all political agitation. The Brahmins, for instance,

understood this fact. With the help of a religious organisation, they secured to themselves the power of nominating kings for the people, while
their sentiments prompted them to keep apart and outside, as men with
a higher and super-regal mission. At the same time religion gives induce-
ment and opportunity to some of the subjects to qualify themselves for
future ruling and commanding: the slowly ascending ranks and classes,
in which, through fortunate marriage customs, volitional power and
delight in self-control are on the increase. To them religion offers sufficient incentives and temptations to aspire to higher intellectuality, and
to experience the sentiments of authoritative self-control, of silence, and
of solitude. Asceticism and Puritanism are almost indispensable means
of educating and ennobling a race which seeks to rise above its hereditary
baseness and work itself upward to future supremacy. And finally, to
ordinary men, to the majority of the people, who exist for service and
general utility, and are only so far entitled to exist, religion gives invaluable
contentedness with their lot and condition, peace of heart, ennoblement
of obedience, additional social happiness and sympathy, with something
of transfiguration and embellishment, something of justification of all
the commonplaceness, all the meanness, all the semi-animal poverty of
their souls. Religion, together with the religious significance of life,
sheds sunshine over such perpetually harassed men, and makes even their
own aspect endurable to them; it operates upon them as the Epicurean
philosophy usually operates upon sufferers of a higher order, in a refresh-
ing and refining manner, almost *turning* suffering *to account,* and in the
end even hallowing and vindicating it. There is perhaps nothing so admirable in Christianity and Buddhism as their art of teaching even the
lowest to elevate themselves by piety to a seemingly higher order of
things, and thereby to retain their satisfaction with the actual world in
which they find it difficult enough to live—this very difficulty being
necessary.

VI

To be sure—to make also the bad counter-reckoning against such
religions, and to bring to light their secret dangers—the cost is always
excessive and terrible when religions do *not* operate as an educational
and disciplinary medium in the hands of the philosopher, but rule voluntarily and *paramountly,* when they wish to be the final end, and not a
means along with other means. Among men, as among all other animals,
there is a surplus of defective, diseased, degenerating, infirm, and necessarily suffering individuals; the successful cases, among men also, are
always the exception; and in view of the fact that man is *the animal not
yet properly adapted to his environment,* the rare exception. But worse
still. The higher the type a man represents, the greater is the improbability

that he will *succeed;* the accidental, the law of irrationality in the general
constitution of mankind, manifests itself most terribly in its destructive
effect on the higher orders of men, the conditions of whose lives are
delicate, diverse, and difficult to determine. What, then, is the attitude
of the two greatest religions above-mentioned to the *surplus* of failures
in life? They endeavour to preserve and keep alive whatever can be preserved; in fact, as the religions *for sufferers,* they take the part of these
upon principle; they are always in favour of those who suffer from life
as from a disease, and they would fain treat every other experience of
life as false and impossible. However highly we may esteem this indulgent
and preservative care (inasmuch as in applying to others, it has applied,
and applies also to the highest and usually the most suffering type of man),
the hitherto *paramount* religions—to give a general appreciation of them
—are among the principal causes which have kept the type of "man"
upon a lower level—they have preserved too much *that which should have
perished.* One has to thank them for invaluable services; and who is
sufficiently rich in gratitude not to feel poor at the contemplation of all
that the "spiritual men" of Christianity have done for Europe hitherto!
But when they had given comfort to the sufferers, courage to the oppressed
and despairing, a staff and support to the helpless, and when they had
allured from society into convents and spiritual penitentiaries the broken-
hearted and distracted: what else had they to do in order to work systematically in that fashion, and with a good conscience, for the preservation
of all the sick and suffering, which means, in deed and in truth, to work
for *the deterioration of the European race?* To *reverse* all estimates of value
—*that* is what they had to do! And to shatter the strong, to spoil great
hopes, to cast suspicion on the delight in beauty, to break down everything
autonomous, manly, conquering, and imperious—all instincts which are
natural to the highest and most successful type of "man"—into uncer-
tainty, distress of conscience, and self-destruction; forsooth, to invert all
love of the earthly and of supremacy over the earth, into hatred of the
earth and earthly things—*that* is the task the Church imposed on itself,
and was obliged to impose, until, according to its standard of value, "un-
worldliness," "unsensuousness," and "higher man" fused into one sentiment. If one could observe the strangely painful, equally coarse and refined
comedy of European Christianity with the derisive and impartial eye of
an Epicurean god, I should think one would never cease marvelling and
laughing; does it not actually seem that some single will has ruled over
Europe for eighteen centuries in order to make a *sublime abortion* of man?
He, however, who, with opposite requirements (no longer Epicurean) and
with some divine hammer in his hand, could approach this almost voluntary degeneration and stunting of mankind, as exemplified in the European Christian (Pascal, for instance), would he not have to cry aloud with

rage, pity, and horror: "Oh, you bunglers, presumptuous pitiful bunglers, what have you done! Was that a work for your hands? How you have hacked and botched my finest stone! What have *you* presumed to do!" —I should say that Christianity has hitherto been the most portentous of presumptions. Men, not great enough, nor hard enough, to be entitled as artists to take part in fashioning *man;* men, not sufficiently strong and far-sighted to *allow,* with sublime self-constraint, the obvious law of the thousandfold failures and perishings to prevail; men, not sufficiently noble to see the radically different grades of rank and intervals of rank that separate man from man:—*such* men, with their "equality before God," have hitherto swayed the destiny of Europe; until at last a dwarfed, almost ludicrous species has been produced, a gregarious animal, something obliging, sickly, mediocre, the European of the present day.

IV. APOTHEGMS AND INTERLUDES

I

Woman learns how to hate in proportion as she—forgets how to charm.

II

Love to one only is a barbarity, for it is exercised at the expense of all others. Love to God also!

III

The same emotions are in man and woman, but in different *tempo;* on that account man and woman never cease to misunderstand each other.

IV

It is a curious thing that God learned Greek when he wished to turn author—and that he did not learn it better.

V

In the background of all their personal vanity, women themselves have still their impersonal scorn—for "woman."

VI

He who attains his ideal, precisely thereby surpasses it.

VII

With his principles a man seeks either to dominate, or justify, or honour, or reproach, or conceal his habits: two men with the same principles probably seek fundamentally different ends therewith.

VIII

The sexes deceive themselves about each other: the reason is that in reality they honour and love only themselves (or their own ideal, to express it more agreeably). Thus man wishes woman to be peaceable: but in fact woman is *essentially* unpeaceable, like the cat, however well she may have assumed the peaceable demeanour.

IX

The great epochs of our life are at the points when we gain courage to rebaptize our badness as the best in us.

X

When we have to change an opinion about anyone, we charge heavily to his account the inconvenience he thereby causes us.

XI

He who cannot find the way to *his* ideal, lives more frivolously and shamelessly than the man without an ideal.

XII

"You want to prepossess him in your favour? Then you must be embarrassed before him."

XIII

The immense expectation with regard to sexual love, and the coyness in this expectation, spoils all the perspectives of women at the outset.

XIV

Where there is neither love nor hatred in the game woman's play is mediocre.

XV

To him who feels himself preordained to contemplation and not to belief, all believers are too noisy and obtrusive; he guards against them.

XVI

A nation is a detour of nature to arrive at six or seven great men.— Yes, and then to get round them.

XVII

When a woman has scholarly inclinations there is generally something wrong with her sexual nature. Barrenness itself conduces to a certain virility of taste; man, indeed, if I may say so, is "the barren animal."

XVIII

Comparing man and woman generally, one may say that woman would not have the genius for adornment, if she had not the instinct for the *secondary* role.

XIX

He who fights with monsters should be careful lest he thereby become a monster. And if thou gaze long into an abyss, the abyss will also gaze into thee.

XX

In the eyes of all true women science is hostile to the sense of shame. They feel as if one wished to peep under their skin with it—or worse still! under their dress and finery.

V. THE NATURAL HISTORY OF MORALS

I

EVERY SYSTEM of morals is a sort of tyranny against "nature" and also against "reason"; that is, however, no objection, unless one should again decree by some system of morals, that all kinds of tyranny and unreasonableness are unlawful. What is essential and invaluable in every system of morals, is that it is a long constraint. In order to understand Stoicism, or Port-Royal, or Puritanism, one should remember the constraint under which every language has attained to strength and freedom—the metrical constraint, the tyranny of rhyme and rhythm. How much trouble have the poets and orators of every nation given themselves!—not excepting some of the prose writers of to-day, in whose ear dwells an inexorable conscientiousness—"for the sake of a folly," as utilitarian bunglers say, and thereby deem themselves wise—"from submission to arbitrary laws," as the anarchists say, and thereby fancy themselves "free," even free-spirited. The singular fact remains, however, that everything of the nature of freedom, elegance, boldness, dance, and masterly certainty, which exists or has existed, whether it be in thought itself, or in administration, or in speaking and persuading, in art just as in conduct, has only developed by means of the tyranny of such arbitrary law; and in all seriousness, it is not at all improbable that precisely this is "nature" and "natural"—and *not laisser-aller!* Every artist knows how different from the state of letting himself go, is his "most natural" condition, the free arranging, locating, disposing, and constructing in the moments of "inspiration"—and how strictly and delicately he then obeys a thousand laws, which, by their very rigidness and precision, defy all formulation by means of ideas (even the most stable idea has, in comparison therewith, something floating, manifold, and ambiguous in it). The essential thing "in heaven and in earth" is, apparently (to repeat it once more), that there should be long *obedience* in the same direction; there thereby results, and has always resulted in the long run, something which has made life worth living; for instance, virtue, art, music, dancing, reason, spirituality—anything whatever that is transfiguring, refined, foolish, or divine. The long bondage of the spirit, the distrustful constraint in the communicability of ideas, the discipline which the thinker imposed on himself to think in accordance with the rules of a church or a court, or conformable to Aristotelian premises, the persistent spiritual will to interpret everything that happened according to a Christian scheme, and in every occurrence to rediscover and justify the Christian God:—all this violence, arbitrariness, severity, dreadfulness, and unreasonableness has proved itself the disciplinary means whereby the European spirit has attained its strength, its remorseless curiosity and subtle mobility; granted also that much irrecoverable strength and spirit had to be stifled, suffocated, and spoilt in the process (for here, as everywhere, "nature" shows herself as she is, in all her extravagant and *indifferent* magnificence, which is shocking, but nevertheless noble). That for centuries European thinkers only thought in order to prove something— nowadays, on the contrary, we are suspicious of every thinker who "wishes to prove something"—that it was always settled beforehand what *was to be* the result of their strictest thinking, as it was perhaps in the Asiatic astrology of former times, or as it is still at the present day in the innocent, Christian-moral explanation of immediate personal events "for the glory of God," or "for the good of the soul":—this tyranny, this arbitrariness, this severe and magnificent stupidity has *educated* the spirit; slavery, both in the coarser and the finer sense, is apparently an indispensable means even of spiritual education and discipline. One may look at every system of morals in this light: it is "nature" therein which teaches to hate the *laisser-aller,* the too great freedom, and implants the need for limited horizons, for immediate duties—it teaches the *narrowing of perspectives,* and thus, in a certain sense, that stupidity is a condition of life and development. "Thou must obey someone, and for a long time; *otherwise* thou wilt come to grief, and lose all respect for thyself"—this seems to me to be the moral imperative of nature, which is certainly neither "categorical," as old Kant wished (consequently the "otherwise"), nor does it address itself to the individual (what does nature care for the individual!), but to nations, races, ages, and ranks, above all, however, to the animal "man" generally, to *mankind.*

II

The old theological problem of "Faith" and "Knowledge," or more plainly, of instinct and reason—the question whether, in respect to the valuation of things, instinct deserves more authority than rationality, which wants to appreciate and act according to motives, according to a "Why," that is to say, in conformity to purpose and utility—it is always the old moral problem that first appeared in the person of Socrates, and had divided men's minds long before Christianity. Socrates himself, following, of course, the taste of his talent—that of a surpassing dialectician —took first the side of reason; and, in fact, what did he do all his life but laugh at the awkward incapacity of the noble Athenians, who were men of instinct, like all noble men, and could never give satisfactory answers concerning the motives of their actions? In the end, however, though silently and secretly, he laughed also at himself: with his finer conscience and introspection, he found in himself the same difficulty and incapacity. "But why"—he said to himself—"should one on that account separate oneself from the instincts! One must set them right, and the reason *also*—one must follow the instincts, but at the same time persuade the reason to support them with good arguments." This was the real *falseness* of that great and mysterious ironist; he brought his conscience up to the point that he was satisfied with a kind of self-outwitting: in fact, he perceived the irrationality in the moral judgment.—Plato, more innocent in such matters, and without the craftiness of the plebeian, wished to prove to himself, at the expenditure of all his strength—the greatest strength a philosopher had ever expended—that reason and instinct lead spontaneously to one goal, to the good, to "God"; and since Plato, all theologians and philosophers have followed the same path—which means that in matters of morality, instinct (or as Christians call it, "Faith," or as I call it, "the herd") has hitherto triumphed. Unless one should make an exception in the case of Descartes, the father of rationalism (and consequently the grandfather of the Revolution), who recognised only the authority of reason: but reason is only a tool, and Descartes was superficial.

III

Whoever has followed the history of a single science, finds in its development a clue to the understanding of the oldest and commonest processes of all "knowledge and cognisance": there, as here, the premature hypotheses, the fictions, the good stupid will to "belief," and the lack of distrust and patience are first developed—our senses learn late, and never learn completely, to be subtle, reliable, and cautious organs of knowledge. Our eyes find it easier on a given occasion to produce a picture already often produced, than to seize upon the divergence and novelty of an impression: the latter requires more force, more "morality." It is difficult and painful for the ear to listen to anything new; we hear strange music badly. When we hear another language spoken, we involuntarily attempt to form the sounds into words with which we are more familiar and conversant—it was thus, for example, that the Germans modified the spoken word *arcubalista* into *armbrust* (cross-bow). Our senses are also hostile and averse to the new; and generally, even in the "simplest" processes of sensation, the emotions *dominate*—such as fear, love, hatred, and the passive emotion of indolence.—As little as a reader nowadays reads all the single words (not to speak of syllables) of a page—he rather takes about five out of every twenty words at random, and "guesses" the probably appropriate sense to them—just as little do we see a tree correctly and completely in respect to its leaves, branches, colour, and shape; we find it so much easier to fancy the chance of a tree. Even in the midst of the most remarkable experiences, we still do just the same; we fabricate the greater part of the experience, and can hardly be made to contemplate any event, *except* as "inventors" thereof. All this goes to prove that from our fundamental nature and from remote ages we have been—*accustomed to lying*. Or, to express it more politely and hypocritically, in short, more pleasantly—one is much more of an artist than one is aware of.—In an animated conversation, I often see the face of the person with whom I am speaking so clearly and sharply defined before me, according to the thought he expresses, or which I believe to be evoked in his mind, that the degree of distinctness far exceeds the *strength* of my visual faculty—the delicacy of the play of the muscles and of the expression of the eyes *must* therefore be imagined by me. Probably the person put on quite a different expression, or none at all.

IV

The difference among men does not manifest itself only in the difference of their lists of desirable things—in their regarding different good things as worth striving for, and being disagreed as to the greater or less value, the order of rank, of the commonly recognised desirable things:—it manifests itself much more in what they regard as actually *having* and *possessing* a desirable thing. As regards a woman, for instance, the control over her body and her sexual gratification serves as an amply sufficient sign of ownership and possession to the more modest man; another with a more suspicious and ambitious thirst for possession, sees the "questionableness," the mere apparentness of such ownership, and wishes to have finer tests in order to know especially whether the woman not only gives herself to him, but also gives up for his sake what she has or would like to have—only *then* does he look upon her as "possessed." A third, however, has not even here got to the limit of his distrust and his desire for possession: he asks himself whether the woman, when she gives up everything for him, does not perhaps do so for a phantom of him; he wishes first to be thoroughly, indeed, profoundly well known; in order to be loved at all he ventures to let himself be found out. Only then does he feel the beloved one fully in his possession, when she no longer deceives herself about him, when she loves him just as much for the sake of his devilry and concealed insatiability, as for his goodness, patience, and spirituality. One man would like to possess a nation, and he finds all the higher arts of Cagliostro and Catalina suitable for his purpose. Another, with a more refined thirst for possession, says to himself: "One may not deceive where one desires to possess"—he is irritated and impatient at the idea that a mask of him should rule in the hearts of the people: "I must, therefore, *make* myself known, and first of all learn to know myself!" Amongst helpful and charitable people, one almost always finds the awkward craftiness which first gets up suitably him who has to be helped, as though, for instance, he should "merit" help, seek just *their* help, and would show himself deeply grateful, attached, and subservient to them for all help. With these conceits, they take control of the needy as a property, just as in general they are charitable and helpful out of a desire for property. One finds them jealous when they are crossed or forestalled in their charity. Parents involuntarily make something like themselves out of their children—they call that "education"; no mother doubts at the bottom of her heart that the child she has borne is thereby her property, no father hesitates about his right to *his own* ideas and notions of worth. Indeed, in former times fathers deemed it right to use their discretion concerning the life or death of the newly born (as amongst the ancient Germans). And like the father, so also do the teacher, the class, the priest, and the prince still see in every new individual an un-ʋbjectionable opportunity for a new possession. The consequence is . . .

V

All the systems of morals which address themselves with a view to their "happiness," as it is called—what else are they but suggestions for behaviour adapted to the degree of *danger* from themselves in which the individuals live; recipes for their passions, their good and bad propensities, in so far as such have the Will to Power and would like to play the master; small and great expediencies and elaborations, permeated with the musty odour of old family medicines and old-wife wisdom; all of them grotesque and absurd in their form—because they address themselves to "all," because they generalise where generalisation is not authorised; all of them speaking unconditionally, and taking themselves uncondi-tionally; all of them flavoured not merely with one grain of salt, but rather endurable only, and sometimes even seductive, when they are over-spiced and begin to smell dangerously, especially of "the other world." That is all of little value when estimated intellectually, and is far from being "science," much less "wisdom"; but, repeated once more, and three times repeated, it is expediency, expediency, expediency, mixed with stupidity, stupidity, stupidity—whether it be the indifference and statuesque cold-ness towards the heated folly of the emotions, which the Stoics advised and fostered; or the no-more-laughing and no-more-weeping of Spinoza, the destruction of the emotions by their analysis and vivisection which he recommended so naïvely; or the lowering of the emotions to an inno-cent mean at which they may be satisfied, the Aristotelianism of morals; or even morality as the enjoyment of the emotions in a voluntary at-tenuation and spiritualisation by the symbolism of art, perhaps as music, or as love of God, and of mankind for God's sake—for in religion the passions are once more enfranchised, provided that . . . ; or, finally, even the complaisant and wanton surrender to the emotions, as has been taught by Hafis and Goethe, the bold letting-go of the reins, the spiritual and corporeal *licentia morum* in the exceptional cases of wise old codgers and drunkards, with whom it "no longer has much danger."

VI

As long as the utility which determines moral estimates is only gregarious utility, as long as the preservation of the community is only kept in view, and the immoral is sought precisely and exclusively in what seems dangerous to the maintenance of the community, there can be no "morality of love to one's neighbour." Granted even that there is already a little constant exercise of consideration, sympathy, fairness, gentleness, and mutual assistance, granted that even in this condition of society all those instincts are already active which are latterly distinguished by honourable names as "virtues," and eventually almost coincide with the conception "morality": in that period they do not as yet belong to the domain of moral valuations—they are still *ultra-moral*. A sympathetic action, for instance, is neither called good nor bad, moral nor immoral, in the best period of the Romans; and should it be praised, a sort of resentful disdain is compatible with this praise, even at the best, directly the sympathetic action is compared with one which contributes to the welfare of the whole, to the *res publica*. After all, "love to our neighbour" is always a secondary matter, partly conventional and arbitrarily manifested in relation to our *fear of our neighbour*. After the fabric of society seems on the whole established and secured against external dangers, it is this fear of our neighbour which again creates new perspectives of moral valuation. Certain strong and dangerous instincts, such as the love of enterprise, foolhardiness, revengefulness, astuteness, rapacity, and love of power, which up till then had not only to be honoured from the point of view of general utility—under other names, of course, than those here given—but had to be fostered and cultivated (because they were perpetually required in the common danger against the common enemies), are now felt in their dangerousness to be doubly strong—when the outlets for them are lacking—and are gradually branded as immoral and given over to calumny. The contrary instincts and inclinations now attain to moral honour; the gregarious instinct gradually draws its conclusions. How much or how little dangerousness to the community or to equality is contained in an opinion, a condition, an emotion, a disposition, or an endowment—that is now the moral perspective; here again fear is the mother of morals. It is by the loftiest and strongest instincts, when they break out passionately and carry the individual far above and beyond the average, and the low level of the gregarious conscience, that the self-reliance of the community is destroyed; its belief in itself, its backbone, as it were, breaks; consequently these very instincts will be most branded and defamed. The lofty independent spirituality, the will to stand alone, and even the cogent reason, are felt to be dangers; everything that elevates the individual above the herd, and is a source of fear to the neighbour, is henceforth called *evil;* the tolerant, unassuming, self-adapting, self-equalising disposition, the *mediocrity* of desires, attains to moral distinction and honour. Finally, under very peaceful circumstances, there is always less opportunity and necessity for training the feelings to severity and rigour; and now every form of severity, even in justice, begins to disturb the conscience; a lofty and rigourous nobleness and self-responsibility almost offends, and awakens distrust, "the lamb," and still more "the sheep," wins respect. There is a point of diseased mellowness and effeminacy in the history of society, at which society itself takes the part of him who injures it, the part of the *criminal,* and does so, in fact, seriously and honestly. To punish, appears to it to be somehow unfair—it is certain that the idea of "punishment" and "the obligation to punish" are then painful and alarming to people. "Is it not sufficient if the criminal be rendered *harmless?* Why should we still punish? Punishment itself is terrible!"—with these questions gregarious morality, the morality of fear, draws its ultimate conclusion. If one could at all do away with danger, the cause of fear, one would have done away with this morality at the same time, it would no longer be necessary, it *would not consider itself* any longer necessary!—Whoever examines the conscience of the present-day European, will always elicit the same imperative from its thousand moral folds and hidden recesses, the imperative of the timidity of the herd: "we wish that some time or other there may be *nothing more to fear!"* Some time or other—the will and the way *thereto* is nowadays called "progress" all over Europe.

VII

Let us at once say again what we have already said a hundred times, for people's ears nowadays are unwilling to hear such truths—*our* truths. We know well enough how offensively it sounds when anyone plainly, and without metaphor, counts man amongst the animals; but it will be accounted to us almost a *crime,* that it is precisely in respect to men of "modern ideas" that we have constantly applied the terms "herd," "herd-instincts," and suchlike expressions. What avail is it? We cannot do otherwise, for it is precisely here that our new insight is. We have found that in all the principal moral judgments Europe has become unanimous, including likewise the countries where European influence prevails: in Europe people evidently *know* what Socrates thought he did not know, and what the famous serpent of old once promised to teach—they "know" to-day what is good and evil. It must then sound hard and be distasteful to the ear, when we always insist that that which here thinks it knows, that which here glorifies itself with praise and blame, and calls itself good, is the instinct of the herding human animal: the instinct which has come and is ever coming more and more to the front, to preponderance and supremacy over other instincts, according to the increasing physiological approximation and resemblance of which it is the symptom. *Morality in Europe at present is herding-animal morality;* and therefore, as we understand the matter, only one kind of human morality, beside which, before which, and after which many other moralities, and above all *higher* moralities, are or should be possible. Against such a "possibility," against such a "should be," however, this morality defends itself with all its strength; it says obstinately and inexorably: "I am morality itself and nothing else is morality!" Indeed, with the help of a religion which has humoured and flattered the sublimest desires of the herding-animal, things have reached such a point that we always find a more visible expression of this morality even in political and social arrangements: the *democratic* movement is the inheritance of the Christian movement. That its *tempo,* however, is much too slow and sleepy for the more impatient ones, for those who are sick and distracted by the herding-instinct, is indicated by the increasingly furious howling, and always less disguised teethgnashing of the anarchist dogs, who are now roving through the highways of European culture. Apparently in opposition to the peacefully industrious democrats and Revolution-ideologues, and still more so to the awkward philosophasters and fraternity-visionaries who call themselves Socialists and want a "free society," those are really at one with them all in their thorough and instinctive hostility to every form of society other than that of the *autonomous* herd (to the extent even of repudiating the notions "master" and "servant"—*ni dieu ni maître,* says a socialist formula); at one in their tenacious opposition to every special claim, every special right and privilege (this means ultimately opposition to *every* right, for when all are equal, no one needs "rights" any longer); at one in their distrust of punitive justice (as though it were a violation of the weak, unfair to the *necessary* consequences of all former society); but equally at one in their religion of sympathy, in their compassion for all that feels, lives, and suffers (down to the very animals, up even to "God"—the extravagance of "sympathy for God" belongs to a democratic age); altogether at one in the cry and impatience of their sympathy, in their deadly hatred of suffering generally, in their almost feminine incapacity for witnessing it or *allowing* it; at one in their involuntary beglooming and heart-softening, under the spell of which Europe seems to be threatened with a new Buddhism; at one in their belief in the morality of *mutual* sympathy, as though it were morality in itself, the climax, the *attained* climax of mankind, the sole hope of the future, the consolation of the present, the great discharge from all the obligations of the past; altogether at one in their belief in the community as the *deliverer,* in the herd, and therefore in "themselves."

VIII

We, who hold a different belief—we, who regard the democratic movement, not only as a degenerating form of political organisation, but as equivalent to a degenerating, a waning type of man, as involving his mediocrising and depreciation: where have *we* to fix our hopes? In *new philosophers*—there is no other alternative: in minds strong and original enough to initiate opposite estimates of value, to transvalue and invert "eternal valuations"; in forerunners, in men of the future, who in the present shall fix the constraints and fasten the knots which will compel millenniums to take *new* paths. To teach man the future of humanity as his *will,* as depending on human will, and to make preparation for vast hazardous enterprises and collective attempts in rearing and educating, in order thereby to put an end to the frightful rule of folly and chance which has hitherto gone by the name of "history" (the folly of the "greatest number" is only its last form)—for that purpose a new type of philosophers and commanders will some time or other be needed, at the very idea of which everything that has existed in the way of occult, terrible, and benevolent beings might look pale and dwarfed. The image of such leaders hovers before *our* eyes:—is it lawful for me to say it aloud, ye free spirits? The conditions which one would partly have to create and partly utilise for their genesis; the presumptive methods and tests by virtue of which a soul should grow up to such an elevation and power as to feel a *constraint* to these tasks; a transvaluation of values, under the new pressure and hammer of which a conscience should be steeled and a heart transformed into brass, so as to bear the weight of such responsibility; and on the other hand the necessity for such leaders, the dreadful danger that they might be lacking, or miscarry and degenerate:—these are *our* real anxieties and glooms, ye know it well, ye free spirits! these are the heavy distant thoughts and storms which sweep across the heaven of *our* life. There are few pains so grievous as to have seen, divined, or experienced how an exceptional man has missed his way and deteriorated; but he who has the rare eye for the universal danger of "man" himself *deteriorating,* he who like us has recognised the extraordinary fortuitousness which has hitherto played its game in respect to the future of mankind—a game in which neither the hand, nor even a "finger of God" has participated!— he who divines the fate that is hidden under the idiotic unwariness and blind confidence of "modern ideas," and still more under the whole of Christo-European morality—suffers from an anguish with which no other is to be compared. He sees at a glance all that could still *be made out of man* through a favourable accumulation and augmentation of human powers and arrangements; he knows with all the knowledge of his conviction how unexhausted man still is for the greatest possibilities, and how often in the past the type man has stood in presence of mysterious decisions and new paths:—he knows still better from his painfulest recollections on what wretched obstacles promising developments of the highest rank have hitherto usually gone to pieces, broken down, sunk, and become contemptible. The *universal degeneracy of mankind* to the level of the "man of the future"—as idealised by the socialistic fools and shallowpates—this degeneracy and dwarfing of man to an absolutely gregarious animal (or as they call it, to a man of "free society"), this brutalising of man into a pigmy with equal rights and claims, is undoubtedly *possible!* He who has thought out this possibility to its ultimate conclusion knows *another* loathing unknown to the rest of mankind—and perhaps also a new *mission!*

VI. WE SCHOLARS

I

AT THE RISK that moralising may also reveal itself here as that which it has always been—namely, resolutely *montrer ses plaies,* according to Balzac— I would venture to protest against an improper and injurious alteration of rank, which quite unnoticed, and as if with the best conscience, threatens nowadays to establish itself in the relations of science and philosophy. I mean to say that one must have the right out of one's own *experience*—experience, as it seems to me, always implies unfortunate experience?—to treat of such an important question of rank, so as not to speak of colour like the blind, or *against* science like women and artists. ("Ah! this dreadful science!" sigh their instinct and their shame, "it always *finds things out!"*) The declaration of independence of the scientific man, his emancipation from philosophy, is one of the subtler after-effects of democratic organisation and disorganisation: the self-glorification and self-conceitedness of the learned man is now everywhere in full bloom, and in its best springtime—which does not mean to imply that in this case self-praise smells sweetly. Here also the instinct of the populace cries, "Freedom from all masters!" and after science has, with the happiest results, resisted theology, whose "handmaid" it had been too long, it now proposes in its wantonness and indiscretion to lay down laws for philosophy, and in its turn to play the "master"—what am I saying! to play the *philosopher* on its own account. My memory—the memory of a scientific man, if you please!—teems with the naïvetés of insolence which I have heard about philosophy and philosophers from young naturalists and old physicians (not to mention the most cultured and most conceited of all learned men, the philologists and schoolmasters, who are both the one and the other by profession). On one occasion it was the specialist and the Jack Horner who instinctively stood on the defensive against all synthetic tasks and capabilities; at another time it was the industrious worker who had got a scent of *otium* and refined luxuriousness in the internal economy of the philosopher, and felt himself aggrieved and belittled thereby. On another occasion it was the colour-blindness of the utilitarian, who sees nothing in philosophy but a series of *refuted* systems, and an extravagant expenditure which "does nobody any good." At another time the fear of disguised mysticism and of the boundary-adjustment of knowledge became conspicuous, at another time the disregard of individual philosophers, which had involuntarily extended to disregard of philosophy generally. In fine, I found most frequently, behind the proud disdain of philosophy in young scholars, the evil after-effect of some particular philosopher, to whom on the whole obedience had been foresworn, without, however, the spell of his scornful estimates of other philosophers having been got rid of—the result being a general ill-will to all philosophy. (Such seems to me, for instance, the after-effect of Schopenhauer on the most modern Germany: by his unintelligent rage against Hegel, he has succeeded in severing the whole of the last generation of Germans from its connection with German culture, which culture, all things considered, has been an elevation and a divining refinement of the *historical sense;* but precisely at this point Schopenhauer himself was poor, irreceptive, and un-German to the extent of ingeniousness.) On the whole, speaking generally, it may just have been the humanness, all-too-humanness of the modern philosophers themselves, in short, their contemptibleness, which has injured most radically the reverence for philosophy and opened the doors to the instinct of the populace. Let it but be acknowledged to what an extent our modern world diverges from the whole style of the world of Heraclites, Plato, Empedocles, and whatever else all the royal and magnificent anchorites of the spirit were called; and with what justice an honest man of science *may* feel himself of a better family and origin, in view of such representatives of philosophy, who, owing to the fashion of the present day, are just as much aloft as they are down below—in Germany, for instance, the two lions of Berlin, the anarchist Eugen Dühring and the amalgamist Eduard von Hartmann. It is especially the sight of those hotchpotch philosophers, who call themselves "realists," or "positivists," which is calculated to implant a dangerous distrust in the soul of a young and ambitious scholar: those philosophers, at the best, are themselves but scholars and specialists, that is very evident! All of them are persons who have been vanquished and *brought back again* under the dominion of science, who at one time or another claimed more from themselves, without having a right to the "more" and its responsibility—and who now, creditably, rancorously, and vindictively, represent in word and deed, *disbelief* in the master-task and supremacy of philosophy. After all, how could it be otherwise? Science flourishes nowadays and has the good conscience clearly visible on its countenance; while that to which the entire modern philosophy has gradually sunk, the remnant of philosophy of the present day, excites distrust and displeasure, if not scorn and pity. Philosophy reduced to a "theory of knowledge," no more in fact than a diffident science of epochs and doctrine of forbearance: a philosophy that never even gets beyond the threshold, and rigourously *denies* itself the right to enter—that is philosophy in its last throes, an end, an agony, something that awakens pity. How could such a philosophy—*rule!*

II

In relation to the genius, that is to say, a being who either *engenders* or *produces*—both words understood in their fullest sense—the man of learning, the scientific average man, has always something of the old maid about him; for, like her, he is not conversant with the two principal functions of man. To both, of course, to the scholar and to the old maid, one concedes respectability, as if by way of indemnification—in these cases one emphasises the respectability—and yet, in the compulsion of this concession, one has the same admixture of vexation. Let us examine more closely: what is the scientific man? Firstly, a commonplace type of man, with commonplace virtues: that is to say, a non-ruling, non-authoritative, and non-self-sufficient type of man; he possesses industry, patient adaptableness to rank and file, equability and moderation in capacity and requirement; he has the instinct for people like himself, and for that which they require—for instance: the portion of independence and green meadow without which there is no rest from labour, the claim to honour and consideration (which first and foremost presupposes recognition and recognisability), the sunshine of a good name, the perpetual ratification of his value and usefulness, with which the inward *distrust* which lies at the bottom of the heart of all dependent men and gregarious animals, has again and again to be overcome. The learned man, as is appropriate, has also maladies and faults of an ignoble kind: he is full of petty envy, and has a lynx-eye for the weak points in those natures to whose elevations he cannot attain. He is confiding, yet only as one who lets himself go, but does not *flow;* and precisely before the man of the great current he stands all the colder and more reserved—his eye is then like a smooth and irresponsive lake, which is no longer moved by rapture or sympathy. The worst and most dangerous thing of which a scholar is capable results from the instinct of mediocrity of his type, from the Jesuitism of mediocrity, which labours instinctively for the destruction of the exceptional man, and endeavours to break—or still better, to relax—every bent bow. To relax, of course, with consideration, and naturally with an indulgent hand—to *relax* with confiding sympathy: that is the real art of Jesuitism, which has always understood how to introduce itself as the religion of sympathy.

III

When a philosopher nowadays makes known that he is not a sceptic, people all hear it impatiently; they regard him on that account with some apprehension, they would like to ask so many, many questions . . . indeed among timid hearers, of whom there are now so many, he is henceforth said to be dangerous. With his repudiation of scepticism, it seems to them as if they heard some evil-threatening sound in the distance, as if a new kind of explosive were being tried somewhere, a dynamite of the spirit, perhaps a newly discovered Russian *nihiline,* a pessimism *bonae voluntatis,* that not only denies, means denial, but—dreadful thought!—*practises* denial. Against this kind of "good will"—a will to the veritable, actual negation of life—there is, as is generally acknowledged nowadays, no better soporific and sedative than scepticism, the mild, pleasing, lulling poppy of scepticism; and Hamlet himself is now prescribed by the doctors of the day as an antidote to the "spirit," and its underground noises. "Are not our ears already full of bad sounds?" say the sceptics, as lovers of repose, and almost as a kind of safety police, "this subterranean Nay is terrible! Be still, ye pessimistic moles!" The sceptic, in effect, that delicate creature, is far too easily frightened; his conscience is schooled so as to start at every Nay, and even at that sharp, decided Yea, and feels something like a bite thereby. Yea! and Nay!—they seem to him opposed to morality; he loves, on the contrary, to make a festival to his virtue by a noble aloofness, while perhaps he says with Montaigne: "What do I know?" Or with Socrates: "I know that I know nothing." Or: "Here I do not trust myself, no door is open to me." Or: "Even if the door were open, why should I enter immediately?" Or: "What is the use of any hasty hypotheses? It might quite well be in good taste to make no hypotheses at all. Are you absolutely obliged to straighten at once what is crooked? to stuff every hole with some kind of oakum? Is there not time enough for that? Has not the time leisure? Oh, ye demons, can ye not at all *wait?* The uncertain also has its charms, the Sphinx, too, is a Circe, and Circe, too, was a philosopher."—Thus does a sceptic console himself; and in truth he needs some consolation. For scepticism is the most spiritual expression of a certain many-sided physiological temperament, which in ordinary language is called nervous debility and sickliness; it arises whenever races or classes which have been long separated, decisively and suddenly blend with one another. In the new generation, which has inherited as it were different standards and valuations in its blood, everything is disquiet, derangement, doubt, and tentative; the best powers operate restrictively, the very virtues prevent each other's growing and becoming strong, equilibrium, ballast, and perpendicular stability are lacking in body and soul. That, however, which is most diseased and degenerated in such nondescripts is the *will;* they are no longer familiar with independence of decision, or the courageous feeling of pleasure in willing— they are doubtful of the "freedom of the will" even in their dreams.

IV

It is always more obvious to me that the philosopher, as a man *indispensable* for the morrow and the day after the morrow, has ever found himself, and *has been obliged* to find himself, in contradiction to the day in which he lives; his enemy has always been the ideal of his day. Hitherto all those extraordinary furtherers of humanity whom one calls philosophers —who rarely regarded themselves as lovers of wisdom, but rather as disagreeable fools and dangerous interrogators—have found their mission, their hard, involuntary, imperative mission (in the end however the greatness of their mission), in being the bad conscience of their age. In putting the vivisector's knife to the breast of the very *virtues of their age,* they have betrayed their own secret; it has been for the sake of a *new* greatness of man, a new untrodden path to his aggrandisement. They have always disclosed how much hypocrisy, indolence, self-indulgence, and self-neglect, how much falsehood was concealed under the most venerated types of contemporary morality, how much virtue was *outlived;* they have always said: "We must remove hence to where *you* are least at home." In face of a world of "modern ideas," which would like to confine every one in a corner, in a "specialty," a philosopher, if there could be philosophers nowadays, would be compelled to place the greatness of man, the conception of "greatness," precisely in his comprehensiveness and multifariousness, in his all-roundness; he would even determine worth and rank according to the amount and variety of that which a man could bear and take upon himself, according to the *extent* to which a man could stretch his responsibility. Nowadays the taste and virtue of the age weaken and attenuate the will; nothing is so adapted to the spirit of the age as weakness of will: consequently, in the ideal of the philosopher, strength of will, sternness and capacity for prolonged resolution, must specially be included in the conception of "greatness"; with as good a right as the opposite doctrine, with its ideal of a silly, renouncing, humble, selfless humanity, was suited to an opposite age—such as the sixteenth century, which suffered from its accumulated energy of will, and from the wildest torrents and floods of selfishness.

V

It is difficult to learn what a philosopher is, because it cannot be taught: one must "know" it by experience—or one should have the pride *not* to know it. The fact that at present people all talk of things of which they *cannot* have any experience, is true more especially and unfortunately as concerns the philosopher and philosophical matters:—the very few

know them, are permitted to know them, and all popular ideas about them
are false. Thus, for instance, the truly philosophical combination of a bold,
exuberant spirituality which runs at *presto* pace, and a dialectic rigour
and necessity which makes no false step, is unknown to most thinkers
and scholars from their own experience, and therefore, should anyone
speak of it in their presence, it is incredible to them. They conceive of
every necessity as troublesome, as a painful compulsory obedience and
state of constraint; thinking itself is regarded by them as something slow
and hesitating, almost as a trouble, and often enough as "worthy of the
sweat of the noble"—but not at all as something easy and divine, closely
related to dancing and exuberance! "To think" and to take a matter
"seriously," "arduously"—that is one and the same thing to them; such
only has been their "experience."—Artists have here perhaps a finer
intuition; they who know only too well that precisely when they no
longer do anything "arbitrarily," and everything of necessity, their feeling of freedom, of subtlety, of power, of creatively fixing, disposing, and
shaping, reaches its climax—in short, that necessity and "freedom of will"
are then the same thing with them. There is, in fine, a gradation of rank
in psychical states, to which the gradation of rank in the problems corresponds; and the highest problems repel ruthlessly every one who ventures
too near them, without being predestined for their solution by the loftiness
and power of his spirituality. Of what use is it for nimble, everyday
intellects, or clumsy, honest mechanics and empiricists to press, in their
plebeian ambition, close to such problems, and as it were into this "holy
of holies"—as so often happens nowadays!

VII. OUR VIRTUES

I

OUR VIRTUES?—It is probable that we, too, have still our virtues, although
naturally they are not those sincere and massive virtues on account of
which we hold our grandfathers in esteem and also at a little distance
from us. We Europeans of the day after to-morrow, we firstlings of the
twentieth century—with all our dangerous curiosity, our multifariousness
and art of disguising, our mellow and seemingly sweetened cruelty in
sense and spirit—we shall presumably, *if* we must have virtues, have those
only which have come to agreement with our most secret and heartfelt
inclinations, with our most ardent requirements: well, then, let us look
for them in our labyrinths!—where, as we know, so many things lose
themselves, so many things get quite lost! And is there anything finer than
to *search* for one's own virtues? Is it not almost to *believe* in one's own

virtues? But this "believing in one's own virtues"—is it not practically the same as what was formerly called one's "good conscience," that long, respectable pigtail of an idea, which our grandfathers used to hang behind their heads, and often enough also behind their understandings? It seems, therefore, that however little we may imagine ourselves to be old-fashioned and grandfatherly respectable in other respects, in one thing we are nevertheless the worthy grandchildren of our grandfathers, we last Europeans with good consciences: we also still wear their pigtail.—Ah! if you only knew how soon, so very soon—it will be different!

II

Now that the praise of the "disinterested person" is so popular one must—probably not without some danger—get an idea of *what* people actually take an interest in, and what are the things generally which fundamentally and profoundly concern ordinary men—including the cultured, even the learned, and perhaps philosophers also, if appearances do not deceive. The fact thereby becomes obvious that the greater part of what interests and charms higher natures, and more refined and fastidious tastes, seems absolutely "uninteresting" to the average man:—if, notwithstanding, he perceive devotion to these interests, he calls it *désintéressé*, and wonders how it is possible to act "disinterestedly." There have been philosophers who could give this popular astonishment a seductive and mystical, other-world expression (perhaps because they did not know the higher nature by experience?), instead of stating the naked and candidly reasonable truth that "disinterested" action is very interesting and "interested" action, provided that . . . "And love?"—What! Even an action for love's sake shall be "unegoistic"? But you fools—! "And the praise of the self-sacrificer?"—But whoever has really offered sacrifice knows that he wanted and obtained something for it—perhaps something from himself for something from himself; that he relinquished here in order to have more there, perhaps in general to be more, or even feel himself "more." But this is a realm of questions and answers in which a more fastidious spirit does not like to stay: for here truth has to stifle her yawns so much when she is obliged to answer. And after all, truth is a woman; one must not use force with her.

III

Wherever sympathy (fellow-suffering) is preached nowadays—and, if I gather rightly, no other religion is any longer preached—let the psychologist have his ears open; through all the vanity, through all the noise which is natural to these preachers (as to all preachers), he will hear a hoarse, groaning, genuine note of *self-contempt*. It belongs to the overshadowing and uglifying of Europe, which has been on the increase for a century (the first symptoms of which are already specified documentarily in a thoughtful letter of Galiani to Madame d'Epinay)—*if it is not really the cause thereof!* The man of "modern ideas," the conceited ape, is excessively dissatisfied with himself—this is perfectly certain. He suffers, and his vanity wants him only "to suffer with his fellows."

IV

Whether it be hedonism, pessimism, utilitarianism, or eudæmonism, all those modes of thinking which measure the worth of things according to *pleasure* and *pain,* that is, according to accompanying circumstances and secondary considerations, are plausible modes of thought and naïvetés, which every one conscious of *creative* powers and an artist's conscience will look down upon with scorn, though not without sympathy. Sympathy for *you!*—to be sure, that is not sympathy as you understand it: it is not sympathy for social "distress," for "society" with its sick and misfortuned, for the hereditarily vicious and defective who lie on the ground around us; still less is it sympathy for the grumbling, vexed, revolutionary slave-classes who strive after power—they call it "freedom." *Our* sympathy is a loftier and further-sighted sympathy:—we see how *man* dwarfs himself, how *you* dwarf him! and there are moments when we view *your* sympathy with an indescribable anguish, when we resist it,—when we regard your seriousness as more dangerous than any kind of levity. You want, if possible—and there is not a more foolish "if possible"—*to do away with suffering;* and we?—it really seems that *we* would rather have it increased and made worse than it has ever been! Well-being, as you understand it—is certainly not a goal; it seems to us an *end;* a condition which at once renders man ludicrous and contemptible—and makes his destruction *desirable!* The discipline of suffering, of *great* suffering—know ye not that it is only *this* discipline that has produced all the elevations of humanity hitherto? The tension of soul in misfortune which communicates to it its energy, its shuddering in view of rack and ruin, its inventiveness and bravery in undergoing, enduring, interpreting, and exploiting misfortune, and whatever depth, mystery, disguise, spirit, artifice, or greatness has been bestowed upon the soul— has it not been bestowed through suffering, through the discipline of great suffering? In man *creature* and *creator* are united: in man there is not only matter, shred, excess, clay, mire, folly, chaos; but there is also the creator, the sculptor, the hardness of the hammer, the divinity of the spectator, and the seventh day—do ye understand this contrast? And that *your* sympathy for the "creature in man" applies to that which has to be fashioned, bruised, forged, stretched, roasted, annealed, refined—to that

which must necessarily *suffer,* and *is meant* to suffer? And *our* sympathy
—do ye not understand what our *reverse* sympathy applies to, when it
resists your sympathy as the worst of all pampering and enervation?—So
it is sympathy *against* sympathy!—But to repeat it once more, there are
higher problems than the problems of pleasure and pain and sympathy;
and all systems of philosophy which deal only with these are naïvetés.

V

We Immoralists.—This world with which *we* are concerned, in
which *we* have to fear and love, this almost invisible, inaudible world of
delicate command and delicate obedience, a world of "almost" in every
respect, captious, insidious, sharp, and tender—yes, it is well protected
from clumsy spectators and familiar curiosity! We are woven into a strong
net and garment of duties, and *cannot* disengage ourselves—precisely
here, we are "men of duty," even we! Occasionally it is true we dance in
our "chains" and betwixt our "swords"; it is none the less true that more
often we gnash our teeth under the circumstances, and are impatient at
the secret hardship of our lot. But do what we will, fools and appearances
say of us: "These are men *without* duty,"—we have always fools and appearances against us!

VI

Honesty, granting that it is the virtue from which we cannot rid ourselves, we free spirits—well, we will labour at it with all our perversity
and love, and not tire of "perfecting" ourselves in *our* virtue, which alone
remains: may its glance some day overspread like a gilded, blue, mocking
twilight this aging civilisation with its dull gloomy seriousness! And if,
nevertheless, our honesty should one day grow weary, and sigh, and
stretch its limbs, and find us too hard, and would fain have it pleasanter,
easier, and gentler, like an agreeable vice, let us remain *hard,* we latest
Stoics, and let us send to its help whatever devilry we have in us:—our
disgust at the clumsy and undefined, our *"nitimur in vetitum,"* our love
of adventure, our sharpened and fastidious curiosity, our most subtle,
disguised, intellectual Will to Power and universal conquest, which
rambles and roves avidiously around all the realms of the future—let us go
with all our "devils" to the help of our "God"!

VII

Woman wishes to be independent, and therefore she begins to enlighten men about "woman as she is"—*this* is one of the worst developments of the general *uglifying* of Europe. For what must these clumsy

attempts of feminine scientificality and self-exposure bring to light! Woman has so much cause for shame; in woman there is so much pedantry, superficiality, schoolmasterliness, petty presumption, unbridledness, and indiscretion concealed—study only woman's behaviour towards children!—which has really been best restrained and dominated hitherto by the *fear* of man. Alas, if ever the "eternally tedious in woman"—she has plenty of it!—is allowed to venture forth! if she begins radically and on principle to unlearn her wisdom and art—of charming, of playing, of frightening away sorrow, of alleviating and taking easily; if she forgets her delicate aptitude for agreeable desires! Female voices are already raised, which, by Saint Aristophanes! make one afraid:—with medical explicitness it is stated in a threatening manner what woman first and last *requires* from man. Is it not in the very worst taste that woman thus sets herself up to be scientific? Enlightenment hitherto has fortunately been men's affair, men's gift—we remained therewith "among ourselves"; and in the end, in view of all that women write about "woman," we may well have considerable doubt as to whether woman really *desires* enlightenment about herself—and *can* desire it. If woman does not thereby seek a new *ornament* for herself—I believe ornamentation belongs to the eternally feminine?—why, then, she wishes to make herself feared: perhaps she thereby wishes to get the mastery. But she does not *want* truth—what does woman care for truth? From the very first nothing is more foreign, more repugnant, or more hostile to woman than truth—her great art is falsehood, her chief concern is appearance and beauty.

VIII

To be mistaken in the fundamental problem of "man and woman," to deny here the profoundest antagonism and the necessity for an eternally hostile tension, to dream here perhaps of equal rights, equal training, equal claims and obligations: that is a *typical* sign of shallow-mindedness; and a thinker who has proved himself shallow at this dangerous spot—shallow in instinct!—may generally be regarded as suspicious, nay more, as betrayed, as discovered; he will probably prove too "short" for all fundamental questions of life, future as well as present, and will be unable to descend into *any* of the depths. On the other hand, a man who has depth of spirit as well as of desires, and has also the depth of benevolence which is capable of severity and harshness, and easily confounded with them, can only think of woman as *Orientals* do: he must conceive of her as a possession, as confinable property, as a being predestined for service and accomplishing her mission therein—he must take his stand in this matter upon the immense rationality of Asia, upon the superiority of the instinct of Asia, as the Greeks did formerly; those best heirs and scholars of Asia—who, as is well known, with their *increasing* culture and amplitude of power, from Homer to the time of Pericles, became gradually *stricter* towards woman, in short, more oriental. *How* necessary, *how* logical, even *how* humanely desirable this was, let us consider for ourselves!

IX

The weaker sex has in no previous age been treated with so much respect by men as at present—this belongs to the tendency and fundamental taste of democracy, in the same way as disrespectfulness to old age—what wonder is it that abuse should be immediately made of this respect? They want more, they learn to make claims, the tribute of respect is at last felt to be well-nigh galling; rivalry for rights, indeed actual strife itself, would be preferred: in a word, woman is losing modesty. And let us immediately add that she is also losing taste. She is unlearning to *fear* man: but the woman who "unlearns to fear" sacrifices her most womanly instincts. That woman should venture forward when the fear-inspiring quality in man—or more definitely, the *man* in man—is no longer either desired or fully developed, is reasonable enough and also intelligible enough; what is more difficult to understand is that precisely thereby—woman deteriorates. This is what is happening nowadays: let us not deceive ourselves about it! Wherever the industrial spirit has triumphed over the military and aristocratic spirit, woman strives for the economic and legal independence of a clerk: "woman as clerkess" is inscribed on the portal of the modern society which is in course of formation. While she thus appropriates new rights, aspires to be "master," and inscribes "progress" of woman on her flags and banners, the very opposite realises itself with terrible obviousness: *woman retrogrades.*

VIII. PEOPLES AND COUNTRIES

I

THERE WAS A TIME when it was customary to call Germans "deep" by way of distinction; but now that the most successful type of new Germanism is covetous of quite other honours, and perhaps misses "smartness" in all that has depth, it is almost opportune and patriotic to doubt whether we did not formerly deceive ourselves with that commendation: in short, whether German depth is not at bottom something different and worse—and something from which, thank God, we are on the point of successfully ridding ourselves. Let us try, then, to relearn with regard to German depth; the only thing necessary for the purpose is a little vivisection of the German soul.—The German soul is above all manifold, varied in its source, aggregated and superimposed, rather than actually built: this is owing to its origin. A German who would embolden himself to assert: "Two souls, alas, dwell in my breast," would make a bad guess at the truth, or, more correctly, he would come far short of the truth about the number of souls. As a people made up of the most extraordinary mixing and mingling of races, perhaps even with a preponderance of the pre-Aryan element, as the "people of the centre" in every sense of the term, the Germans are more intangible, more ample, more contradictory, more unknown, more incalculable, more surprising, and even more terrifying than other peoples are to themselves:—they escape *definition,* and are thereby alone the despair of the French. It is characteristic of the Germans that the question: "What is German?" never dies out among them.

II

The German *drags* at his soul, he drags at everything he experiences. He digests his events badly; he never gets "done" with them; and German depth is often only a difficult, hesitating "digestion." And just as all chronic invalids, all dyspeptics, like what is convenient, so the German loves "frankness" and "honesty"; it is so *convenient* to be frank and honest!—This confidingness, this complaisance, this showing-the-cards of German *honesty,* is probably the most dangerous and most successful disguise which the German is up to nowadays: it is his proper Mephisto-phelean art; with this he can "still achieve much"! The German lets himself go, and thereby gazes with faithful, blue, empty German eyes—and other countries immediately confound him with his dressing-gown!—I meant to say that, let "German depth" be what it will—among ourselves alone we perhaps take the liberty to laugh at it—we shall do well to continue henceforth to honour its appearance and good name, and not barter away too cheaply our old reputation as a people of depth for Prussian "smartness," and Berlin wit and sand. It is wise for a people to pose, and *let* itself be regarded, as profound, clumsy, good-natured, honest, and foolish: it might even be—profound to do so! Finally, we should do honour to our name—we are not called the *"tiusche Volk"* (deceptive people) for nothing. . . .

III

There are two kinds of geniuses: one which above all engenders and seeks to engender, and another which willingly lets itself be fructified and brings forth. And similarly, among the gifted nations, there are those on whom the woman's problem of pregnancy has devolved, and the secret task of forming, maturing, and perfecting—the Greeks, for instance, were a nation of this kind, and so are the French; and others which have to fructify and become the cause of new modes of life—like the Jews, the Romans, and, in all modesty be it asked: like the Germans?—nations tortured and enraptured by unknown fevers and irresistibly forced out of themselves, amorous and longing for foreign races (for such as "let themselves be fructified"), and withal imperious, like everything conscious of being full of generative force, and consequently empowered "by the grace of God." These two kinds of geniuses seek each other like man and woman; but they also misunderstand each other—like man and woman.

IV

They are not a philosophical race—the English: Bacon represents an *attack* on the philosophical spirit generally, Hobbes, Hume, and Locke, an abasement, and a depreciation of the idea of a "philosopher" for more than a century. It was *against* Hume that Kant uprose and raised himself; it was Locke of whom Schelling *rightly* said, *"Je méprise Locke";* in the struggle against the English mechanical stultification of the world, Hegel and Schopenhauer (along with Goethe) were of one accord; the two hostile brother-geniuses in philosophy, who pushed in different directions towards the opposite poles of German thought, and thereby wronged each other as only brothers will do.—What is lacking in England, and has always been lacking, that half-actor and rhetorician knew well enough, the absurd muddle-head, Carlyle, who sought to conceal under passionate grimaces what he knew about himself: namely, what was *lacking* in Carlyle—real *power* of intellect, real *depth* of intellectual perception, in short, philosophy. It is characteristic of such an unphilosophical race to hold on firmly to Christianity—they *need* its discipline for "moralising" and humanising. The Englishman, more gloomy, sensual, headstrong, and brutal than the German—is for that very reason, as the baser of the two, also the most pious: he has all the *more need* of Christianity. To finer nostrils, this English Christianity itself has still a characteristic English taint of spleen and alcoholic excess, for which, owing to good reasons, it is used as an antidote—the finer poison to neutralise the coarser: a finer form of poisoning is in fact a step in advance with coarse-mannered people, a step towards spiritualisation.

V

There are truths which are best recognised by mediocre minds, because they are best adapted for them, there are truths which only possess charms and seductive power for mediocre spirits:—one is pushed to this probably unpleasant conclusion, now that the influence of respectable but mediocre Englishmen—I may mention Darwin, John Stuart Mill, and Herbert Spencer—begins to gain the ascendency in the middle-class region of European taste. Indeed, who could doubt that it is a useful thing for *such* minds to have the ascendency for a time? It would be an error to consider the highly developed and independently soaring minds as specially qualified for determining and collecting many little common facts, and deducing conclusions from them; as exceptions, they are rather from the first in no very favourable position towards those who are "the rules." After all, they have more to do than merely to perceive:—in effect, they have to *be* something new, they have to *signify* something new, they have to *represent* new values!

IX. WHAT IS NOBLE?

I

To REFRAIN MUTUALLY from injury, from violence, from exploitation, and put one's will on a par with that of others: this may result in a certain rough sense in good conduct among individuals when the necessary conditions are given (namely, the actual similarity of the individuals in amount of force and degree of worth, and their co-relation within one organisation). As soon, however, as one wished to take this principle more generally, and if possible even as *the fundamental principle of society,* it would immediately disclose what it really is—namely, a Will to the *denial* of life, a principle of dissolution and decay. Here one must think profoundly to the very basis and resist all sentimental weakness: life itself is *essentially* appropriation, injury, conquest of the strange and weak, suppression, severity, obtrusion of peculiar forms, incorporation, and at the least, putting it mildest, exploitation;—but why should one for ever use precisely these words on which for ages a disparaging purpose has been stamped? Even the organisation within which, as was previously supposed, the individuals treat each other as equal—it takes place in every healthy aristocracy—must itself, if it be a living and not a dying organisation, do all that towards other bodies, which the individuals within it refrain from doing to each other: it will have to be the in-carnated Will to Power, it will endeavour to grow, to gain ground, attract to itself and acquire ascendency—not owing to any morality or immorality, but because it *lives,* and because life *is* precisely Will to Power.

II

In a tour through the many finer and coarser moralities which have hitherto prevailed or still prevail on the earth, I found certain traits recurring regularly together, and connected with one another, until finally two primary types revealed themselves to me, and a radical distinction was brought to light. There is *master-morality* and *slave-morality;*—I would at once add, however, that in all higher and mixed civilisations, there are also attempts at the reconciliation of the two moralities; but one finds still oftener the confusion and mutual misunderstanding of them, indeed, sometimes their close juxtaposition—even in the same man, within one soul. The distinctions of moral values have either originated in a ruling caste, pleasantly conscious of being different from the ruled—or among the ruled class, the slaves and dependents of all sorts. In the first case, when it is the rulers who determine the conception "good," it is the exalted, proud disposition which is regarded as the distinguishing feature, and that which determines the order of rank. The noble type of man separates from himself the beings in whom the opposite of this exalted, proud disposition displays itself: he despises them. Let it at once be noted that in this first kind of morality the antithesis "good" and "bad" means practically the same as "noble" and "despicable";—the antithesis "good" and *"evil"* is of a different origin.

III

It is otherwise with the second type of morality, *slave-morality*. Supposing that the abused, the oppressed, the suffering, the unemancipated, the weary, and those uncertain of themselves, should moralise, what will be the common element in their moral estimates? Probably a pessimistic suspicion with regard to the entire situation of man will find expression, perhaps a condemnation of man, together with his situation. The slave has an unfavourable eye for the virtues of the powerful; he has a scepticism and distrust, a *refinement* of distrust of everything "good" that is there honoured—he would fain persuade himself that the very happiness there is not genuine. On the other hand, *those* qualities which serve to alleviate the existence of sufferers are brought into prominence and flooded with light; it is here that sympathy, the kind, helping hand, the warm heart, patience, diligence, humility, and friendliness attain to honour; for here these are the most useful qualities, and almost the only means of supporting the burden of existence. Slave-morality is essentially the morality of utility. Here is the seat of the origin of the famous antithesis "good" and "evil":—power and dangerousness are assumed to reside in the evil, a certain dreadfulness, subtlety, and strength, which do not admit of being despised. According to slave-morality, therefore, the "evil" man arouses fear; according to master-morality, it is precisely the "good" man who arouses fear and seeks to arouse it, while the bad man is regarded as the despicable being.

PRAGMATISM

by

WILLIAM JAMES

CONTENTS

Pragmatism

WILLIAM JAMES

1842–1910

WILLIAM JAMES, born in New York City on January 11, 1842, was the son of the Swedenborgian theologian, Henry James, and the brother of the famous American novelist by the same name. In 1870 he was graduated from Harvard University with the degree of M.D. and two years later received an appointment as lecturer in psychology and anatomy at his alma mater. Later this appointment was transferred to the department of psychology and philosophy. These last two fields became his consuming interest. By 1880 he was assistant professor of philosophy, and five years later he became full professor in that field. In 1889 we find him raised to a full professorship in psychology.

His work and his writings in both these departments made him world-famous. He established at Harvard the first laboratory of experimental psychology in this country. In 1890 he published a two-volume work, *Principles of Psychology,* and became almost immediately the recognized leader of the physical school of psychologists.

James's most important work, however, was done in the field of philosophy. The quintessence of his genius in this field is to be found in his book of lectures on *Pragmatism.* He developed a philosophic point of view which tended to dominate American, and a great deal of European, thought during the first quarter of the twentieth century, and which is the basis for much present-day philosophic thinking and writing. The complete title of his book is *Pragmatism—A New Name for Old Ways of Thinking.*

The writing of James is the healthy work of a sick man. For many years he suffered from a weak heart. One day, while on his vacation in the Adirondacks, he lost his way. His exertion to find the road brought about his collapse. From that time on, he was never himself again.

In 1907 he was obliged, because of his ill health, to resign from the Harvard faculty. He took a trip to Europe. It was a triumphant tour for the "Great Professor Weelyam Yames." But upon his return (in the summer of 1910) he suffered another attack. This attack proved fatal.

The philosophy of William James is based upon a foundation of three cardinal points:

Meliorism, Pluralism, Pragmatism.

1—*Meliorism.* This term is derived from the Latin word *melior,* which means *better.* The philosophy of *meliorism* is the philosophy of *betterment,* or *improvement.* It stands halfway between *optimism,* the credo that all's right with the world, and *pessimism,* the theory that all's wrong with the world. The meliorist admits that the world is full of evil, but he believes that man is put into it in order to eliminate the evil and to make the world better.

For the world is not a *singular* world—that is, a finished unit, but a *plural* world—that is, "an aggregation of separate and contradictory (and imperfect) elements." This is the doctrine of

2—*Pluralism.* It is our business, in this plural world, to conquer the evil elements and to establish the good elements. Is success certain? No. Is it possible? Yes. And it is this possibility of success that makes life worth living. It is a joy to fight this good fight—with hope as the guiding star, and with God as the inspiring guide.

Let us then, with God's help, struggle on to shape the world nearer to our heart's desire. Let us live the *practical* life. And this brings us to

3—*Pragmatism.* The world we live in is a pragmatic—or practical—world. This is the fact to which we have to adapt ourselves. Let us accept those truths which enable us to make the world better for ourselves and for our neighbors. The pragmatism of James is a sensible urge to co-operation among free members of a democratic society. The meaning of life, he believed, lies not in an isolated struggle between individual and individual or between group and group, but in a united struggle of all individuals and of all groups against the forces that would hold back the general progress of mankind.

PRAGMATISM

LECTURE I: THE PRESENT DILEMMA IN PHILOSOPHY

IN PHILOSOPHY we have a contrast expressed in the pair of terms 'rationalist' and 'empiricist,' 'empiricist' meaning your lover of facts in all their crude variety, 'rationalist' meaning your devotee to abstract and eternal principles. No one can live an hour without both facts and principles, so it is a difference rather of emphasis; yet it breeds antipathies of the most pungent character between those who lay the emphasis differently; and we shall find it extraordinarily convenient to express a certain contrast in men's ways of taking their universe, by talking of the 'empiricist' and of the 'rationalist' temper.

Historically we find the terms 'intellectualism' and 'sensationalism' used as synonyms of 'rationalism' and 'empiricism.' Well, nature seems to combine most frequently with intellectualism an idealistic and optimistic tendency. Empiricists on the other hand are not uncommonly materialistic, and their optimism is apt to be decidedly conditional and tremulous. Rationalism is always monistic. It starts from wholes and universals, and makes much of the unity of things. Empiricism starts from the parts, and makes of the whole a collection—is not averse therefore to calling itself pluralistic. Rationalism usually considers itself more religious than empiricism, but there is much to say about this claim, so I merely mention it. It is a true claim when the individual rationalist is what is called a man of feeling, and when the individual empiricist prides himself on being hard-headed. In that case the rationalist will usually also be in favor of what is called free-will, and the empiricist will be a fatalist—I use the terms most popularly current. The rationalist finally will be of dogmatic temper in his affirmations, while the empiricist may be more sceptical and open to discussion.

I will write these traits down in two columns. I think you will practically recognize the two types of mental make-up that I mean if I head the columns by the titles 'tender-minded' and 'tough-minded' respectively.

The Tender-minded	The Tough-minded
Rationalistic (going by 'principles'),	Empiricist (going by 'facts'),
Intellectualistic,	Sensationalistic,
Idealistic,	Materialistic,
Optimistic,	Pessimistic,
Religious,	Irreligious,
Free-willist,	Fatalistic,
Monistic,	Pluralistic,
Dogmatical.	Sceptical.

Most of us have a hankering for the good things on both sides of the line. Facts are good, of course—give us lots of facts. Principles are good —give us plenty of principles. The world is indubitably one if you look at it in one way, but as indubitably is it many, if you look at it in another. And so forth—your ordinary philosophic layman never being a radical, never straightening out his system, but living vaguely in one plausible compartment of it or another to suit the temptations of successive hours.

But some of us are more than mere laymen in philosophy. We are worthy of the name of amateur athletes, and are vexed by too much inconsistency and vacillation in our creed. We cannot preserve a good intellectual conscience so long as we keep mixing incompatibles from opposite sides of the line.

Never were as many men of a decidedly empiricist proclivity in existence as there are at the present day. Our children, one may say, are almost born scientific. But our esteem for facts has not neutralized in us all religiousness. It is itself almost religious. Our scientific temper is devout. Now take a man of this type, and let him be also a philosophic amateur, unwilling to mix a hodge-podge system after the fashion of a common layman, and what does he find his situation to be? He wants facts; he wants science; but he also wants a religion.

Now what kinds of philosophy do you find actually offered to meet your need? You find an empirical philosophy that is not religious enough, and a religious philosophy that is not empirical enough for your purpose. If you look to the quarter where facts are most considered you find the whole tough-minded program in operation, and the 'conflict between science and religion' in full blast.

If now, on the other hand, you turn to the religious quarter for consolation, and take counsel of the tender-minded philosophies, what do you find?

Religious philosophy in our day and generation is, among us English-reading people, of two main types. One of these is more radical and aggressive, the other has more the air of fighting a slow retreat. By the more radical wing of religious philosophy I mean the so-called transcendental idealism of the Anglo-Hegelian school, the philosophy of such men as Green, the Cairds, Bosanquet, and Royce. This philosophy has greatly influenced the more studious members of our Protestant ministry. It is pantheistic, and undoubtedly it has already blunted the edge of the traditional theism in Protestantism at large.

That theism remains, however. It is the lineal descendant, through one stage of concession after another, of the dogmatic scholastic theism still taught rigorously in the seminaries of the Catholic Church. For a long time it used to be called among us the philosophy of the Scottish school.

These two systems are what you have to choose between if you turn to the tender-minded school. And if you are the lovers of facts I have supposed you to be, you find the trail of the serpent of rationalism, of intellectualism, over everything that lies on that side of the line. You escape indeed the materialism that goes with the reigning empiricism; but you pay for your escape by losing contact with the concrete parts of life.

It is at this point that my own solution begins to appear. I offer the oddly named thing pragmatism as a philosophy that can satisfy both kinds of demand. It can remain religious like the rationalisms, but at the same time, like the empiricisms, it can preserve the richest intimacy with facts.

If any of you here are professional philosophers, and some of you I know to be such, you will doubtless have felt my discourse so far to have been crude in an unpardonable, nay, in an almost incredible degree. Tender-minded and tough-minded, what a barbaric disjunction!

Believe me, I feel the full force of the indictment. The picture I have given is indeed monstrously over-simplified and rude. But like all abstractions, it will prove to have its use. If philosophers can treat the life of the universe abstractly, they must not complain of an abstract treatment of the life of philosophy itself. In point of fact the picture I have given is, however coarse and sketchy, literally true. Temperaments with their cravings and refusals do determine men in their philosophies, and always will. The details of systems may be reasoned out piecemeal, and when the student is working at a system, he may often forget the forest for the single tree. But when the labor is accomplished, the mind always performs its big summarizing act, and the system forthwith stands over against one like a living thing, with that strange simple note of individuality which haunts our memory, like the wraith of the man, when a friend or enemy of ours is dead.

Our work over the details of his system is indeed what gives us our resultant impression of the philosopher, but it is on the resultant impression itself that we react. Expertness in philosophy is measured by the definiteness of our summarizing reactions, by the immediate perceptive epithet with which the expert hits such complex objects off. But great expertness is not necessary for the epithet to come. Few people have definitely articulated philosophies of their own. But almost every one has his own peculiar sense of a certain total character in the universe, and of the inadequacy fully to match it of the peculiar systems that he knows. They don't just cover *his* world.

One word more—namely about philosophies necessarily being abstract outlines. There are outlines and outlines, outlines of buildings that are *fat,* conceived in the cube by their planner, and outlines of buildings invented flat on paper, with the aid of ruler and compass. These remain skinny and emaciated even when set up in stone and mortar, and the outline already suggests that result. An outline in itself is meagre, truly, but it does not necessarily suggest a meagre thing. It is the essential meagreness of *what is suggested* by the usual rationalistic philosophies that moves empiricists to their gesture of rejection. The case of Herbert Spencer's system is much to the point here. Rationalists feel his fearful array of insufficiencies, yet the half of England wants to bury him in Westminster Abbey.

Why? Simply because we feel his heart to be *in the right place* philosophically. His principles may be all skin and bone, but at any rate his books try to mould themselves upon the particular shape of this particular world's carcase. The noise of facts resounds through all his chapters, the citations of fact never cease, he emphasizes facts, turns his face towards their quarter; and that is enough. It means the right *kind* of thing for the empiricist mind.

The pragmatistic philosophy of which I hope to begin talking in my next lecture preserves as cordial a relation with facts, and, unlike Spencer's philosophy, it neither begins nor ends by turning positive religious constructions out of doors—it treats them cordially as well.

LECTURE II: WHAT PRAGMATISM MEANS

THE PRAGMATIC METHOD is primarily a method of settling metaphysical disputes that otherwise might be interminable. Is the world one or many? —fated or free?—material or spiritual?—here are notions either of which may or may not hold good of the world; and disputes over such notions are unending. The pragmatic method in such cases is to try to interpret each notion by tracing its respective practical consequences. What difference would it practically make to anyone if this notion rather than that notion were true? If no practical difference whatever can be traced, then the alternatives mean practically the same thing, and all dispute is idle. Whenever a dispute is serious, we ought to be able to show some practical difference that must follow from one side or the other's being right.

It is astonishing to see how many philosophical disputes collapse into insignificance the moment you subject them to this simple test of tracing a concrete consequence. There can *be* no difference anywhere that doesn't *make* a difference elsewhere—no difference in abstract truth that doesn't express itself in a difference in concrete fact and in conduct consequent upon that fact, imposed on somebody, somehow, somewhere, and somewhen. The whole function of philosophy ought to be to find out what definite difference it will make to you and me, at definite instants of our life, if this world-formula or that world-formula be the true one.

Pragmatism represents a perfectly familiar attitude in philosophy, the empiricist attitude, but it represents it, as it seems to me, both in a more radical and in a less objectionable form than it has ever yet assumed.

At the same time it does not stand for any special results. It is a method only. But the general triumph of that method would mean an enormous change in what I called in my last lecture the 'temperament' of philosophy. It appears less as a solution than as a program for more work, and more particularly as an indication of the ways in which existing realities may be *changed*.

Theories thus become instruments, not answers to enigmas, in which we can rest. We don't lie back upon them, we move forward, and, on occasion, make nature over again by their aid. Pragmatism unstiffens all our theories, limbers them up and sets each one at work. Being nothing essentially new, it harmonizes with many ancient philosophic tendencies.

No particular results then, so far, but only an attitude of orientation, is what the pragmatic method means. *The attitude of looking away from first things, principles, 'categories,' supposed necessities; and of looking towards last things, fruits, consequences, facts.*

So much for the pragmatic method! The word pragmatism has come to be used in a still wider sense, as meaning also a certain *theory of truth*.

One of the most successfully cultivated branches of philosophy in our time is what is called inductive logic, the study of the conditions under which our sciences have evolved. Writers on this subject have begun to show a singular unanimity as to what the laws of nature and elements of fact mean, when formulated by mathematicians, physicists, and chemists. When the first mathematical, logical, and natural uniformities, the first *laws,* were discovered, men were so carried away by the clearness, beauty, and simplification that resulted, that they believed themselves to have deciphered authentically the eternal thoughts of the Almighty.

But as the sciences have developed farther, the notion has gained ground that most, perhaps all, of our laws are only approximations. The laws themselves, moreover, have grown so numerous that there is no counting them; and so many rival formulations are proposed in all the branches of science that investigators have become accustomed to the notion that no theory is absolutely a transcript of reality, but that any one of them may from some point of view be useful. Thus human arbitrariness has driven divine necessity from scientific logic.

Riding now on the front of this wave of scientific logic, Messrs. Schiller and Dewey appear with their pragmatistic account of what truth everywhere signifies. Everywhere, these teachers say, 'truth' in our ideas and beliefs means the same thing that it means in science. It means, they say, nothing but this, *that ideas (which themselves are but parts of our experience) become true just in so far as they help us to get into satisfactory relation with other parts of our experience,* to summarize them and get about among them by conceptual short-cuts instead of following the interminable succession of particular phenomena. Any idea upon which we can ride, so to speak; any idea that will carry us prosperously from any one part of our experience to any other part, linking things satisfactorily, working securely, simplifying, saving labor; is true for just so much, true in so far forth, true *instrumentally.* This is the 'instrumental' view of truth.

The observable process which Schiller and Dewey particularly singled out for generalization is the familiar one by which any individual settles into *new opinions.* The process here is always the same. The individual has a stock of old opinions already, but he meets a new experience that puts them to a strain. The result is an inward trouble to which his mind till then had been a stranger, and from which he seeks to escape by modifying his previous mass of opinions. He saves as much of it as he can, for in this matter of belief we are all extreme conservatives. So he tries to change first this opinion, and then that (for they resist change very variously), until at last some new idea comes up which he can graft upon the ancient stock with a minimum of disturbance of the latter, some idea that mediates between the stock and the new experience and runs them into one another most felicitously and expediently.

This new idea is then adopted as the true one. It preserves the older stock of truths with a minimum of modification, stretching them just enough to make them admit the novelty, but conceiving that in ways as familiar as the case leaves possible.

The point I now urge you to observe particularly is the part played by the older truths. Failure to take account of it is the source of much of the unjust criticism levelled against pragmatism. Their influence is absolutely controlling. Loyalty to them is the first principle—in most cases it is the only principle; for by far the most usual way of handling phenomena so novel that they would make for a serious rearrangement of our preconception is to ignore them altogether, or to abuse those who bear witness for them.

A new opinion counts as 'true' just in proportion as it gratifies the individual's desire to assimilate the novel in his experience to his beliefs in stock. It must both lean on old truth and grasp new fact; and its success in doing this is a matter for the individual's appreciation. When old truth grows, then, by new truth's addition, it is for subjective reasons. We are in the process and obey the reasons. That new idea is truest which performs most felicitously its function of satisfying our double urgency. It makes itself true, gets itself classed as true, by the way it works; grafting itself then upon the ancient body of truth, which thus grows much as a tree grows by the activity of a new layer of cambium.

Such then would be the scope of pragmatism—first, a method; and second, a genetic theory of what is meant by truth.

But enough of this at present. The justification of what I say must be postponed. I wish now to add a word in further explanation of the claim I made at our last meeting, that pragmatism may be a happy harmonizer of empiricist ways of thinking with the more religious demands of human beings.

Men who are strongly of the fact-loving temperament are liable to be kept at a distance by the small sympathy with facts which that philosophy from the present-day fashion of idealism offers them. It is far too intellectualistic. Aspirants to a philosophic religion turn, as a rule, more hopefully nowadays towards idealistic pantheism than towards the older dualistic theism, in spite of the fact that the latter still counts able defenders.

But the brand of pantheism offered is hard for them to assimilate if they are lovers of facts, or empirically minded. It is the absolutistic brand, spurning the dust and reared upon pure logic. It keeps no connexion whatever with concreteness. Affirming the Absolute Mind, which is its substitute for God, to be the rational presupposition of all particulars of fact, whatever they may be, it remains supremely indifferent to what the particular facts in our world actually are. Be they what they may, the Absolute will father them.

Far be it from me to deny the majesty of this conception, or its capacity to yield religious comfort to a most respectable class of minds. But from the human point of view, no one can pretend that it doesn't suffer from the faults of remoteness and abstractness. It is eminently a product of what I have ventured to call the rationalistic temper. It disdains empiricism's needs.

Now pragmatism, devoted though she be to facts, has no such materialistic bias as ordinary empiricism labors under. Moreover, she has no objection whatever to the realizing of abstractions, so long as you get about among particulars with their aid and they actually carry you somewhere. Interested in no conclusions but those which our minds and our experiences work out together, she has no *a priori* prejudices against theology. *If theological ideas prove to have a value for concrete life, they will be true, for pragmatism, in the sense of being good for so much. For how much more they are true, will depend entirely on their relations to the other truths that also have to be acknowledged.*

I am well aware how odd it must seem to some of you to hear me say that an idea is 'true' so long as to believe it is profitable to our lives. That it is *good,* for as much as it profits, you will gladly admit. If what we do by its aid is good, you will allow the idea itself to be good in so far forth, for we are the better for possessing it. But is it not a strange misuse of the word truth, you will say, to call ideas also 'true' for this reason?

To answer this difficulty fully is impossible at this stage of my account. Let me now say only this, that truth is *one species of good,* and not, as is usually supposed, a category distinct from good, and co-ordinate with it. *The true is the name of whatever proves itself to be good in the way of belief, and good, too, for definite, assignable reasons.*

You see by this what I meant when I called pragmatism a mediator and reconciler and said, borrowing the word from Papini, that she 'unstiffens' our theories. She has in fact no prejudices whatever, no obstructive dogmas, no rigid canons of what shall count as proof. She is completely genial. She will entertain any hypothesis, she will consider any evidence. It follows that in the religious field she is at a great advantage both over positivistic empiricism, with its anti-theological bias, and over religious rationalism, with its exclusive interest in the remote, the noble, the simple, and the abstract in the way of conception.

In short, she widens the field of search for God. Rationalism sticks to logic and the empyrean. Empiricism sticks to the external senses. Pragmatism is willing to take anything, to follow either logic or the senses and to count the humblest and most personal experiences. She will count mystical experiences if they have practical consequences. She will take a God who lives in the very dirt of private fact—if that should seem a likely place to find him.

Her only test of probable truth is what works best in the way of leading us, what fits every part of life best and combines with the collectivity of experience's demands, nothing being omitted. If theological ideas should do this, if the notion of God, in particular, should prove to do it, how could pragmatism possibly deny God's existence? She could see no meaning in treating as 'not true' a notion that was pragmatically so successful. What other kind of truth could there be, for her, than all this agreement with concrete reality?

LECTURE III: SOME METAPHYSICAL PROBLEMS
PRAGMATICALLY CONSIDERED

I AM NOW to make the pragmatic method more familiar by giving you some illustrations of its application to particular problems. I will begin with what is driest, and the first thing I shall take will be the problem of *Substance*. Here is a bit of blackboard crayon. Its modes, attributes, properties, accidents, or affections,—use which term you will,—are whiteness, friability, cylindrical shape, insolubility in water, etc., etc. But the bearer of these attributes is so much *chalk*, which thereupon is called the substance in which they inhere.

Now it was very early seen that all *we know* of the chalk is the whiteness, friability, etc. A group of attributes is what each substance here is known as, they form its sole cash-value for our actual experience.

Material substance was criticised by Berkeley with such telling effect that his name has reverberated through all subsequent philosophy. So far from denying the external world which we know, Berkeley corroborated it. It was the scholastic notion of a material substance unapproachable by us, *behind* the external world, deeper and more real than it, and needed to support it, which Berkeley maintained to be the most effective of all reducers of the external world to unreality. Abolish that substance, he said, believe that God, whom you can understand and approach, sends you the sensible world directly, and you confirm the latter and back it up by his divine authority. Berkeley's criticism of 'matter' was consequently absolutely pragmatistic. Matter is known as our sensations of colour, figure, hardness, and the like. They are the cash-value of the term. The difference matter makes to us by truly being is that we then get such sensations; by not being, is that we lack them. These sensations then are its sole meaning. Berkeley doesn't deny matter, then; he simply tells us what it consists of. It is a true name for just so much in the way of sensations.

What do we *mean* by matter? What practical difference can it make *now* that the world should be run by matter or by spirit?

It makes not a single jot of difference so far as the *past* of the world goes, whether we deem it to have been the work of matter or whether we think a divine spirit was its author. Both theories have shown all their consequences and, by the hypothesis we are adopting, these are identical. The pragmatist must consequently say that the two theories, in spite of their different-sounding names, mean exactly the same thing, and that the dispute is purely verbal.

Thus if no future detail of experience or conduct is to be deduced from our hypothesis, the debate between materialism and theism becomes quite idle and insignificant. Matter and God in that event mean exactly the same thing—the power, namely, neither more nor less, that could make just this completed world—and the wise man is he who in such a case would turn his back on such a supererogatory discussion.

But philosophy is prospective also, and, after finding what the world has been and done, and yielded, still asks the further question, 'What does the world *promise?*'

Theism and materialism, so indifferent when taken retrospectively, point, when we take them prospectively, to wholly different outlooks of experience. For, according to the theory of mechanical evolution, the laws of redistribution of matter and motion, though they are certainly to thank for all the good hours which our organisms have ever yielded us and for all the ideals which our minds now frame, are yet fatally certain to undo their work again, and to redissolve everything that they have once evolved.

Materialism means simply the denial that the moral order is eternal, and the cutting off of ultimate hopes; spiritualism means the affirmation of an eternal moral order and the letting loose of hope. Surely here is an issue genuine enough, for anyone who feels it; and, as long as men are men, it will yield matter for a serious philosophic debate.

Let me take up another well-worn controversy, *the free-will problem.* Most persons who believe in what is called their free will do so after the rationalistic fashion. It is a principle, a positive faculty or virtue added to man, by which his dignity is enigmatically augmented. He ought to believe it for this reason. Determinists, who deny it, who say that individual men originate nothing, but merely transmit to the future the whole push of the past cosmos of which they are so small an expression, diminish man. He is less admirable, stripped of this creative principle.

Free will pragmatically means *novelties in the world,* the right to expect that in its deepest elements as well as in its surface phenomena, the future may not identically repeat and imitate the past. Free will is thus a general cosmological theory of *promise.*

LECTURE IV: THE ONE AND THE MANY

WE SAW in the last lecture that the pragmatic method, in its dealings with certain concepts, instead of ending with admiring contemplation, plunges forward into the river of experience with them and prolongs the perspective by their means.

In this present hour I wish to illustrate the pragmatic method by one more application. I wish to turn its light upon the ancient problem of 'the one and the many.'

Philosophy has often been defined as the quest or the vision of the world's unity. Few persons ever challenge this definition, which is true as far as it goes, for philosophy has indeed manifested above all things its interest in unity. But how about the *variety* in things? Is that such an irrelevant matter? If instead of using the term philosophy, we talk in general of our intellect and its needs, we quickly see that unity is only one of them. What our intellect really aims at is neither variety nor unity taken singly, but *totality*. In this, acquaintance with reality's diversities is as important as understanding their connexion. Curiosity goes *pari passu* with the systematizing passion.

'The world is One!'—the formula may become a sort of number-worship. 'Three' and 'seven' have, it is true, been reckoned sacred numbers; but, abstractly taken, why is 'one' more excellent than 'forty-three,' or than 'two million and ten'? In this first vague conviction of the world's unity, there is so little to take hold of that we hardly know what we mean by it.

The only way to get forward with our notion is to treat it pragmatically. Granting the oneness to exist, what facts will be different in consequence? What will the unity be known as? The world is One— yes, but *how* one? What is the practical value of the oneness for *us*?

Asking such questions, we pass from the vague to the definite, from the abstract to the concrete. Many distinct ways in which a oneness predicated of the universe might make a difference, come to view. I will note successively the more obvious of these ways.

1. First, the world is at least *one subject of discourse*. If its manyness were so irremediable as to permit *no* union whatever of its parts, not even our minds could 'mean' the whole of it at once: they would be like eyes trying to look in opposite directions. Well, let things be one in so far forth! You can then fling such a word as universe at the whole collection of them, but what matters it? It still remains to be ascertained whether they are one in any further or more valuable sense.

2. Are they, for example, *continuous*? Can you pass from one to another, keeping always in your one universe without any danger of falling out? In other words, do the parts of our universe *hang together,* instead of being like detached grains of sand?

Even grains of sand hang together through the space in which they are embedded, and if you can in any way move through such space, you can pass continuously from number one of them to number two. Space and time are thus vehicles of continuity by which the world's parts hang together. The practical difference to us, resultant from these forms of union, is immense. Our whole motor life is based upon them.

3. There are innumerable other paths of practical continuity among things. Lines of *influence* can be traced by which they hang together. Following any such line you pass from one thing to another till you may have covered a good part of the universe's extent.

Human efforts are daily unifying the world more and more in definite systematic ways. The result is innumerable little hangings-together of the world's parts within the larger hangings-together, little worlds, not only of discourse but of operation, within the wider universe. Each system exemplifies one type or grade of union, its parts being strung on that peculiar kind of relation, and the same part may figure in many different systems, as a man may hold various offices and belong to several clubs. From this 'systematic' point of view, therefore, the pragmatic value of the world's unity is that all these definite networks actually and practically exist.

4. All these systems of influence may be listed under the general problem of the world's *causal unity*. If the minor causal influences among things should converge towards one common causal origin of them in the past, one great first cause for all that is, one might then speak of the absolute causal unity of the world. Against this notion of the unity of origin of all things there has always stood the pluralistic notion of an eternal self-existing many in the shape of atoms or even of spiritual units of some sort.

5. The most important sort of union that obtains among things, pragmatically speaking, is their *generic unity*. Things exist in kinds, there are many specimens in each kind, and what the 'kind' implies for one specimen, it implies also for every other specimen of that kind. We can easily conceive that every fact in the world might be singular, that is, unlike any other fact and sole of its kind. In such a world of singulars our logic would be useless, for logic works by predicating of the single instance what is true of all its kind. With no two things alike in the world, we should be unable to reason from our past experiences to our future ones. The existence of so much generic unity in things is thus perhaps the most momentous pragmatic specification of what it may mean to say 'the world is One.' *Absolute* generic unity would obtain if there were one *summum genus* under which all things without exception could be eventually subsumed. 'Beings,' 'thinkables,' 'experiences,' would be candidates for this position.

6. Another specification of what the phrase 'the world is One' may mean is *unity of purpose*. An enormous number of things in the world subserve a common purpose. All the man-made systems, administrative, industrial, military, or what not, exist each for its controlling purpose.

Our different purposes are at war with each other. Where one can't crush the other out, they compromise; and the result is again different from what anyone distinctly proposed beforehand. Vaguely and generally, much of what was purposed may be gained; but everything makes strongly for the view that our world is incompletely unified teleologically and is still trying to get its unification better organized.

7. *Æsthetic union* among things also obtains, and is very analogous to teleological union. Things tell a story. Their parts hang together so as to work out a climax. They play into each other's hands expressively.

8. The *great* monistic *denkmittel* for a hundred years past has been the notion of *the one Knower*. The many exist only as objects for his thought—exist in his dream, as it were; and *as he knows* them, they have one purpose, form one system, tell one tale for him. This notion of an *all-enveloping noetic unity* in things is the sublimest achievement of intellectualist philosophy.

'The world is One,' therefore, just so far as we experience it to be concatenated, One by as many definite conjunctions as appear. But then also *not* One by just as many definite *dis*-junctions as we find. The oneness and the manyness of it thus obtain in respects which can be separately named. It is neither a universe pure and simple nor a multiverse pure and simple. And its various manners of being One suggest, for their accurate ascertainment, so many distinct programs of scientific work. Thus the pragmatic question 'What is the oneness known as? What practical difference will it make?' saves us from all feverish excitement over it as a principle of sublimity and carries us forward into the stream of experience with a cool head. The stream may indeed reveal far more connexion and union than we now suspect, but we are not entitled on pragmatic principles to claim absolute oneness in any respect in advance.

Pragmatism, pending the final empirical ascertainment of just what the balance of union and disunion among things may be, must obviously range herself upon the pluralistic side. Some day, she admits, even total union, with one knower, one origin, and a universe consolidated in every conceivable way, may turn out to be the most acceptable of all hypotheses. Meanwhile the opposite hypothesis, of a world imperfectly unified still, and perhaps always to remain so, must be sincerely entertained. This latter hypothesis is pluralism's doctrine. Since absolute monism forbids its being even considered seriously, branding it as irrational from the start, it is clear that pragmatism must turn its back on absolute monism, and follow pluralism's more empirical path.

This leave us with the common-sense world, in which we find things partly joined and partly disjoined. 'Things,' then, and their 'conjunctions' —what do such words mean, pragmatically handled? In my next lecture, I will apply the pragmatic method to the stage of philosophizing known as Common Sense.

LECTURE V: PRAGMATISM AND COMMON SENSE

OUR KNOWLEDGE GROWS *in spots*. The spots may be large or small, but the knowledge never grows all over: some old knowledge always remains what it was. Your knowledge of pragmatism, let us suppose, is growing now. Later, its growth may involve considerable modification of opinions which you previously held to be true. But such modifications are apt to be gradual.

New truths are resultants of new experiences and of old truths combined and mutually modifying one another. And since this is the case in the changes of opinion of to-day, there is no reason to assume that it has not been so at all times. It follows that very ancient modes of thought may have survived through all the later changes in men's opinions.

My thesis now is this, that *our fundamental ways of thinking about things are discoveries of exceedingly remote ancestors, which have been able to preserve themselves throughout the experience of all subsequent time.* They form one great stage of equilibrium in the human mind's development, the stage of *common sense*. Other stages have grafted themselves upon this stage, but have never succeeded in displacing it. Let us consider this common-sense stage first, as if it might be final.

In practical talk, a man's common sense means his good judgment, his freedom from excentricity, his *gumption,* to use the vernacular word. In philosophy it means something entirely different, it means his use of certain intellectual forms or categories of thought. Were we lobsters, or bees, it might be that our organization would have led to our using quite different modes from these of apprehending our experiences. It *might* be too that such categories, unimaginable by us to-day, would have proved on the whole as serviceable for handling our experiences mentally as those which we actually use.

The old common-sense way of rationalizing your sense-impressions is by a set of concepts of which the most important are these:

Thing;
The same or different;
Kinds;
Minds;
Bodies;
One Time;
One Space;
Subjects and attributes;
Causal influences;
The fancied;
The real.

We are now so familiar with the order that these notions have woven for us out of the everlasting weather of our perceptions that we find it hard to realize how little of a fixed routine the perceptions follow when taken by themselves.

Common sense appears thus as a perfectly definite stage in our understanding of things, a stage that satisfies in an extraordinarily successful way the purposes for which we think. 'Things' do exist, even when we do not see them. Their 'kinds' also exist. Their 'qualities' are what they act by, and are what we act on; and these also exist.

But when we look back, and speculate as to how the common-sense categories may have achieved their wonderful supremacy, no reason appears why it may not have been by a process just like that by which the conceptions due to Democritus, Berkeley, or Darwin achieved their similar triumphs in more recent times.

The peripatetic philosophy, obeying rationalist propensities, has tried to eternalize the common-sense categories by treating them very technically and articulately. A 'thing' for instance is a being, or *ens*. An *ens* is a subject in which qualities 'inhere.' A subject is a substance. Substances are of kinds, and kinds are definite in number, and discrete. These distinctions are fundamental and eternal. As terms of *discourse* they are indeed magnificently useful, but what they mean, apart from their use in steering our discourse to profitable issues, does not appear. If you ask a scholastic philosopher what a substance may be in itself, apart from its being the support of attributes, he simply says that your intellect knows perfectly what the word means.

But what the intellect knows clearly is only the word itself and its steering function. So it comes about that intellects *sibi permissi,* intellects only curious and idle, have forsaken the common-sense level for what in general terms may be called the 'critical' level of thought. Not merely *such* intellects either—your Humes and Berkeleys and Hegels; but practical observers of facts, your Galileos, Daltons, Faradays, have found it impossible to treat the *naïfs* sense-termini of common sense as ultimately real. As common sense interpolates her constant 'things' between our intermittent sensations, so science *extra*polates her world of 'primary' qualities, her atoms, her ether, her magnetic fields, and the like, beyond the common-sense world. The 'things' are now invisible impalpable things; and the old visible common-sense things are supposed to result from the mixture of these invisibles. Or else the whole *naïf* conception of thing gets superseded, and a thing's name is interpreted as denoting only the law or *regel der verbindung* by which certain of our sensations habitually succeed or coexist.

Science and critical philosophy thus burst the bounds of common sense. With science *naïf* realism ceases: 'Secondary' qualities become unreal; primary ones alone remain. With critical philosophy, havoc is made of everything. The common-sense categories one and all cease to represent anything in the way of *being;* they are but sublime tricks of human thought, our ways of escaping bewilderment in the midst of sensation's irremediable flow.

But the scientific tendency in critical thought, though inspired at first by purely intellectual motives, has opened an entirely unexpected range of practical utilities to our astonished view.

The philosophic stage of criticism, much more thorough in its negations than the scientific stage, so far gives us no new range of practical power. Locke, Hume, Berkeley, Kant, Hegel, have all been utterly sterile, so far as shedding any light on the details of nature goes, and I can think of no invention or discovery that can be directly traced to anything in their peculiar thought, for neither with Berkeley's tar-water nor with Kant's nebular hypothesis had their respective philosophic tenets anything to do. The satisfactions they yield to their disciples are intellectual, not practical; and even then we have to confess that there is a large minus-side to the account.

There are thus at least three well-characterized levels, stages, or types of thought about the world we live in, and the notions of one stage have one kind of merit, those of another stage another kind. It is impossible, however, to say that any stage as yet in sight is absolutely more *true* than any other. Common sense is the more *consolidated* stage, because it got its innings first, and made all language into its ally. Whether it or science be the more *august* stage may be left to private judgment. But neither consolidation nor augustness are decisive marks of truth.

There is no *ringing* conclusion possible when we compare these types of thinking, with a view to telling which is the more absolutely true. Their naturalness, their intellectual economy, their fruitfulness for practice, all start up as distinct tests of their veracity, and as a result we get confused. Common sense is *better* for one sphere of life, science for another, philosophic criticism for a third; but whether either be *truer* absolutely, Heaven only knows.

There are only two points that I wish you to retain from the present lecture. The first one relates to common sense. We have seen reason to suspect it, to suspect that in spite of their being so venerable, of their being so universally used and built into the very structure of language, its categories may after all be only a collection of extraordinarily successful hypotheses by which our forefathers have from time immemorial unified and straightened the discontinuity of their immediate experiences, and put themselves into an equilibrium with the surface of nature so satisfactory for ordinary practical purposes that it certainly would have lasted forever, but for the excessive intellectual vivacity of Democritus,

Archimedes, Galileo, Berkeley, and of other excentric geniuses whom the example of such men inflamed.

The other point is this. Ought not the existence of the various types of thinking which we have reviewed, each so splendid for certain purposes, yet all conflicting still, and neither one of them able to support a claim of absolute veracity, to awaken a presumption favorable to the pragmatistic view that all our theories are *instrumental,* are mental modes of *adaptation* to reality, rather than revelations or gnostic answers to some divinely instituted world-enigma?

LECTURE VI: PRAGMATISM'S CONCEPTION OF TRUTH

TRUTH, as any dictionary will tell you, is a property of certain of our ideas. It means their 'agreement,' as falsity means their disagreement, with 'reality.' Pragmatists and intellectualists both accept this definition as a matter of course. They begin to quarrel only after the question is raised as to what may precisely be meant by the term 'agreement,' and what by the term 'reality,' when reality is taken as something for our ideas to agree with.

Pragmatism asks its usual· question. 'Grant an idea or belief to be true,' it says, 'what concrete difference will its being true make in any one's actual life?'

The moment pragmatism asks this question, it sees the answer: *True ideas are those that we can assimilate, validate, corroborate and verify. False ideas are those that we can not.* That is the practical difference it makes to us to have true ideas; that, therefore, is the meaning of truth, for it is all that truth is known as.

This thesis is what I have to defend. The truth of an idea is not a stagnant property inherent in it. Truth *happens* to an idea. It *becomes* true, is *made* true by events. Its verity *is* in fact an event, a process: the process namely of its verifying itself, its veri-*fication.* Its validity is the process of its valid-*ation.*

But what do the words verification and validation themselves pragmatically mean? They again signify certain practical consequences of the verified and validated idea. It is hard to find any one phrase that characterizes these consequences better than the ordinary agreement-formula —just such consequences being what we have in mind whenever we say that our ideas 'agree' with reality. They lead us, namely, through the acts and other ideas which they instigate, into or up to, or towards, other parts of experience with which we feel all the while—such feeling being among our potentialities—that the original ideas remain in agreement. The connexions and transitions come to us from point to point as being progressive, harmonious, satisfactory. This function of agreeable leading is what we mean by an idea's verification.

The importance to human life of having true beliefs about matters of fact is a thing too notorious. We live in a world of realities that can be infinitely useful or infinitely harmful. Ideas that tell us which of them to expect count as the true ideas in all this primary sphere of verification, and the pursuit of such ideas is a primary human duty. The possession of truth, so far from being here an end in itself, is only a preliminary means towards other vital satisfactions. True is the name for whatever idea starts the verification-process, useful is the name for its completed function in experience. True ideas would never have been singled out as such, would never have acquired a class-name, least of all a name suggesting value, unless they had been useful from the outset in this way.

From this simple cue pragmatism gets her general notion of truth as something essentially bound up with the way in which one moment in our experience may lead us towards other moments which it will be worth while to have been led to. Primarily, and on the common-sense level, the truth of a state of mind means this function of *a leading that is worth while*. When a moment in our experience, of any kind whatever, inspires us with a thought that is true, that means that sooner or later we dip by that thought's guidance into the particulars of experience again and make advantageous connexion with them.

To 'agree' in the widest sense with a reality *can only mean to be guided either straight up to it or into its surroundings, or to be put into such working touch with it as to handle either it or something connected with it better than if we disagreed.* Better either intellectually or practically! And often agreement will only mean the negative fact that nothing contradictory from the quarter of that reality comes to interfere with the way in which our ideas guide us elsewhere. To copy a reality is, indeed, one very important way of agreeing with it, but it is far from being essential. The essential thing is the process of being guided. Any idea that helps us to *deal,* whether practically or intellectually, with either the reality or its belongings, that doesn't entangle our progress in frustrations, that *fits,* in fact, and adapts our life to the reality's whole setting, will agree sufficiently to meet the requirement. It will hold true of that reality.

Such is the large loose way in which the pragmatist interprets the word agreement. He treats it altogether practically. He lets it cover any process of conduction from a present idea to a future terminus, provided only it run prosperously. It is only thus that 'scientific' ideas, flying as they do beyond common sense, can be said to agree with their realities. It is, as I have already said, *as if* reality were made of ether, atoms, or electrons, but we mustn't think so literally. The term 'energy' doesn't even pretend to stand for anything 'objective.' It is only a way of measuring the surface of phenomena so as to string their changes on a simple formula.

LECTURE VII: PRAGMATISM AND HUMANISM

WHAT hardens the heart of every one I approach with the view of truth sketched in my last lecture is that typical idol of the tribe, the notion of *the* Truth, conceived as the one answer, determinate and complete, to the one fixed enigma which the world is believed to propound. It never occurs to most of us that the question 'What is *the* truth?' is no real question and that the whole notion of *the* truth is an abstraction from the fact of truths in the plural, a mere useful summarizing phrase like *the* Latin Language or *the* Law.

Laws and languages are man-made things. Mr. Schiller applies the analogy to beliefs, and proposes the name of 'Humanism' for the doctrine that to an unascertainable extent our truths are man-made products too. Human motives sharpen all our questions, human satisfactions lurk in all our answers, all our formulas have a human twist. This element is so inextricable in the products that Mr. Schiller sometimes seems almost to leave it an open question whether there be anything else. 'The world,' he says, 'is what we make it. It is fruitless to define it by what it originally was or by what it is apart from us; it *is* what is made of it. Hence . . . the world *is plastic.*' He adds that we can learn the limits of the plasticity only by trying, and that we ought to start as if it were wholly plastic, acting methodically on that assumption, and stopping only when we are decisively rebuked.

Lotze has in several places made a deep suggestion. We naïvely assume, he says, a relation between reality and our minds which may be just the opposite of the true one. Reality, we naturally think, stands ready-made and complete, and our intellects supervene with the one simple duty of describing it as it is already. But may not our descriptions, Lotze asks, be themselves important additions to reality? And may not previous reality itself be there, far less for the purpose of reappearing unaltered in our knowledge, than for the very purpose of stimulating our minds to such additions as shall enhance the universe's total value. *'Die erhöhung des vorgefundenen daseins'* is a phrase used by Professor Eucken somewhere, which reminds one of this suggestion by the great Lotze.

It is identically our pragmatistic conception. In our cognitive as well as in our active life we are creative. We *add,* both to the subject and to the predicate part of reality. The world stands really malleable, waiting to receive its final touches at our hands. Like the kingdom of heaven, it suffers human violence willingly. Man *engenders* truths upon it.

The import of the difference between pragmatism and rationalism is now in sight throughout its whole extent. The essential contrast is that *for rationalism reality is ready-made and complete from all eternity, while for pragmatism it is still in the making, and awaits part of its complexion from the future.* On the one side the universe is absolutely secure, on the other it is still pursuing its adventures.

The alternative between pragmatism and rationalism, in the shape in which we now have it before us, is no longer a question in the theory of knowledge, it concerns the structure of the universe itself.

On the pragmatist side we have only one edition of the universe, unfinished, growing in all sorts of places, especially in the places where thinking beings are at work.

On the rationalist side we have a universe in many editions, one real one, the infinite folio, or *édition de luxe,* eternally complete; and then the various finite editions, full of false readings, distorted and mutilated each in its own way.

LECTURE VIII: PRAGMATISM AND RELIGION

ON PRAGMATIC PRINCIPLES we cannot reject any hypothesis if consequences useful to life flow from it. Universal conceptions, as things to take account of, may be as real for pragmatism as particular sensations are.

The use of the Absolute is proved by the whole course of men's religious history. The eternal arms are then beneath. Remember Vivekananda's use of the Atman—not indeed a scientific use, for we can make no particular deductions from it. It is emotional and spiritual altogether.

It is always best to discuss things by the help of concrete examples. Let me read therefore some of those verses entitled 'To You' by Walt Whitman—'You' of course meaning the reader or hearer of the poem whosover he or she may be.

Whoever you are, now I place my hand upon you that you be my poem;
I whisper with my lips close to your ear,
I have loved many men and women and men, but I love none better than you.

O I have been dilatory and dumb;
I should have made my way to you long ago;
I should have blabbed nothing but you, I should have chanted nothing but you.

I will leave all and come and make the hymns of you;
None have understood you, but I understand you;
None have done justice to you—you have not done justice to yourself;
None but have found you imperfect—I only find no imperfection in you.

O I could sing such glories and grandeurs about you;
You have not known what you are—you have slumbered upon yourself all your
    life;
What you have done returns already in mockeries.

But the mockeries are not you;
Underneath them and within them, I see you lurk;
I pursue you where none else has pursued you.
Silence, the desk, the flippant expression, the night, the accustomed routine, if
    these conceal you from others, or from yourself, they do not conceal you
    from me;
The shaved face, the unsteady eye, the impure complexion, if these balk others,
    they do not balk me;
The pert apparel, the deformed attitude, drunkenness, greed, premature death,
    all these I part aside.

There is no endowment in man or woman that is not tallied in you;
There is no virtue, no beauty, in man or woman, but as good is in you;
No pluck nor endurance in others, but as good is in you;
No pleasure waiting for others, but an equal pleasure waits for you.

Whoever you are! claim your own at any hazard!
These shows of the east and west are tame, compared with you;
These immense meadows—these interminable rivers—you are immense and
    interminable as they;
You are he or she who is master or mistress over them,
Master or mistress in your own right over Nature, elements, pain, passion, dis-
    solution.

The hopples fall from your ankles—you find an unfailing sufficiency;
Old or young, male or female, rude, low, rejected by the rest whatever you are
    promulges itself;
Through birth, life, death, burial, the means are provided, nothing is scanted;
Through angers, losses, ambition, ignorance, ennui, what you are picks its way.

Verily a fine and moving poem, in any case, but there are two ways of
taking it, both useful.

One is the monistic way, the mystical way of pure cosmic emotion.
The glories and grandeurs, they are yours absolutely, even in the midst
of your defacements. Whatever may happen to you, whatever you may
appear to be, inwardly you are safe.

But pragmatism sees another way to be respected also, the pluralistic
way of interpreting the poem. The you so glorified, to which the hymn
is sung, may mean your better possibilities phenomenally taken, or the
specific redemptive effects even of your failures, upon yourself or others.
It may mean your loyalty to the possibilities of others whom you admire
and love so that you are willing to accept your own poor life, for it is that
glory's partner. You can at least appreciate, applaud, furnish the audience,
of so brave a total world. Forget the low in yourself, then, think only of
the high. Identify your life therewith; then, through angers, losses, ignorance, ennui, whatever you thus make yourself, whatever you thus most
deeply are, picks its way.

Noble enough is either way of reading the poem; but plainly the
pluralistic way agrees with the pragmatic temper best, for it immedi-

ately suggests an infinitely larger number of the details of future experience to our mind. It sets definite activities in us at work. Although this second way seems prosaic and earth-born in comparison with the first way, yet no one can accuse it of tough-mindedness in any brutal sense of the term. Yet if, as pragmatists, you should positively set up the second way *against* the first way, you would very likely be misunderstood. You would be accused of denying nobler conceptions, and of being an ally of tough-mindedness in the worst sense.

Is then this you of yous, this absolutely real world, this unity that yields the moral inspiration and has the religious value, to be taken monistically or pluralistically? Is it *ante rem* or *in rebus*? Is it a principle or an end, an absolute or an ultimate, a first or a last? Does it make you look forward or lie back? It is certainly worth while not to clump the two things together, for if discriminated, they have decidedly diverse meanings for life.

Please observe that the whole dilemma revolves pragmatically about the notion of the world's possibilities. It is necessary therefore to begin by focusing upon that word. What may the word 'possible' definitely mean? To unreflecting men it means a sort of third estate of being, less real than existence, more real than non-existence, a twilight realm, a hybrid status, a limbo into which and out of which realities ever and anon are made to pass.

Such a conception is of course too vague and nondescript to satisfy us. Here, as elsewhere, the only way to extract a term's meaning is to use the pragmatic method on it. When you say that a thing is possible, what difference does it make?

It makes at least this negative difference that if the statement be true, it follows that *there is nothing extant capable of preventing* the possible thing. The absence of real grounds of interference may thus be said to make things *not impossible,* possible therefore in the *bare* or *abstract* sense.

But most possibles are not bare, they are concretely grounded, or well grounded, as we say. What does this mean pragmatically? It means not only that there are no preventive conditions present, but that some of the conditions of production of the possible thing actually are here.

Let us apply this notion to the salvation of the world. What does it pragmatically mean to say that this is possible? It means that some of the conditions of the world's deliverance do actually exist. The more of them there are existent, the fewer preventing conditions you can find, the better grounded is the salvation's possibility, the more *probable* does the fact of the deliverance become.

There are unhappy men who think the salvation of the world impossible. Theirs is the doctrine known as pessimism.

Optimism in turn would be the doctrine that thinks the world's salvation inevitable.

Midway between the two there stands what may be called the doctrine of meliorism, though it has hitherto figured less as a doctrine than as an attitude in human affairs. Meliorism treats salvation as neither necessary nor impossible. It treats it as a possibility, which becomes more and more of a probability the more numerous the actual conditions of salvation become.

It is clear that pragmatism must incline towards meliorism. Some conditions of the world's salvation are actually extant, and she cannot possibly close her eyes to this fact: and should the residual conditions come, salvation would become an accomplished reality. Naturally the terms I use here are exceedingly summary. You may interpret the word 'salvation' in any way you like, and make it as diffuse and distributive, or as climacteric and integral a phenomenon as you please.

Take, for example, any one of us in this room with the ideals which he cherishes and is willing to live and work for. Every such ideal realized will be one moment in the world's salvation. But these particular ideals are not bare abstract possibilities. They are grounded, they are *live* possibilities, for we are their live champions and pledges, and if the complementary conditions come and add themselves, our ideals will become actual things. What now are the complementary conditions? They are first such a mixture of things as will in the fulness of time give us a chance, a gap that we can spring into, and, finally, *our act*.

Does our act then *create* the world's salvation so far as it makes room for itself, so far as it leaps into the gap? Does it create, not the whole world's salvation of course, but just so much of this as itself covers of the world's extent?

Here I take the bull by the horns, and in spite of the whole crew of rationalists and monists, of whatever brand they be, I ask *why not?* Our acts, our turning-places, where we seem to ourselves to make ourselves and grow, are the parts of the world to which we are closest, the parts of which our knowledge is the most intimate and complete. Why should we not take them at their face value? Why may they not be the actual turning-places and growing-places which they seem to be, of the world— why not the workshop of being, where we catch fact in the making, so that nowhere may the world grow in any other kind of way than this?

Take the hypothesis seriously and as a live one. Suppose that the world's author put the case to you before creation, saying: 'I am going to make a world not certain to be saved, a world the perfection of which shall be conditional merely, the condition being that each several agent does its own "level best." I offer you the chance of taking part in such a world. Its safety, you see, is unwarranted. It is a real adventure, with real danger, yet it may win through. It is a social scheme of co-operative work genuinely to be done. Will you join the procession? Will you trust yourself and trust the other agents enough to face the risk?'

Most of us would welcome the proposition and add our *fiat* to the *fiat* of the creator. Yet perhaps some would not; for there are morbid minds in every human collection, and to them the prospect of a universe with only a fighting chance of safety would probably make no appeal. There are moments of discouragement in us all, when we are sick of self and tired of vainly striving. Our own life breaks down, and we fall into the attitude of the prodigal son. We mistrust the chances of things. We want a universe where we can just give up, fall on our father's neck, and be absorbed into the absolute life as a drop of water melts into the river or the sea.

So we see concretely two types of religion in sharp contrast. Using our old terms of comparison, we may say that the absolutistic scheme appeals to the tender-minded while the pluralistic scheme appeals to the tough.

May not the claims of tender-mindedness go too far? May not the notion of a world already saved *in toto* anyhow, be too saccharine to stand? May not religious optimism be too idyllic? Must *all* be saved? Is *no* price to be paid in the work of salvation? Is the last word sweet? Is all 'yes, yes' in the universe? Doesn't the fact of 'no' stand at the very core of life? Doesn't the very 'seriousness' that we attribute to life mean that ineluctable noes and losses form a part of it, that there are genuine sacrifices somewhere, and that something permanently drastic and bitter always remains at the bottom of its cup?

I cannot speak officially as a pragmatist here; all I can say is that my own pragmatism offers no objection to my taking sides with this more moralistic view, and giving up the claim of total reconciliation. The possibility of this is involved in the pragmatistic willingness to treat pluralism as a serious hypothesis. In the end it is our faith and not our logic that decides such questions, and I deny the right of any pretended logic to veto my own faith. I find myself willing to take the universe to be really dangerous and adventurous, without therefore backing out and crying 'no play.' I am willing to think that the prodigal-son attitude, open to us as it is in many vicissitudes, is not the right and final attitude towards the whole of life. I am willing that there should be real losses and real losers, and no total preservation of all that is. I can believe in the ideal as an ultimate, not as an origin, and as an extract, not the whole. When the cup is poured off, the dregs are left behind for ever, but the possibility of what is poured off is sweet enough to accept.

I fear that my previous lectures, confined as they have been to human and humanistic aspects, may have left the impression on many of you that pragmatism means methodically to leave the superhuman out. I have shown small respect indeed for the Absolute, and I have until this moment spoken of no other superhuman hypothesis but that. But I trust that you see sufficiently that the Absolute has nothing but its superhumanness in common with the theistic God. On pragmatistic principles, if the hypothesis of God works satisfactorily in the widest sense of the word, it is true. Now whatever its residual difficulties may be, experience shows that it certainly does work, and that the problem is to build it out and determine it so that it will combine satisfactorily with all the other working truths. I firmly disbelieve, myself, that our human experience is the highest form of experience extant in the universe. I believe rather that we stand in much the same relation to the whole of the universe as our canine and feline pets do to the whole of human life. They inhabit our drawing-rooms and libraries. They take part in scenes of whose significance they have no inkling. They are merely tangent to curves of history the beginnings and ends and forms of which pass wholly beyond their ken. So we are tangent to the wider life of things. But, just as many of the dog's and cat's ideals coincide with our ideals, and the dogs and cats have daily living proof of the fact, so we may well believe, on the proofs that religious experience affords, that higher powers exist and are at work to save the world on ideal lines similar to our own.

You see that pragmatism can be called religious, if you allow that religion can be pluralistic or merely melioristic in type. But whether you will finally put up with that type of religion or not is a question that only you yourself can decide. Pragmatism has to postpone dogmatic answer, for we do not yet know certainly which type of religion is going to work best in the long run. The various overbeliefs of men, their several faith-ventures, are in fact what are needed to bring the evidence in. You will probably make your own ventures severally. If radically tough, the hurly-burly of the sensible facts of nature will be enough for you, and you will need no religion at all. If radically tender, you will take up with the more monistic form of religion: the pluralistic form, with its reliance on possibilities that are not necessities, will not seem to afford you security enough.

But if you are neither tough nor tender in an extreme and radical sense, but mixed as most of us are, it may seem to you that the type of pluralistic and moralistic religion that I have offered is as good a religious synthesis as you are likely to find. Between the two extremes of crude naturalism on the one hand and transcendental absolutism on the other, you may find that what I take the liberty of calling the pragmatistic or melioristic type of theism is exactly what you require.

CREATIVE EVOLUTION

by

HENRI BERGSON

CONTENTS

Creative Evolution

HENRI BERGSON

1859–1941

BORN IN Paris on October 18, 1859, Bergson entered the
École Normale Supérieure at the age of seventeen. His interests at that time were definitely scientific. There is no Provi-
dence in life, he believed, no purpose, no reason for hope. His
fellow students called him "the atheist."

Upon his graduation from the normal school he accepted
a teaching position in the country town of Clermont-Ferrand.
Here he took long walks and found the opportunity to "think
things out." These beautiful hills, this majestic sunset, this
rhythmical rippling of the times and the tides, were they the
result of mere chance? Were they not rather the revealing
figures of a definite design—a moving and evolving pattern
of eternal creation?

This "poetical realization" of an endlessly creative impulse gradually permeated "every fiber of his body and every
cell of his mind." Bergson had come to Clermont a skeptic.
He returned to Paris an idealist. He had lost his interest in the
"microscopic explanation of the parts" and began to direct
his intellect to the "philosophic contemplation of the whole."
Once in a lecture, referring to the difference between scientific
research and philosophical insight, he said: "You have all
handled a microscope. Suppose you examine through it some
anatomical preparation. . . . Slip the glass along and observe
how one cell succeeds another cell, each clearly distinguishable. But what is the object, and what have you seen? If you
want to get the answer to this question, you will be obliged
to abandon the microscope and to consider as a whole, with
your naked eye, that ugly spider's foot."

Bergson's way of looking at life—with the inner rather

than with the outer eye—met with the popular fancy. In 1900 he was appointed professor of philosophy at the Collège de France. Throngs flocked to his lectures, and to the bookstalls to buy his books—*Time and Free Will, Matter and Memory, Mind Energy, Laughter and Metaphysics,* and *Creative Evolution.* For forty years he enchanted his audiences with the beauty of his mind and the simplicity of his heart. And then, in 1940, the Hitler-dominated French Government passed an order that all Jewish professors in France must resign from their positions in the state universities. Bergson was offered an exemption from this order. But he refused the favor. He was willing to share the fate of his coreligionists. He resigned from the Collège de France. The following year he died.

Bergson's philosophy is based upon the principle of *creative evolution*—a term which he employed to express his theory that the creation of the world was not a single act of the past, but is a progressive action that continues to the present day. Evolution, maintains Bergson, is not a mechanical process but a designed purpose. And man is not the plaything of a blind struggle for existence but the cocreator, along with God, of his own destiny, of the whole world's destiny.

For the drama of creation is being written eternally, and man partakes of the nature both of the actor and of the playwright. The play goes on; and at every moment it promises, with the help of man, to blossom into something new and unforeseeable and grand.

The creative impulse—Bergson calls it the *élan vital,* the vital spark—lies within us all. It is the energy that gives birth to every noble thought, every beautiful emotion, every generous act. It is the urge that impels life ever onward and upward, from the lowest plant to the highest man. "The animal takes its stand upon the plant, man bestrides animality, and the whole of humanity, in space and time, is one immense army galloping beside and before and behind each of us in an overwhelming charge able to beat down every resistance and to clear every obstacle" not only in life, but even in death. For through the power of creative evolution, this vital spark in God and man, life conquers death.

CREATIVE EVOLUTION

I: THE EVOLUTION OF LIFE—MECHANISM AND TELEOLOGY

THE EXISTENCE of which we are most assured and which we know best is unquestionably our own, for of every other object we have notions which may be considered external and superficial, whereas, of ourselves, our perception is internal and profound. What, then, do we find? In this privileged case, what is the precise meaning of the word "exist"?

I find, first of all, that I pass from state to state. But this is not saying enough. Change is far more radical than we are at first inclined to suppose.

For I speak of each of my states as if it formed a block and were a separate whole. I say indeed that I change, but the change seems to me to reside in the passage from one state to the next: of each state, taken separately, I am apt to think that it remains the same during all the time that it prevails. Nevertheless, a slight effort of attention would reveal to me that there is no feeling, no idea, no volition which is not undergoing change every moment: if a mental state ceased to vary, its duration would cease to flow.

For our duration is not merely one instant replacing another; if it were, there would never be anything but the present—no prolonging of the past into the actual, no evolution, no concrete duration. Duration is the continuous progress of the past which gnaws into the future and which swells as it advances. And as the past grows without ceasing, so also there is no limit to its preservation. Memory is not a faculty of putting away recollections in a drawer, or of inscribing them in a register. There is no register, no drawer; there is not even, properly speaking, a faculty, for a faculty works intermittently, when it will or when it can, whilst the piling up of the past upon the past goes on without relaxation. In reality, the past is preserved by itself, automatically. In its entirety, probably, it follows us at every instant; all that we have felt, thought, and willed from our earliest infancy is there, leaning over the present which is about to join it, pressing against the portals of consciousness that would fain leave it outside.

From this survival of the past it follows that consciousness cannot go through the same state twice. The circumstances may still be the same, but they will act no longer on the same person, since they find him at a new moment of his history. Our personality, which is being built up each instant with its accumulated experience, changes without ceasing. By changing, it prevents any state, although superficially identical with another, from ever repeating it in its very depth. That is why our duration is irreversible. We could not live over again a single moment, for we should have to begin by effacing the memory of all that had followed. Even could we erase this memory from our intellect, we could not from our will.

Thus our personality shoots, grows, and ripens without ceasing. Each of its moments is something new added to what was before. We may go further: it is not only something new, but something unforeseeable. Doubtless, my present state is explained by what was in me and by what was acting on me a moment ago. In analyzing it I should find no other elements. But even a superhuman intelligence would not have been able to foresee the simple indivisible form which gives to these purely abstract elements their concrete organization. For to foresee consists of projecting into the future what has been perceived in the past, or of imagining for a later time a new grouping, in a new order, of elements already perceived. But that which has never been perceived, and which is at the same time simple, is necessarily unforeseeable. It is then right to say that what we do depends on what we are; but it is necessary to add also that we are, to a certain extent, what we do, and that we are creating ourselves continually. This creation of self by self is the more complete, the more one reasons on what one does. But we need not go more deeply into this. We are seeking only the precise meaning that our consciousness gives to this word "exist," and we find that, for a conscious being, to exist is to change, to change is to mature, to mature is to go on creating oneself endlessly. Should the same be said of existence in general?

A material object, of whatever kind, presents opposite characters to those which we have just been describing. Either it remains as it is, or else, if it changes under the influence of an external force, our idea of this change is that of a displacement of parts which themselves do not change. If these parts took to changing, we should split them up in their turn. We should thus descend to the molecules of which the fragments are made, to the atoms that make up the molecules, to the corpuscles that generate the atoms, to the "imponderable" within which the corpuscle is perhaps a mere vortex. In short, we should push the division or analysis as far as necessary. But we should stop only before the unchangeable.

All our belief in objects, all our operations on the systems that science isolates, rest in fact on the idea that time does not bite into them. The abstract time t attributed by science to a material object or to an isolated system consists only in a certain number of simultaneities or more generally of correspondences, and this number remains the same, whatever be the nature of the intervals between the correspondences. With these intervals we are never concerned when dealing with inert matter; or, if they are considered, it is in order to count therein fresh correspondences, between which again we shall not care what happens. Common sense, which is occupied with detached objects, and also science, which considers isolated systems, are concerned only with the ends of the intervals and not with the intervals themselves. Therefore the flow of time might assume an infinite rapidity, the entire past, present, and future of material objects or of isolated systems might be spread out all at once in space, without there being anything to change.either in the formulae of the scientist or even in the language of common sense. The number t would always stand for the same thing; it would still count the same number of correspondences between the states of the objects or systems and the points of the line, ready drawn, which would be then the "course of time."

Yet succession is an undeniable fact, even in the material world. Though our reasoning on isolated systems may imply that their history, past, present, and future, might be instantaneously unfurled like a fan, this history, in point of fact, unfolds itself gradually, as if it occupied a duration like our own.

Certainly, the operation by which science isolates and closes a system is not altogether artificial. If it had no objective foundation, we could not explain why it is clearly indicated in some cases and impossible in others. We shall see that matter has a tendency to constitute *isolable* systems, that can be treated geometrically. In fact, we shall define matter by just this tendency. But it is only a tendency. Matter does not go to the end, and the isolation is never complete.

There is no reason, therefore, why a duration, and so a form of existence like our own, should not be attributed to the systems that science isolates, provided such systems are reintegrated into the Whole. But they must be so reintegrated.

Now, we have considered material objects generally. Are there not some objects privileged? The bodies we perceive are, so to speak, cut out of the stuff of nature by our *perception,* and the scissors follow, in some way, the marking of lines along which *action* might be taken. But the body which is to perform this action, the body which marks out upon matter the design of its eventual actions even before they are actual, the body that has only to point its sensory organs on the flow of the real in order to make that flow crystallize into definite forms and thus to create all the other bodies—in short, the *living* body—is this a body as others are?

Doubtless it, also, consists in a portion of extension bound up with the rest of extension, an intimate part of the Whole, subject to the same physical and chemical laws that govern any and every portion of matter. But, while the subdivision of matter into separate bodies is relative to our perception, while the building up of closed-off systems of material points is relative to our science, the living body has been separated and closed off by nature herself. It is composed of unlike parts that complete each other. It performs diverse functions that involve each other. It is an *individual,* and of no other object, not even of the crystal, can this be said, for a crystal has neither difference of parts nor diversity of functions. No doubt, it is hard to decide, even in the organized world, what is individual and what is not. The difficulty is great, even in the animal kingdom; with plants it is almost insurmountable. The biologist who proceeds as a geometrician is too ready to take advantage here of our inability to give a precise and general definition of individuality. A perfect definition applies only to a *completed* reality; now, vital properties are never entirely realized, though always on the way to become so; they are not so much *states* as *tendencies.* And a tendency achieves all that it aims at only if it is not thwarted by another tendency. How, then, could this occur in the domain of life, where the interaction of antagonistic tendencies is always implied? In particular, it may be said of individuality that, while the tendency to individuate is everywhere present in the organized world, it is everywhere opposed by the tendency towards reproduction. For the individuality to be perfect, it would be necessary that no detached part of the organism could live separately. But then reproduction would be impossible. For what is reproduction, but the building up of a new organism with a detached fragment of the old? Individuality therefore harbors its enemy at home. Its very need of perpetuating itself in time condemns it never to be complete in space. The biologist must take due account of both tendencies in every instance, and it is therefore useless to ask him for a definition of individuality that shall fit all cases and work automatically.

But too often one reasons about the things of life in the same way as about the conditions of crude matter. Nowhere is the confusion so evident as in discussions about individuality. Generally speaking, unorganized bodies, which are what we have need of in order that we may act, and on which we have modelled our fashion of thinking, are regulated by this simple law: *the present contains nothing more than the past, and what is found in the effect was already in the cause.* But suppose that the distinctive feature of the organized body is that it grows and changes without ceasing, as indeed the most superficial observation testifies, there would be nothing astonishing in the fact that it was *one* in the first instance, and afterwards *many.* True, in the more complex animals, nature localizes in the almost independent sexual cells the power of producing the whole anew. But something of this power may remain diffused in the rest of the organism, as the facts of regeneration prove, and it is conceivable that in certain privileged cases the faculty may persist integrally in a latent condition and manifest itself on the first opportunity. In truth, that I may have the right to speak of individuality, it is not necessary that the organism should be without the power to divide into fragments that are able to live. It is sufficient that it should have presented a certain systematization of parts before the division, and that the same systematization tend to be reproduced in each separate portion afterwards. Now, that is precisely what we observe in the organic world. We may conclude, then, that individuality is never perfect, and that it is often difficult, sometimes impossible, to tell what is an individual, and what is not, but that life nevertheless manifests a search for individuality, as if it strove to constitute systems naturally isolated, naturally closed.

By this is a living being distinguished from all that our perception or our science isolates or closes artificially. It would therefore be wrong to compare it to an *object*. Should we wish to find a term of comparison in the inorganic world, it is not to a determinate material object, but much rather to the totality of the material universe that we ought to compare the living organism. Like the universe as a whole, like each conscious being taken separately, the organism which lives is a thing that *endures*. Its past, in its entirety, is prolonged into its present, and abides there, actual and acting. How otherwise could we understand that it passes through distinct and well-marked phases, that it changes its age—in short, that it has a history? Once more, there is no universal biological law which applies precisely and automatically to every living thing. There are only *directions* in which life throws out species in general. Each particular species, in the very act by which it is constituted, affirms its independence, follows its caprice, deviates more or less from the straight line, sometimes even remounts the slope and seems to turn its back on its original direction. It is easy enough to argue that a tree never grows old, since the tips of its branches are always equally young, always equally capable of engendering new trees by budding. But in such an organism—which is, after all, a society rather than an individual—*something* ages, if only the leaves and the interior of the trunk. And each cell, considered separately, evolves in a specific way. *Wherever anything lives, there is, open somewhere, a register in which time is being inscribed.*

True, biologists are not agreed on what is gained and what is lost between the day of birth and the day of death. There are those who hold to the continual growth in the volume of protoplasm from the birth of the cell right on to its death. More probable and more profound is the theory according to which the diminution bears on the quantity of nutritive substance contained in that "inner environment" in which the organism is being renewed, and the increase on the quantity of unexcreted residual substances which, accumulating in the body, finally "crust it over." Must we however—with an eminent bacteriologist—declare any explanation of growing old insufficient that does not take account of phagocytosis? We do not feel qualified to settle the question. But the fact that the two theories agree in affirming the constant accumulation or loss of a certain kind of matter, even though they have little in common as to what is gained and lost, shows pretty well that the frame of the explanation has been furnished *a priori.*

The cause of growing old must lie deeper. We hold that there is unbroken continuity between the evolution of the embryo and that of the complete organism. The impetus which causes a living being to grow larger, to develop and to age, is the same that has caused it to pass through the phases of the embryonic life. The development of the embryo is a perpetual change of form. Anyone who attempts to note all its successive aspects becomes lost in an infinity, as is inevitable in dealing with a continuum. Life does but prolong this prenatal evolution. In short, what is properly vital in growing old is the insensible, infinitely graduated, continuance of the change of form. Now, this change is undoubtedly accompanied by phenomena of organic destruction: to these, and to these alone, will a mechanistic explanation of aging be confined. It will note the facts of sclerosis, the gradual accumulation of residual substances, the growing hypertrophy of the protoplasm of the cell. But under these visible effects an inner cause lies hidden. The evolution of the living being, like that of the embryo, implies a continual recording of duration, a persistence of the past in the present, and so an appearance, at least, of organic memory.

The present state of an unorganized body depends exclusively on what happened at the previous instant; and likewise the position of the material points of a system defined and isolated by science is determined by the position of these same points at the moment immediately before. In other words, the laws that govern unorganized matter are expressible, in principle, by differential equations in which time (in the sense in which the mathematician takes this word) would play the role of independent variable. Is it so with the laws of life? Does the state of a living body find its complete explanation in the state immediately before? Yes, if it is agreed *a priori* to liken the living body to other bodies, and to identify it, for the sake of the argument, with the artificial systems on which the chemist, physicist, and astronomer operate. But in astronomy, physics, and chemistry the proposition has a perfectly definite meaning: it signifies that certain aspects of the present, important for science, are calculable as functions of the immediate past. Nothing of the sort in the domain of life. Here calculation touches, at most, certain phenomena of organic *destruction.* Organic *creation,* on the contrary, the evolutionary phenomena which properly constitute life, we cannot in any way subject to a mathematical treatment. It will be said that this impotence is due only to our ignorance.

But it may equally well express the fact that the present moment of a living body does not find its explanation in the moment immediately before, that *all* the past of the organism must be added to that moment, its heredity—in fact, the whole of a very long history. In the second of these two hypotheses, not in the first, is really expressed the present state of the biological sciences, as well as their direction. As for the idea that the living body might be treated by some superhuman calculator in the same mathematical way as our solar system, this has gradually arisen from a metaphysic which has taken a more precise form since the physical discoveries of Galileo, but which was always the natural metaphysic of the human mind. Its apparent clearness, our impatient desire to find it true, the enthusiasm with which so many excellent minds accept it without proof—all the seductions, in short, that it exercises on our thought, should put us on our guard against it. The attraction it has for us proves well enough that it gives satisfaction to an innate inclination. But, as will be seen further on, the intellectual tendencies innate to-day, which life must have created in the course of its evolution, are not at all meant to supply us with an explanation of life: they have something else to do.

Any attempt to distinguish between an artificial and a natural system, between the dead and the living, runs counter to this tendency at once. Thus it happens that we find it equally difficult to imagine that the organized has duration and that the unorganized has not. When we say that the state of an artificial system depends exclusively on its state at the moment before, does it not seem as if we were bringing time in, as if the system had something to do with real duration? And, on the other hand, though the whole of the. past goes into the making of the living being's present moment, does not organic memory press it into the moment immediately before the present, so that the moment immediately before becomes the sole cause of the present one?—To speak thus is to ignore the cardinal difference between *concrete* time, along which a real system develops, and that *abstract* time which enters into our speculations on artificial systems. What does it mean, to say that the state of an artificial system depends on what it was at the moment immediately before? There is no instant immediately before another instant; there could not be, any more than there could be one mathematical point touching another. The instant "immediately before" is, in reality, that which is connected with the present instant by the interval dt. All that you mean to say, therefore, is that the present state of the system is defined by equations into which differential coefficients enter, such as ds/dt, dv/dt, that is to say, at bottom, *present* velocities and *present* accelerations. You are therefore really speaking only of the present—a present, it is true, considered along with its *tendency*. The systems science works with are, in fact, in an instantaneous present that is always being renewed; such systems are never in that real, concrete duration in which the past remains bound up with the present. When the mathematician calculates the future state of a system at the end of a time t, there is nothing to prevent him from supposing that the universe vanishes from this moment till that, and suddenly reappears. It is the t-th moment only that counts—and that will be a mere instant. What will flow on in the interval—that is to say, real time—does not count, and cannot enter into the calculation. If the mathematician says that he puts himself inside this interval, he means that he is placing himself at a certain point, at a particular moment, therefore at the extremity again of a certain time t'; with the interval up to T' he is not concerned. If he divides the interval into infinitely small parts by considering the differential dt, he thereby expresses merely the fact that he will consider accelerations and velocities—that is to say, numbers which denote tendencies and enable him to calculate the state of the system at a given moment. But he is always speaking of a given moment—a static moment, that is—and not of flowing time. In short, *the world the mathematician deals with is a world that dies and is reborn at every instant—the world which Descartes was thinking of when he spoke of continued creation.* But, in time thus conceived, how could evolution, which is the very essence of life, ever take place? Evolution implies a real persistence of the past in the present, a duration which is, as it were, a hyphen, a connecting link. In other words, to know a living being or *natural system* is to get at the very interval of duration, while the knowledge of an *artificial* or *mathematical system* applies only to the extremity.

Continuity of change, preservation of the past in the present, real duration—the living being seems, then, to share these attributes with consciousness. Can we go further and say that life, like conscious activity, is invention, is unceasing creation?

The idea of transformism is already in germ in the natural classification of organized beings. The naturalist, in fact, brings together the organisms that are like each other, then divides the group into sub-groups within which the likeness is still greater, and so on: all through the operation, the characters of the group appear as general themes on which each of the sub-groups performs its particular variation. Now, such is just the relation we find, in the animal and in the vegetable world between the generator and the generated: on the canvas which the ancestor passes on, and which his descendants possess in common, each puts his own original embroidery. True, the differences between the descendant and the ancestor are slight, and it may be asked whether the same living matter presents enough plasticity to take in turn such different forms as those of a fish, a reptile, and a bird. But, to this question, observation gives a peremptory answer. It shows that up to a certain period in its development the embryo of the bird is hardly distinguishable from that of the reptile, and that the individual develops, throughout the embryonic life in general, a series of transformations comparable to those through which, according to the theory of evolution, one species passes into another. A single cell, the result of the combination of two cells, male and female, accomplishes this work by dividing. Every day, before our eyes, the highest forms of life are springing from a very elementary form. Experience, then, shows that the most complex has been able to issue from the most simple by way of evolution. Now, has it arisen so, as a matter of fact? Paleontology, in spite of the insufficiency of its evidence, invites us to believe it has; for, where it makes out the order of succession of species with any precision, this order is just what considerations drawn from embryogeny and comparative anatomy would lead anyone to suppose, and each new paleontological discovery brings transformism a new confirmation. Thus, the proof drawn from mere observation is ever being strengthened, while, on the other hand, experiment is removing the objections one by one. The recent experiments of H. de Vries, for instance, by showing that important variations can be produced suddenly and transmitted regularly, have overthrown some of the greatest difficulties raised by the theory. They have enabled us greatly to shorten the time biological evolution seems to demand. They also render us less exacting toward paleontology. So that, all things considered, the transformist hypothesis looks more and more like a close approximation to the truth. It is not rigorously demonstrable; but, failing the certainty of theoretical or experimental demonstration, there is a probability which is continually growing, due to evidence which, while coming short of direct proof, seems to point persistently in its direction: such is the kind of probability that the theory of transformism offers.

So we come back, by a somewhat roundabout way, to the idea we started from, that of an *original impetus* of life, passing from one generation of germs to the following generation of germs through the developed organisms which bridge the interval between the generations. This impetus, sustained right along the lines of evolution among which it gets divided, is the fundamental cause of variations, at least of those that are regularly passed on, that accumulate and create new species. In general, when species have begun to diverge from a common stock, they accentuate their divergence as they progress in their evolution. Yet, in certain definite points, they may evolve identically; in fact, they must do so if the hypothesis of a common impetus be accepted.

II: THE DIVERGENT DIRECTIONS OF THE EVOLUTION OF LIFE—TORPOR, INTELLIGENCE, INSTINCT

THE EVOLUTION MOVEMENT would be a simple one, and we should soon have been able to determine its direction, if life had described a single course, like that of a solid ball shot from a cannon. But it proceeds rather like a shell, which suddenly bursts into fragments, which fragments, being themselves shells, burst in their turn into fragments destined to burst again, and so on for a time incommensurably long. We perceive only what is nearest to us, namely, the scattered movements of the pulverized explosions. From them we have to go back, stage by stage, to the original movement.

When a shell bursts, the particular way it breaks is explained both by the explosive force of the powder it contains and by the resistance of the metal. So of the way life breaks into individuals and species. It depends, we think, on two series of causes: the resistance life meets from inert matter, and the explosive force—due to an unstable balance of tendencies —which life bears within itself.

The resistance of inert matter was the obstacle that had first to be overcome. Life seems to have succeeded in this by dint of humility, by making itself very small and very insinuating, bending to physical and chemical forces, consenting even to go a part of the way with them, like the switch that adopts for a while the direction of the rail it is endeavoring to leave. Of phenomena in the simplest forms of life, it is hard to say whether they are still physical and chemical or whether they are already vital.

But the real and profound causes of division were those which life bore within its bosom. For life is tendency, and the essence of a tendency is to develop in the form of a sheaf, creating, by its very growth, divergent directions among which its impetus is divided.

So our study of the evolution movement will have to unravel a certain number of divergent directions, and to appreciate the importance of what has happened along each of them—in a word, to determine the nature of the dissociated tendencies and estimate their relative proportion. Combining these tendencies, then, we shall get an approximation, or rather an imitation, of the indivisible motor principle whence their impetus proceeds. Evolution will thus prove to be something entirely different from a series of adaptations to circumstances, as mechanism claims; entirely different also from the realization of a plan of the whole, as maintained by the doctrine of finality.

That adaptation to environment is the necessary condition of evolution we do not question for a moment. It is quite evident that a species would disappear, should it fail to bend to the conditions of existence which are imposed on it. But it is one thing to recognize that outer circumstances are forces evolution must reckon with, another to claim that they are the directing causes of evolution. This latter theory is that of mechanism. It excludes absolutely the hypothesis of an original impetus,

I mean an internal push that has carried life, by more and more complex forms, to higher and higher destinies. Yet this impetus is evident, and a ⁻mere glance at fossil species shows us that life need not have evolved at all, or might have evolved only in very restricted limits, if it had chosen the alternative, much more convenient to itself, of becoming anchylosed in its primitive forms.

But, if the evolution of life is something other than a series of adaptations to accidental circumstances, so also it is not the realization of a plan. A plan is given in advance. It is represented, or at least representable, before its realization. The complete execution of it may be put off to a distant future, or even indefinitely; but the idea is none the less formulable at the present time, in terms actually given. If, on the contrary, evolution is a creation unceasingly renewed, it creates, as it goes on, not only the forms of life, but the ideas that will enable the intellect to understand it, the terms which will serve to express it. That is to say that its future overflows its present, and cannot be sketched out therein in an idea.

There is the first error of finalism. It involves another, yet more serious.

If life realizes a plan, it ought to manifest a greater harmony the further it advances, just as the house shows better and better the idea of the architect as stone is set upon stone. If, on the contrary, the unity of life is to be found solely in the impetus that pushes it along the road of time, the harmony is not in front, but behind.

To begin with the second point, let us say that no definite characteristic distinguishes the plant from the animal. Attempts to define the two kingdoms strictly have always come to naught. There is not a single property of vegetable life that is not found, in some degree, in certain animals; not a single characteristic feature of the animal that has not been seen in certain species or at certain moments in the vegetable world. Naturally, therefore, biologists enamored of clean-cut concepts have regarded the distinction between the two kingdoms as artificial. They would be right, if definition in this case must be made, as in the mathematical and physical sciences, according to certain statical attributes which belong to the object defined and are not found in any other. Very different, in our opinion, is the kind of definition which befits the sciences of life. There is no manifestation of life which does not contain, in a rudimentary state—either latent or potential,—the essential characters of most other manifestations. The difference is in the proportions. But this very difference of proportion will suffice to define the group, if we can establish that it is not accidental, and that the group as it evolves, tends more and more to emphasize these particular characters. In a word, *the group must not be defined by the possession of certain characters, but by its tendency to emphasize them.* From this point of view, taking tendencies rather than states into account, we find that vegetables and animals may be precisely defined and distinguished, and that they correspond to two divergent developments of life.

Now, it seems to us most probable that the animal cell and the vegetable cell are derived from a common stock, and that the first living organisms oscillated between the vegetable and animal form, participating in both at once. Ordinarily, one of the two tendencies covers or crushes down the other, but in exceptional circumstances the suppressed one starts up and regains the place it had lost. The mobility and consciousness of the vegetable cell are not so sound asleep that they cannot rouse themselves when circumstances permit or demand it; and, on the other hand, the evolution of the animal kingdom has always been retarded, or stopped, or dragged back, by the tendency it has kept toward the vegetative life. However full, however overflowing the activity of an animal species may appear, torpor and unconsciousness are always lying in wait for it. It keeps up its rôle only by effort, at the price of fatigue. Along the route on which the animal has evolved, there have been numberless shortcomings and cases of decay, generally associated with parasitic habits; they are so many shuntings on to the vegetative life. Thus, everything bears out the belief that vegetable and animal are descended from a common ancestor which united the tendencies of both in a rudimentary state.

But the two tendencies mutually implied in this rudimentary form became dissociated as they grew. Hence the world of plants with its fixity and insensibility, hence the animals with their mobility and consciousness. There is no need, in order to explain this dividing into two, to bring in any mysterious force. It is enough to point out that the living being leans naturally toward what is most convenient to it, and that vegetables and animals have chosen two different kinds of convenience in the way of procuring the carbon and nitrogen they need. Vegetables continually and mechanically draw these elements from an environment that continually provides it. Animals, by action that is discontinuous, concentrated in certain moments, and conscious, go to find these bodies in organisms that have already fixed them. They are two different ways of being industrious, or perhaps we may prefer to say, of being idle. For this very reason we doubt whether nervous elements, however rudimentary, will ever be found in the plant. What corresponds in it to the directing will of the animal is, we believe, the direction in which it bends the energy of the solar radiation when it uses it to break the connection of the carbon with the oxygen in carbonic acid. What corresponds in it to the sensibility of the animal is the impressionability, quite of its kind, of its chlorophyl to light. Now, a nervous system being pre-eminently a mechanism which serves as intermediary between sensations and volitions, the true "nervous system" of the plant seems to be the mechanism or rather chemicism *sui generis* which serves as intermediary between the impressionability of its chlorophyl to light and the producing of starch: which amounts to saying that the plant can have no nervous elements, and that *the same impetus that has led the animal to give itself nerves and nerve centres must have ended, in the plant, in the chlorophyllian function.*

It must not be forgotten that the force which is evolving throughout the organized world is a limited force, which is always seeking to transcend itself and always remains inadequate to the work it would fain produce.

From the bottom to the top of the organized world we do indeed find one great effort; but most often this effort turns short, sometimes paralyzed by contrary forces, sometimes diverted from what it should do by what it does, absorbed by the form it is engaged in taking, hypnotized by it as by a mirror. Even in its most perfect works, though it seems to have triumphed over external resistances and also over its own, it is at the mercy of the materiality which it has had to assume.

Vegetative torpor, instinct, and intelligence—these, then, are the elements that coincided in the vital impulsion common to plants and animals, and which, in the course of a development in which they were made manifest in the most unforeseen forms, have been dissociated by the very fact of their growth. *The cardinal error which, from Aristotle onwards, has vitiated most of the philosophies of nature, is to see in vegetative, instinctive, and rational life, three successive degrees of the development of one and the same tendency, whereas they are three divergent directions of an activity that has split up as it grew.* The difference between them is not a difference of intensity, nor, more generally, of degree, but of kind.

It is important to investigate this point. We have seen in the case of vegetable and animal life how they are at once mutually complementary and mutually antagonistic. Now we must show that intelligence and instinct also are opposite and complementary. But let us first explain why we are generally led to regard them as activities of which one is superior to the other and based upon it, whereas in reality they are not things of the same order: they have not succeeded one another, nor can we assign to them different grades.

It is because intelligence and instinct, having originally been interpenetrating, retain something of their common origin. Neither is ever found in a pure state. We said that in the plant the consciousness and mobility of the animal, which lie dormant, can be awakened; and that the animal lives under the constant menace of being drawn aside to the vegetative life. The two tendencies—that of the plant and that of the animal— were so thoroughly interpenetrating, to begin with, that there has never been a complete severance between them: they haunt each other continually; everywhere we find them mingled; it is the proportion that differs.

So with intelligence and instinct. There is no intelligence in which some traces of instinct are not to be discovered, more especially no instinct that is not surrounded with a fringe of intelligence. It is this fringe of intelligence that has been the cause of so many misunderstandings. From the fact that instinct is always more or less intelligent, it has been concluded that instinct and intelligence are things of the same kind, that there is only a difference of complexity or perfection between them, and, above all, that one of the two is expressible in terms of the other. In reality, they accompany each other only because they are complementary, and they are complementary only because they are different, what is instinctive in instinct being opposite to what is intelligent in intelligence.

III: ON THE MEANING OF LIFE—THE ORDER OF NATURE AND THE FORM OF INTELLIGENCE

IN THE COURSE of our first chapter we traced a line of demarcation between the inorganic and the organized, but we pointed out that the division of unorganized matter into separate bodies is relative to our senses and to our intellect, and that matter, looked at as an undivided whole, must be a flux rather than a thing. In this we were preparing the way for a reconciliation between the inert and the living.

On the other side, we have shown in our second chapter that the same opposition is found again between instinct and intelligence, the one turned to certain determinations of life, the other molded on the configuration of matter. But instinct and intelligence, we have also said, stand out from the same background, which, for want of a better name, we may call consciousness in general, and which must be coextensive with universal life. In this way, we have disclosed the possibility of showing the genesis of intelligence in setting out from general consciousness, which embraces it.

We are now, then, to attempt a genesis of intellect at the same time as a genesis of material bodies—two enterprises that are evidently correlative, if it be true that the main lines of our intellect mark out the general form of our action on matter, and that the detail of matter is ruled by the requirements of our action. Intellectuality and materiality have been constituted, in detail, by reciprocal adaptation. Both are derived from a wider and higher form of existence. It is there that we must replace them, in order to see them issue forth.

From this point of view, the general considerations we have presented concerning the evolution of life will be cleared up and completed. We will distinguish more sharply what is accidental from what is essential in this evolution.

The impetus of life, of which we are speaking, consists in a need of creation. It cannot create absolutely, because it is confronted with matter, that is to say with the movement that is the inverse of its own. But it seizes upon this matter, which is necessity itself, and strives to introduce into it the largest possible amount of indetermination and liberty. How does it go to work?

An animal high in the scale may be represented in a general way, we said, as a sensori-motor nervous system imposed on digestive, respiratory, circulatory systems, etc. The function of these latter is to cleanse, repair, and protect the nervous system, to make it as independent as possible of external circumstances, but, above all, to furnish it with energy to be expended in movements. The increasing complexity of the organism is therefore due theoretically (in spite of innumerable exceptions due to accidents of evolution) to the necessity of complexity in the nervous system. No doubt, each complication of any part of the organism involves many others in addition, because this part itself must live, and every change in one point of the body reverberates, as it were, throughout. The complication may therefore go on to infinity in all directions; but it is the complication of the nervous system which conditions the others in right, if not always in fact. Now, in what does the progress of the nervous system itself consist? In a simultaneous development of automatic activity and of voluntary activity, the first furnishing the second with an appropriate instrument. Thus, in an organism such as ours, a considerable number of motor mechanisms are set up in the medulla and in the spinal cord, awaiting only a signal to release the corresponding act: the will is employed, in some cases, in setting up the mechanism itself, and in the others in choosing the mechanisms to be released, the manner of combining them, and the moment of releasing them. The will of an animal is the more effective and the more intense, the greater the number of the mechanisms it can choose from, the more complicated the switchboard on which all the motor paths cross, or, in other words, the more developed its brain. Thus, the progress of the nervous system assures to the act increasing precision, increasing variety, increasing efficiency and independence. The organism behaves more and more like a machine for action, which reconstructs itself entirely for every new act, as if it were made of india-rubber and could, at any moment, change the shape of all its parts. But, prior to the nervous system, prior even to the organism properly so called, already in the undifferentiated mass of the amoeba, this essential property of animal life is found. The amoeba deforms itself in varying directions; its entire mass does what the differentiation of parts will localize in a sensori-motor system in the developed animal. Doing it only in a rudimentary manner, it is dispensed from the complexity of the higher organisms; there is no need here of the auxiliary elements that pass on to motor elements the energy to expend; the animal moves as a whole, and, as a whole also, procures energy by means of the organic substances it assimilates. Thus, whether low or high in the animal scale, we always find that animal life consists (1) in procuring a provision of energy; (2) in expending it, by means of a matter as supple as possible, in directions variable and unforeseen.

Now, whence comes the energy? From the ingested food, for food is a kind of explosive, which needs only the spark to discharge the energy it stores. Who has made this explosive? The food may be the flesh of an animal nourished on animals and so on; but in the end it is to the vegetable we always come back. Vegetables alone gather in the solar energy, and the animals do but borrow it from them, either directly or by some passing it on to others. How then has the plant stored up this energy? Chiefly by the chlorophyllian function, a chemicism *sui generis* of which we do not possess the key, and which is probably unlike that of our laboratories. The process consists in using solar energy to fix the carbon of carbonic acid, and thereby to store this energy as we should store that of a water-carrier by employing him to fill an elevated reservoir: the water, once brought up, can set in motion a mill or a turbine, as we will and when we will. Each atom of carbon fixed represents something like the elevation of the weight of water, or like the stretching of an elastic thread uniting the carbon to the oxygen in the carbonic acid. The elastic is relaxed, the weight falls back again, in short the energy held in reserve is restored, when, by a simple release, the carbon is permitted to rejoin its oxygen.

So that all life, animal and vegetable, seems in its essence like an effort to accumulate energy and then to let it flow into flexible channels, changeable in shape, at the end of which it will accomplish infinitely varied kinds of work. That is what the *vital impetus,* passing through matter, would fain do all at once. It would succeed, no doubt, if its power were unlimited, or if some reinforcement could come to it from without. But the impetus is finite, and it has been given once for all. It cannot overcome all obstacles. The movement it starts is sometimes turned aside, sometimes divided, always opposed; and the evolution of the organized world is the unrolling of this conflict. The first great scission that had to be effected was that of the two kingdoms, vegetable and animal, which thus happen to be mutually complementary, without, however, any agreement having been made between them. It is not for the animal that the plant accumulates energy, it is for its own consumption; but its expenditure on itself is less discontinuous, and less concentrated, and therefore less efficacious, than was required by the initial impetus of life, essentially directed toward free actions: the same organism could not with equal force sustain the two functions at once, of gradual storage and sudden use. Of themselves, therefore, and without any external intervention, simply by the effect of the duality of the tendency involved in the original impetus and of the resistance opposed by matter to this impetus, the organisms leaned some in the first direction, others in the second. To this scission there succeeded many others. Hence the diverging lines of evolution, at least what is essential in them. But we must take into account retrogressions, arrests, accidents of every kind. And we must remember, above all, that each species behaves as if the general movement of life stopped at it instead of passing through it. It thinks only of itself, it lives only for itself. Hence the numberless struggles that we behold in nature. Hence a discord, striking and terrible, but for which the original principle of life must not be held responsible.

The part played by contingency in evolution is therefore great. Contingent, generally, are the forms adopted, or rather invented. Contingent, relative to the obstacles encountered in a given place and at a given moment, is the dissociation of the primordial tendency into such and such complementary tendencies which create divergent lines of evolution. Contingent the arrests and set-backs; contingent, in large measure, the adaptations. Two things only are necessary: (1) a gradual accumulation of energy; (2) an elastic canalization of this energy in variable and indeterminable directions, at the end of which are free acts.

This twofold result has been obtained in a particular way on our planet. But it might have been obtained by entirely different means. It was not necessary that life should fix its choice mainly upon the carbon of carbonic acid. What was essential for it was to store solar energy; but, instead of asking the sun to separate, for instance, atoms of oxygen and carbon, it might (theoretically at least, and, apart from practical difficulties possibly insurmountable) have put forth other chemical elements, which would then have had to be associated or dissociated by entirely different physical means. And if the element characteristic of the substances that supply energy to the organism had been other than carbon, the element characteristic of the plastic substances would probably have been other than nitrogen, and the chemistry of living bodies would then have been radically different from what it is. The result would have been living forms without any analogy to those we know, whose anatomy would have been different, whose physiology also would have been different. Alone, the sensori-motor function would have been preserved, if not in its mechanism, at least in its effects. It is therefore probable that life goes on in other planets, in other solar systems also, under forms of which we have no idea, in physical conditions to which it seems to us, from the point of view of our physiology, to be absolutely opposed. If its essential aim is to catch up usable energy in order to expend it in explosive actions, it probably chooses, in each solar system and on each planet, as it does on the earth, the fittest means to get this result in the circumstances with which it is confronted. That is at least what reasoning by analogy leads to, and we use analogy the wrong way when we declare life to be impossible wherever the circumstances with which it is confronted are other than those on the earth. The truth is that life is possible wherever energy descends the incline indicated by Carnot's law and where a cause of inverse direction can retard the descent—that is to say, probably, in all the worlds suspended from all the stars. We go further: it is not even necessary that life should be concentrated and determined in organisms properly so called, that is, in definite bodies presenting to the flow of energy ready-made though elastic canals. It can be conceived (although it can hardly be imagined) that energy might be saved up, and then expended on varying lines running across a matter not yet solidified. Every essential of life would still be there, since there would still be slow accumulation of energy and sudden release. There would hardly be more difference between this vitality, vague and formless, and the definite vitality we know, than there is, in our psychical life, between the state of dream and the state of waking. Such may have been the condition of life in our nebula before the condensation of matter was complete, if it be true that life springs forward at the very moment when, as the effect of an inverse movement, the nebular matter appears.

It is therefore conceivable that life might have assumed a totally different outward appearance and designed forms very different from those we know. With another chemical substratum, in other physical conditions, the impulsion would have remained the same, but it would have split up very differently in course of progress; and the whole would have traveled another road—whether shorter or longer who can tell? In any case, in the entire series of living beings no term would have been what it now is. Now, was it necessary that there should be a series, or terms? Why should not the unique impetus have been impressed on a unique body, which might have gone on evolving?

This question arises, no doubt, from the comparison of life to an impetus. And it must be compared to an impetus, because no image borrowed from the physical world can give more nearly the idea of it. But it is only an image. In reality, life is of the psychological order, and it is of the essence of the psychical to enfold a confused plurality of interpenetrating terms. In space, and in space only, is distinct multiplicity possible: a point is absolutely external to another point. But pure and empty unity, also, is met with only in space; it is that of a mathematical point. Abstract unity and abstract multiplicity are determinations of space or categories of the understanding, whichever we will, spatiality and intellectuality being molded on each other. But what is of psychical nature cannot entirely correspond with space, nor enter perfectly into the categories of the understanding. Is my own person, at a given moment, one or manifold? If I declare it one, inner voices arise and protest—those of the sensations, feelings, ideas, among which my individuality is distributed. But, if I make it distinctly manifold, my consciousness rebels quite as strongly; it affirms that my sensations, my feelings, my thoughts are abstractions which I effect on myself, and that each of my states implies all the others. I am then (we must adopt the language of the understanding, since only the understanding has a language) a unity that is multiple and a multiplicity that is one; but unity and multiplicity are only views of my personality taken by an understanding that directs its categories at me; I enter neither into one nor into the other nor into both at once, although both, united, may give a fair imitation of the mutual interpenetration and continuity that I find at the base of my own self. Such is my inner life, and such also is life in general. While, in its contact with matter, life is comparable to an impulsion or an impetus, regarded in itself it is an immensity of potentiality, a mutual encroachment of thousands and thousands of tendencies which nevertheless are "thousands and thousands" only when once regarded as outside of each other, that is, when spatialized. Contact with matter is what determines this dissociation. Matter divides actually what was but potentially manifold; and, in this sense, individuation is in part the work of matter, in part the result of life's own inclination. Thus, a poetic sentiment, which bursts into distinct verses, lines, and words, may be said to have already contained this multiplicity of individuated elements, and yet, in fact, it is the materiality of language that creates it.

But through the words, lines, and verses runs the simple inspiration which is the whole poem. So, among the dissociated individuals, one life goes on moving: everywhere the tendency to individualize is opposed and at the same time completed by an antagonistic and complementary tendency to associate, as if the manifold unity of life, drawn in the direction of multiplicity, made so much the more effort to withdraw itself on to itself. A part is no sooner detached than it tends to reunite itself, if not to all the rest, at least to what is nearest to it. Hence, throughout the whole realm of life, a balancing between individuation and association. Individuals join together into a society; but the society, as soon as formed, tends to melt the associated individuals into a new organism, so as to become itself an individual, able in its turn to be part and parcel of a new association. At the lowest degree of the scale of organisms we already find veritable associations, microbial colonies, and in these associations, according to a recent work, a tendency to individuate by the constitution of a nucleus. The same tendency is met with again at a higher stage, in the protophytes, which, once having quitted the parent cell by way of division, remain united to each other by the gelatinous substance that surrounds them—also in those protozoa which begin by mingling their pseudopodia and end by welding themselves together. The "colonial" theory of the genesis of higher organisms is well known. The protozoa, consisting of one single cell, are supposed to have formed, by assemblage, aggregates which, relating themselves together in their turn, have given rise to aggregates of aggregates; so organisms more and more complicated, and also more and more differentiated, are born of the association of organisms barely differentiated and elementary. In this extreme form, the theory is open to grave objections: more and more the idea seems to be gaining ground, that polyzoism is an exceptional and abnormal fact. But it is none the less true that things happen *as if* every higher organism was born of an association of cells that have subdivided the work between them. Very probably it is not the cells that have made the individual by means of association; it is rather the individual that has made the cells by means of dissociation. But this itself reveals to us, in the genesis of the individual, a haunting of the social form, as if the individual could develop only on the condition that its substance should be split up into elements having themselves an appearance of individuality and united among themselves by an appearance of sociality. There are numerous cases in which nature seems to hesitate between the two forms, and to ask herself if she shall make a society or an individual. The slightest push is enough, then, to make the balance weigh on one side or the other. If we take an infusorian sufficiently large, such as the Stentor, and cut it into two halves each containing a part of the nucleus, each of the two halves will generate an independent Stentor; but if we divide it incompletely, so that a protoplasmic communication is left between the two halves, we shall see them execute, each from its side, corresponding movements: so that in this case it is enough that a thread should be maintained or cut in order that life should affect the social or the individual form. Thus, in rudimentary organisms consisting of a single cell, we already find that the apparent individuality of the whole is the composition of an *undefined* number of potential individualities potentially associated. But, from top to bottom of the series of living beings, the same law is manifested. And it is this that we express when we say that unity and multiplicity are categories of inert matter, that the vital impetus is neither pure unity nor pure multiplicity, and that if the matter to which it communicates itself compels it to choose one of the two, its choice will never be definitive: it will leap from one to the other indefinitely. The evolution of life in the double direction of individuality and association has therefore nothing accidental about it: it is due to the very nature of life.

Essential also is the progress to reflexion. If our analysis is correct, it is consciousness, or rather supra-consciousness, that is at the origin of life. Consciousness, or supra-consciousness, is the name for the rocket whose extinguished fragments fall back as matter; consciousness, again, is the name for that which subsists of the rocket itself, passing through the fragments and lighting them up into organisms. But this consciousness, which is a *need of creation,* is made manifest to itself only where creation is possible. It lies dormant when life is condemned to automatism; it wakens as soon as the possibility of a choice is restored. That is why, in organisms unprovided with a nervous system, it varies according to the power of locomotion and of deformation of which the organism disposes. And in animals with a nervous system, it is proportional to the complexity of the switchboard on which the paths called sensory and the paths called motor intersect—that is, of the brain. How must this solidarity between the organism and consciousness be understood?

We will not dwell here on a point that we have dealt with in former works. Let us merely recall that a theory such as that according to which consciousness is attached to certain neurons, and is thrown off from their work like a phosphorescence, may be accepted by the scientist for the detail of analysis; it is a convenient mode of expression. But it is nothing else. In reality, a living being is a centre of action. It represents a certain sum of contingency entering into the world, that is to say, a certain quantity of possible action—a quantity variable with individuals and especially with species. The nervous system of an animal marks out the flexible lines on which its action will run (although the potential energy is accumulated in the muscles rather than in the nervous system itself); its nervous centres indicate, by their development and their configuration, the more or less extended choice it will have among more or less numerous and complicated actions. Now, since the awakening of consciousness in a living creature is the more complete, the greater the latitude of choice allowed to it and the larger the amount of action bestowed upon it, it is clear that the development of consciousness will appear to be dependent on that of the nervous centres. On the other hand, every state of consciousness being, in one aspect of it, a question put to the motor activity and even the beginning of a reply, there is no psychical event that does not imply the entry into play of the cortical mechanisms. Everything seems, therefore, to happen *as if* consciousness sprang from the brain, and *as if* the detail of conscious activity were modeled on that of the cerebral activity. In reality, consciousness does not spring from the brain; but brain and consciousness correspond because equally they measure, the one by the complexity of its structure and the other by the intensity of its awareness, the quantity of *choice* that the living being has at its disposal.

It is precisely because a cerebral state expresses simply what there is of nascent action in the corresponding psychical state, that the psychical state tells us more than the cerebral state. The consciousness of a living being, as we have tried to prove elsewhere, is inseparable from its brain in the sense in which a sharp knife is inseparable from its edge: the brain is the sharp edge by which consciousness cuts into the compact tissue of events, but the brain is no more coextensive with consciousness than the edge is with the knife. Thus, from the fact that two brains, like that of the ape and that of the man, are very much alike, we cannot conclude that the corresponding consciousnesses are comparable or commensurable.

But the two brains may perhaps be less alike than we suppose. How can we help being struck by the fact that, while man is capable of learning any sort of exercise, of constructing any sort of object, in short of acquiring any kind of motor habit whatsoever, the faculty of combining new movements is strictly limited in the best-endowed animal, even in the ape? The cerebral characteristic of man is there. The human brain is made, like every brain, to set up motor mechanisms and to enable us to choose among them, at any instant, the one we shall put in motion by the pull of a trigger. But it differs from other brains in this, that the number of mechanisms it can set up, and consequently the choice that it gives as to which among them shall be released, is unlimited. Now, from the limited to the unlimited there is all the distance between the closed and the open. It is not a difference of degree, but of kind.

Radical therefore, also, is the difference between animal consciousness, even the most intelligent, and human consciousness. For consciousness corresponds exactly to the living being's power of choice; it is coextensive with the fringe of possible action that surrounds the real action: consciousness is synonymous with invention and with freedom. Now, in the animal, invention is never anything but a variation on the theme of routine. Shut up in the habits of the species, it succeeds, no doubt, in enlarging them by its individual initiative; but it escapes automatism only for an instant, for just the time to create a new automatism. The gates of its prison close as soon as they are opened; by pulling at its chain it succeeds only in stretching it. With man, consciousness breaks the chain. In man, and in man alone, it sets itself free. The whole history of life until man has been that of the effort of consciousness to raise matter, and of the more or less complete overwhelming of consciousness by the matter which has fallen back on it. The enterprise was paradoxical, if, indeed, we may speak here otherwise than by metaphor of enterprise and of effort. It was to create with matter, which is necessity itself, an instrument of freedom, to make a machine which should triumph over mechanism, and to use the determinism of nature to pass through the meshes of the net which this very determinism had spread. But, everywhere except in man, consciousness has let itself be caught in the net whose meshes it tried to pass through: it has remained the captive of the mechanisms it has set up. Automatism, which it tries to draw in the direction of freedom, winds about it and drags it down. It has not the power to escape, because the energy it has provided for acts is almost all employed in maintaining the infinitely subtle and essentially unstable equilibrium into which it has brought matter. But man not only maintains his machine, he succeeds in using it as he pleases. Doubtless he owes this to the superiority of his brain, which enables him to build an unlimited number of motor mechanisms, to oppose new habits to the old ones unceasingly, and, by dividing automatism against itself, to rule it. He owes it to his language, which furnishes consciousness with an immaterial body in which to incarnate itself and thus exempts it from dwelling exclusively on material bodies, whose flux would soon drag it along and finally swallow it up. He owes it to social life, which stores and preserves efforts as language stores thought, fixes thereby a mean level to which individuals must raise themselves at the outset, and by this initial stimulation prevents the average man from slumbering and drives the superior man to mount still higher. But our brain, our society, and our language are only the external and various signs of one and the same internal superiority. They tell, each after its manner, the unique, exceptional success which life has won at a given moment of its evolution. They express the difference of kind, and not only of degree, which separates man from the rest of the animal world. They let us guess that, while at the end of the vast spring-board from which life has taken its leap, all the others have stepped down, finding the cord stretched too high, man alone has cleared the obstacle.

It is in this quite special sense that man is the "term" and the "end" of evolution. Life, we have said, transcends finality as it transcends the other categories. It is essentially a current sent through matter, drawing from it what it can. There has not, therefore, properly speaking, been any project or plan. On the other hand, it is abundantly evident that the rest of nature is not for the sake of man: we struggle like the other species, we have struggled against other species. Moreover, if the evolution of life had encountered other accidents in its course, if, thereby, the current of life had been otherwise divided, we should have been, physically and morally, far different from what we are. For these various reasons it would be wrong to regard humanity, such as we have it before our eyes, as pre-figured in the evolutionary movement. It cannot even be said to be the outcome of the whole of evolution, for evolution has been accomplished on several divergent lines, and while the human species is at the end of one of them, other lines have been followed with other species at their end. It is in a quite different sense that we hold humanity to be the ground of evolution.

From our point of view, life appears in its entirety as an immense wave which, starting from a centre, spreads outwards, and which on almost the whole of its circumference is stopped and converted into oscillation: at one single point the obstacle has been forced, the impulsion has passed freely. It is this freedom that the human form registers. Everywhere but in man, consciousness has had to come to a stand; in man alone it has kept on its way. Man, then, continues the vital movement indefinitely, although he does not draw along with him all that life carries in itself. On other lines of evolution there have traveled other tendencies which life implied, and of which, since everything interpenetrates, man has, doubtless, kept something, but of which he has kept only very little. *It is as if a vague and formless being, whom we may call, as we will,* man or superman, *had sought to realize himself, and had succeeded only by abandoning a part of himself on the way.* The losses are represented by the rest of the animal world, and even by the vegetable world, at least in what these have that is positive and above the accidents of evolution.

From this point of view, the discordances of which nature offers us the spectacle are singularly weakened. The organized world as a whole becomes as the soil on which was to grow either man himself or a being who morally must resemble him. The animals, however distant they may be from our species, however hostile to it, have none the less been useful traveling companions, on whom consciousness has unloaded whatever encumbrances it was dragging along, and who have enabled it to rise, in man, to heights from which it sees an unlimited horizon open again before it.

It is true that it has not only abandoned cumbersome baggage on the way; it has also had to give up valuable goods. Consciousness, in man, is pre-eminently intellect. It might have been, it ought, so it seems, to have been also intuition. Intuition and intellect represent two opposite directions of the work of consciousness: intuition goes in the very direction of life, intellect goes in the inverse direction, and thus finds itself naturally in accordance with the movement of matter. A complete and perfect humanity would be that in which these two forms of conscious activity should attain their full development. And, between this humanity and ours, we may conceive any number of possible stages, corresponding to all the degrees imaginable of intelligence and of intuition. In this lies the part of contingency in the mental structure of our species. A different evolution might have led to a humanity either more intellectual still or more intuitive. In the humanity of which we are a part, intuition is, in fact, almost completely sacrificed to intellect. It seems that to conquer matter, and to reconquer its own self, consciousness has had to exhaust the best part of its power. This conquest, in the particular conditions in which it has been accomplished, has required that consciousness should adapt itself to the habits of matter and concentrate all its attention on them, in fact determine itself more especially as intellect. Intuition is there, however, but vague and above all discontinuous. It is a lamp almost extinguished, which only glimmers now and then, for a few moments at most. But it glimmers wherever a vital interest is at stake. On our personality, on our liberty, on the place we occupy in the whole of nature, on our origin and perhaps also on our destiny, it throws a light feeble and vacillating, but which none the less pierces the darkness of the night in which the intellect leaves us.

These fleeting intuitions, which light up their object only at distant intervals, philosophy ought to seize, first to sustain them, then to expand them and so unite them together. The more it advances in this work, the more will it perceive that intuition is mind itself, and, in a certain sense, life itself: the intellect has been cut out of it by a process resembling that which has generated matter. Thus is revealed the unity of the spiritual life. We recognize it only when we place ourselves in intuition in order to go from intuition to the intellect, for from the intellect we shall never pass to intuition.

Philosophy introduces us thus into the spiritual life. And it shows us at the same time the relation of the life of the spirit to that of the body. The great error of the doctrines on the spirit has been the idea that by isolating the spiritual life from all the rest, by suspending it in space as high as possible above the earth, they were placing it beyond attack, as if they were not thereby simply exposing it to be taken as an effect of mirage! Certainly they are right to listen to conscience when conscience affirms human freedom; but the intellect is there, which says that the cause determines its effect, that like conditions like, that all is repeated and that all is given. They are right to believe in the absolute reality of the person and in his independence toward matter; but science is there, which shows the interdependence of conscious life and cerebral activity. They are right to attribute to man a privileged place in nature, to hold that the distance is infinite between the animal and man; but the history of life is there, which makes us witness the genesis of species by gradual transformation, and seems thus to reintegrate man in animality. When a strong instinct assures the probability of personal survival, they are right not to close their ears to its voice; but if there exist "souls" capable of an independent life, whence do they come? When, how, and why do they enter into this body which we see arise, quite naturally, from a mixed cell derived from the bodies of its two parents? All these questions will remain unanswered, a philosophy of intuition will be a negation of science, will be sooner or later swept away by science, if it does not resolve to see the life of the body just where it really is, on the road that leads to the life of the spirit. But it will then no longer have to do with definite living beings. Life as a whole, from the initial impulsion that thrust it into the world, will appear as a wave which rises, and which is opposed by the descending movement of matter. On the greater part of its surface, at different heights, the current is converted by matter into a vortex. At one point alone it passes freely, dragging with it the obstacle which will weigh on its progress but will not stop it. At this point is humanity; it is our privileged situation. On the other hand, this rising wave is consciousness, and, like all consciousness, it includes potentialities without number which interpenetrate and to which consequently neither the category of unity nor that of multiplicity is appropriate, made as they both are for inert matter. The matter that it bears along with it, and in the interstices of which it inserts itself, alone can divide it into distinct individualities. On flows the current, running through human generations, subdividing itself into individuals. This subdivision was vaguely indicated in it, but could not have been made clear without matter. Thus souls are continually being created, which, nevertheless, in a certain sense pre-existed. They are nothing else than the little rills into which the great river of life divides itself, flowing through the body of humanity. The movement of the stream is distinct from the river bed, although it must adopt its winding course. Consciousness is distinct from the organism it animates, although it must undergo its vicissitudes. As the possible actions which a state of consciousness indicates are at every instant beginning to be carried out in the nervous centres, the brain underlies at every instant the motor indications of the state of consciousness; but the interdependency of consciousness and brain is limited to this; the destiny of consciousness is not bound up on that account with the destiny of cerebral matter. Finally, consciousness is essentially free; it is freedom itself; but it cannot pass through matter without settling on it, without adapting itself to it: this adaptation is what we call intellectuality; and the intellect, turning itself back toward active, that is to say free, consciousness, naturally makes it enter into the conceptual forms into which it is accustomed to see matter fit. It will therefore always perceive freedom in the form of necessity; it will always neglect the part of novelty or of creation inherent in the free act; it will always substitute for action itself an imitation artificial, approximative, obtained by compounding the old with the old and the same with the same. Thus, to the eyes of a philosophy that attempts to reabsorb intellect in intuition, many difficulties vanish or become light. But such a doctrine does not only facilitate speculation; it gives us also more power to act and to live. For, with it, we feel ourselves no longer isolated in humanity, humanity no longer seems isolated in the nature that it dominates. As the smallest grain of dust is bound up with our entire solar system, drawn along with it in that undivided movement of descent which is materiality itself, so all organized beings, from the humblest to the highest, from the first origins of life to the time in which we are, and in all places as in all times, do but evidence a single impulsion, the inverse of the movement of matter, and in itself indivisible. All the living hold together, and all yield to the same tremendous push. The animal takes its stand on the plant, man bestrides animality, and the whole of humanity, in space and in time, is one immense army galloping beside and before and behind each of us in an overwhelming charge able to beat down every resistance and clear the most formidable obstacles, perhaps even death.

IV: THE CINEMATOGRAPHICAL MECHANISM OF THOUGHT AND THE MECHANISTIC ILLUSION

MATTER OR MIND, reality has appeared to us as a perpetual becoming. It makes itself or it unmakes itself, but it is never something made. Such is the intuition that we have of mind when we draw aside the veil which is interposed between our consciousness and ourselves. This, also, is what our intellect and senses themselves would show us of matter, if they could obtain a direct and disinterested idea of it. But, preoccupied before everything with the necessities of action, the intellect, like the senses, is limited to taking, at intervals, views that are instantaneous and by that very fact immobile of the becoming of matter. Consciousness, being in its turn formed on the intellect, sees clearly of the inner life what is already made, and only feels confusedly the making. Thus, we pluck out of duration those moments that interest us, and that we have gathered along its course. These alone we retain. And we are right in so doing, while action only is in question. But when, in *speculating* on the *nature* of the real, we go on regarding it as our practical interest requires us to regard it, we become unable to perceive the true evolution, the radical becoming. Of becoming we perceive only states, of duration only instants, and even when we speak of duration and of becoming, it is of another thing that we are thinking. Such is the most striking of the two illusions we wish to examine. It consists in supposing that we can think the unstable by means of the stable, the moving by means of the immobile.

The other illusion is near akin to the first. It has the same origin, being also due to the fact that we import into speculation a procedure made for practice. All action aims at getting something that we feel the want of, or at creating something that does not yet exist. In this very special sense, it fills a void, and goes from the empty to the full, from an absence to a presence, from the unreal to the real. Now the unreality which is here in question is purely relative to the direction in which our attention is engaged, for we are immersed in realities and cannot pass out of them; only, if the present reality is not the one we are seeking, we speak of the *absence* of this sought-for reality wherever we find the *presence* of another. We thus express what we have as a function of what we want. This is quite legitimate in the sphere of action. But, whether we will or no, we keep to this way of speaking, and also of thinking, when we speculate on the nature of things independently of the interest they have for us. Thus arises the second of the two illusions. We propose to examine this first. It is due, like the other, to the static habits that our intellect contracts when it prepares our action on things. Just as we pass through the immobile to go to the moving, so we make use of the void in order to think the full.

For a mind which should follow purely and simply the thread of experience, there would be no void, no nought, even relative or partial, no possible negation. Such a mind would see facts succeed facts, states succeed states, things succeed things. What it would note at each moment would be things existing, states appearing, events happening. It would live in the actual, and, if it were capable of judging, it would never affirm anything except the existence of the present.

Endow this mind with memory, and especially with the desire to dwell on the past; give it the faculty of dissociating and of distinguishing: it will no longer only note the present state of the passing reality; it will represent the passing as a change, and therefore as a contrast between what has been and what is. And as there is no essential difference between a past that we remember and a past that we imagine, it will quickly rise to the idea of the "possible" in general.

It will thus be shunted on to the siding of negation. And especially it will be at the point of representing a disappearance. But it will not yet have reached it. To represent that a thing has disappeared, it is not enough to perceive a contrast between the past and the present; it is necessary besides to turn our back on the present, to dwell on the past, and to think the contrast of the past with the present in terms of the past only, without letting the present appear in it.

The idea of annihilation is therefore not a pure idea; it implies that we regret the past or that we conceive it as regrettable, that we have some reason to linger over it. The idea arises when the phenomenon of substitution is cut in two by a mind which considers only the first half, because that alone interests it. Suppress all interest, all feeling, and there is nothing left but the reality that flows, together with the knowledge ever renewed that it impresses on us of its present state.

From annihilation to negation, which is a more general operation, there is now only a step. All that is necessary is to represent the contrast of what is, not only with what has been, but also with all that might have been. And we must express this contrast as a function of what might have been, and not of what is; we must affirm the existence of the actual while looking only at the possible. The formula we thus obtain no longer expresses merely a disappointment of the individual; it is made to correct or guard against an error, which is rather supposed to be the error of another. In this sense, negation has a pedagogical and social character.

Now, once negation is formulated, it presents an aspect symmetrical with that of affirmation; if affirmation affirms an objective reality, it seems that negation must affirm a non-reality equally objective, and, so to say, equally real. In which we are both right and wrong: wrong, because negation cannot be objectified, in so far as it is negative; right, however, in that the negation of a thing implies the latent affirmation of its replacement by something else, which we systematically leave on one side. But the negative form of negation benefits by the affirmation at the bottom of it. Bestriding the positive solid reality to which it is attached, this phantom objectifies itself. Thus is formed the idea of the void or of a partial nought, a thing being supposed to be replaced, not by another thing, but by a void which it leaves, that is, by the negation of itself. Now, as this operation works on anything whatever, we suppose it performed on each thing in turn, and finally on all things in block. We thus obtain the idea of absolute Nothing. If now we analyze this idea of Nothing, we find that it is, at bottom, the idea of Everything, together with a movement of the mind that keeps jumping from one thing to another, refuses to stand still, and concentrates all its attention on this refusal by never determining its actual position except by relation to that which it has just left. It is therefore an idea eminently comprehensive and full, as full and comprehensive as the idea of *All,* to which it is very closely akin.

How then can the idea of Nought be opposed to that of All? Is it not plain that this is to oppose the full to the full, and that the question, "Why does something exist?" is consequently without meaning, a pseudo-problem raised about a pseudo-idea? Yet we must say once more why this phantom of a problem haunts the mind with such obstinacy. In vain do we show that in the idea of an "annihilation of the real" there is only the image of all realities expelling one another endlessly, in a circle; in vain do we add that the idea of non-existence is only that of the expulsion of an imponderable existence, or a "merely possible" existence, by a more substantial existence which would then be the true reality; in vain do we find in the *sui generis* form of negation an element which is not intellectual —negation being the judgment of a judgment, an admonition given to someone else or to oneself, so that it is absurd to attribute to negation the power of creating ideas of a new kind, viz., ideas without content; —in spite of all, the conviction persists that before things, or at least under things, there is "Nothing." If we seek the reason of this fact, we shall find it precisely in the feeling, in the social and, so to speak, practical element, that gives its specific form to negation. The greatest philosophic difficulties arise, as we have said, from the fact that the forms of human action venture outside of their proper sphere. We are made in order to act as much as, and more than, in order to think—or rather, when we follow the bent of our nature, it is in order to act that we think. It is therefore no wonder that the habits of action give their tone to those of thought, and that our mind always perceives things in the same order in which we are accustomed to picture them when we propose to act on them. Now, it is unquestionable, as we remarked above, that every human action has its starting-point in a dissatisfaction, and thereby in a feeling of absence. We should not act if we did not set before ourselves an end, and we seek a thing only because we feel the lack of it. Our action proceeds thus from "nothing" to "something," and its very essence is to embroider "something" on the canvas of "nothing." The truth is that the "nothing" concerned here is the absence not so much of a thing as of a utility. If I bring a visitor into a room that I have not yet furnished, I say to him that "there is nothing in it." Yet I know the room is full of air; but, as we do not sit on air, the room truly contains nothing that at this moment, for the visitor and for myself, counts for anything. In a general way, human work consists in creating utility; and, as long as the work is not done, there is "nothing"—nothing that we want. Our life is thus spent in filling voids, which our intellect conceives under the influence, by no means intellectual, of desire and of regret, under the pressure of vital necessities; and if we mean by void an absence of utility and not of things, we may say, in this quite relative sense, that we are constantly going from the void to the full: such is the direction which our action takes. Our speculation cannot help doing the same; and, naturally, it passes from the relative sense to the absolute sense, since it is exercised on things themselves and not on the utility they have for us. Thus is implanted in us the idea that reality fills a void, and that Nothing, conceived as an absence of everything, pre-exists before all things in right, if not in fact. It is this illusion that we have tried to remove by showing that the idea of Nothing, if we try to see in it that of an annihilation of all things, is self-destructive and reduced to a mere word; and that if, on the contrary, it is truly an idea, then we find in it as much matter as in the idea of All.

Now, if we try to characterize more precisely our natural attitude towards Becoming, this is what we find. Becoming is infinitely varied. That which goes from yellow to green is not like that which goes from green to blue: they are different *qualitative* movements. That which goes from flower to fruit is not like that which goes from larva to nymph and from nymph to perfect insect: they are different *evolutionary* movements.

The action of eating or of drinking is not like the action of fighting: they are different *extensive* movements. And these three kinds of movement themselves—qualitative, evolutionary, extensive—differ profoundly. The trick of our perception, like that of our intelligence, like that of our language, consists in extracting from these profoundly different becomings the single representation of becoming *in general,* undefined becoming, a mere abstraction which by itself says nothing and of which, indeed, it is very rarely that we think. To this idea, always the same, and always obscure or unconscious, we then join, in each particular case, one or several clear images that represent *states* and which serve to distinguish all becomings from each other. It is this composition of a specified and definite state with change general and undefined that we substitute for the specific change. An infinite multiplicity of becomings variously colored, so to speak, passes before our eyes: we manage so that we see only differences of color, that is to say, differences of state, beneath which there is supposed to flow, hidden from our view, a becoming always and everywhere the same, invariably colorless.

Suppose we wish to portray on a screen a living picture, such as the marching past of a regiment. There is one way in which it might first occur to us to do it. That would be to cut out jointed figures representing the soldiers, to give to each of them the movement of marching, a movement varying from individual to individual although common to the human species, and to throw the whole on the screen. We should need to spend on this little game an enormous amount of work, and even then we should obtain but a very poor result: how could it, at its best, reproduce the suppleness and variety of life? Now, there is another way of proceeding, more easy and at the same time more effective. It is to take a series of snapshots of the passing regiment and to throw these instantaneous views on the screen, so that they replace each other very rapidly. This is what the cinematograph does. With photographs, each of which represents the regiment in a fixed attitude, it reconstitutes the mobility of the regiment marching. It is true that if we had to do with photographs alone, however much we might look at them, we should never see them animated: with immobility set beside immobility, even endlessly, we could never make movement. In order that the pictures may be animated, there must be movement somewhere. The movement does indeed exist here; it is in the apparatus. It is because the film of the cinematograph unrolls, bringing in turn the different photographs of the scene to continue each other, that each actor of the scene recovers his mobility; he strings all his successive attitudes on the invisible movement of the film. The process then consists in extracting from all the movements peculiar to all the figures an impersonal movement abstract and simple, *movement in general,* so to speak: we put this into the apparatus, and we reconstitute the individuality of each particular movement by combining this nameless movement with the personal attitudes. Such is the contrivance of the cinematograph. And such is also that of our knowledge. Instead of attaching ourselves to the inner becoming of things, we place ourselves outside them in order to recompose their becoming artificially. We take snapshots, as it were, of the passing reality, and, as these are characteristic of the reality, we have only to string them on a becoming, abstract, uniform, and invisible, situated at the back of the apparatus of knowledge, in order to imitate what there is that is characteristic in this becoming itself. Perception, intellection, language so proceed in general. Whether we would think becoming, or express it, or even perceive it, we hardly do anything else than set going a kind of cinematograph inside us. We may therefore sum up what we have been saying in the conclusion that the *mechanism of our ordinary knowledge is of a cinematographical kind.*

Of the altogether practical character of this operation there is no possible doubt. Each of our acts aims at a certain insertion of our will into the reality. There is, between our body and other bodies, an arrangement like that of the pieces of glass that compose a kaleidoscopic picture. Our activity goes from an arrangement to a re-arrangement, each time no doubt giving the kaleidoscope a new shake, but not interesting itself in the shake, and seeing only the new picture. Our knowledge of the operation of nature must be exactly symmetrical, therefore, with the interest we take in our own operation. In this sense we may say, if we are not abusing this kind of illustration, that *the cinematographical character of our knowledge of things is due to the kaleidoscopic character of our adaptation to them.*

The cinematographical method is therefore the only practical method, since it consists in making the general character of knowledge form itself on that of action, while expecting that the detail of each act should depend in its turn on that of knowledge. In order that action may always be enlightened, intelligence must always be present in it; but intelligence, in order thus to accompany the progress of activity and ensure its direction, must begin by adopting its rhythm. Action is discontinuous, like every pulsation of life; discontinuous, therefore, is knowledge. The mechanism of the faculty of knowing has been constructed on this plan. Essentially practical, can it be of use, such as it is, for speculation? Let us try with it to follow reality in its windings, and see what will happen.

I take of the continuity of a particular becoming a series of views, which I connect together by "becoming in general." But of course I cannot stop there. What is not determinable is not representable: of "becoming in general" I have only a verbal knowledge. As the letter *x* designates a certain unknown quantity, whatever it may be, so my "becoming in general," always the same, symbolizes here a certain transition of which I have taken some snapshots; of the transition itself it teaches me nothing. Let me then concentrate myself wholly on the transition, and, between any two snapshots, endeavor to realize what is going on. As I apply the same method, I obtain the same result; a third view merely slips in between the two others. I may begin again as often as I will, I may set views alongside of views for ever, I shall obtain nothing else. The application of the cinematographical method therefore leads to a perpetual recommencement, during which the mind, never able to satisfy itself and never finding where to rest, persuades itself, no doubt, that it imitates by its instability the very movement of the real. But though, by straining itself to the point of giddiness, it may end by giving itself the illusion of mobility, its operation has not advanced it a step, since it remains as far as ever from its goal. In order to advance with the moving reality, you must replace yourself within it. Install yourself within change, and you will grasp at once both change itself and the successive states in which *it might* at any instant be immobilized. But with these successive states, perceived from without as real and no longer as potential immobilities, you will never reconstitute movement. Call them *qualities, forms, positions,* or *intentions,* as the case may be, multiply the number of them as you will, let the interval between two consecutive states be infinitely small: before the intervening movement you will always experience the disappointment of the child who tries by clapping his hands together to crush the smoke. The movement slips through the interval, because every attempt to reconstitute change out of states implies the absurd proposition, that movement is made of immobilities.

Catalog

If you are interested in a list of fine Paperback
books, covering a wide range of subjects
and interests, send your name and address,
requesting your free catalog, to:

McGraw-Hill Paperbacks
1221 Avenue of Americas
New York, N.Y. 10020